Buildings and Ideas 1933–83

BUILDINGS & IDEAS
1933-83

FROM THE STUDIO OF
LESLIE MARTIN
AND HIS ASSOCIATES

CAMBRIDGE UNIVERSITY PRESS

CAMBRIDGE

LONDON   NEW YORK   NEW ROCHELLE   MELBOURNE   SYDNEY

Published by the Press Syndicate of the University of Cambridge
The Pitt Building, Trumpington Street, Cambridge CB2 1RP
32 East 57th Street, New York, NY 10022, USA
296 Beaconsfield Parade, Middle Park, Melbourne 3206, Australia

First published 1983

Printed in Great Britain at
The University Press, Cambridge

Library of Congress catalogue card number: 82–4359

British library cataloguing in publication data
Martin, J. L.
Buildings and ideas 1933–83
1. Martin, J. L.   2. Architecture, Modern –
20th century
I. Title
720'.92'4   NA997.M/
ISBN 0 521 23107 8

This book is dedicated to those
institutions and individuals who,
over the years, were kind enough
to give me the opportunity to design
buildings. I have always valued and
enjoyed those friendly associations.

Contents

Colleagues

It is now some years since Professor Trevor Dannatt suggested that I should compile this book. I am grateful to him for his continued encouragement since then, for his editing of the script and for his Foreword.

In particular I wish to mention those who have worked with me as associated architects. Their names and the buildings on which we worked in association are listed below:

Trevor Dannatt: College Hall, Knighton, University of Leicester.

Colin St J. Wilson: University layouts: Leicester, Hull and Royal Holloway College, Egham. King's Hostel, Harvey Court and the Stone Building, Peterhouse, all in Cambridge. Manor Road Library Group, Oxford, and British Museum first scheme.

Patrick Hodgkinson: Harvey Court, Cambridge, and Library Group, Oxford.

Douglas Lanham: The Library Group and the Zoology/Psychology building, both in Oxford.

Colen Lumley: Middleton Hall and Arts building, Hull. New halls and adjoining development, Glasgow, schemes 1971–7. Music School, Cambridge, Stage I. McGowan Library, Pembroke College, Oxford.

David Owers: Balliol and St Anne's, postgraduate residence, Oxford. Wellington Square, Oxford. Kettle's Yard, Cambridge, Stage I. Government centre, Taif.

Ivor Richards: Music School, Cambridge, all stages. New halls and adjoining development, Glasgow, 1979–82. Schemes for a college social building and linked auditoria. Royal Scottish Academy of Music and Drama, Glasgow. Gallery of Contemporary Art, Lisbon.

Many others who have assisted in the studio at various times have contributed to the work illustrated. I owe a special debt to Patrick Hodgkinson for his contribution in the early days. Lionel March initiated research,

worked on the 1968 scheme for the new halls and central development in Glasgow and later, with Jeremy Taylor, produced valuable work on the Whitehall project. My wife, Sadie Speight, has made her own very special contribution to my work throughout the whole of my professional career. She has also produced the format and the general layout of this book.

In the case of major schemes built at some distance from the studio we have worked with associated colleagues. In particular in the case of the Gallery of Contemporary Art in Lisbon, I would like to thank all those who made this building possible: Dr Perdigao, the Chairman of the Gulbenkian Foundation, engineer Sr Luis Lobato, architect Jose Sommer Ribeiro and their staff. Dr Azzam was responsible for asking me, and indeed a number of architects from various parts of the world, to help with projects in the Middle East, and in the case of the Government building in Taif we had the competent support of Messrs ETEC of Beirut and Paris. At Glasgow on the building for the Royal Scottish Academy of Music and Drama we are working with Messrs Nimmo and Partners, Glasgow.

My period of work in the public service is mentioned briefly in the appendix. I am grateful to Robert Matthew who as architect to the LCC gave me the opportunity to work on the Royal Festival Hall. Later during my period as architect to the Council I worked closely with several colleagues and when specific schemes are referred to I have mentioned the names of my principal associates in the text.

In addition to some of my own drawings, special drawings for the book have been made by Susan Mason and Ivor Richards. Jacqui Arbon has typed innumerable drafts of the text and the final script. I am also indebted to Michael Black, Lyn Chatterton, John Trevitt and their colleagues at the Cambridge University Press for constant help and advice.

Foreword

Trevor Dannatt

When Leslie Martin was chosen as the recipient of the Royal Gold Medal in 1973, the citation paid tribute to 'a truly outstanding contribution to architecture and planning, both through his private and public practice, and most notably as a leading figure in architectural teaching and research'. That was the judgement of his professional colleagues. One writer commented that:

> He could have won the medal for his architecture alone, or his research, or his contribution to education; but it is perhaps his attitude to the whole range of his endeavours and skills that is his most important facet. Leslie Martin manages always to maintain a consistent philosophy that holds true for the entire range of his involvements.[1] It is his thought that is central.

In a long career in practice, he has worked with a number of associated architects and colleagues and he would be the first to acknowledge the part that they have played in the work of the studio that is included here. But colleagues have come and gone, and the continuing element, Leslie Martin himself, provides the consistency of thought and attitude that is demonstrated throughout this book and which, in the last few years, has flourished into one of his most creative and productive periods.

The idea and nature of this book has been discussed and developed over the last two years, and its structure is such that it demonstrates the architect's wide range of concern for the discipline of architecture in theory and practice. It represents his own rigorous selection of material both written and visual, and provides a comprehensive record, demonstrating the close correlation of idea and realisation in his work.

In one of his lectures Leslie Martin stated that he thought 'every critic certainly and perhaps every lecturer has a duty to outline his own position in relation to his subject'. I feel I should do so in relation to this introduction: I write primarily as an architect who, as a student in the late thirties and early forties, was stimulated by the first published buildings of J. L. Martin (as he then credited himself) – two or three houses and the Northwich School. I had *The Flat Book*[2] and, more important, *Circle* (where perhaps I 'read' the illustrations with more understanding than the text). He was one of the architects for whom I wanted to work, and did – followed by an association in work, friendship and shared interests over some thirty years, a period which has seen the development of a grave and eloquent architectural language, personal yet within the developing movement (now a tradition) of constructive architecture.

Recently the ideas and the buildings of the movement have been under attack, and although some critiques at least may have exposed the corrupt slogans and thin arguments of the 'social architecture' wing, yet they have left – in my view – the central ideas (and major buildings) more than relevant. At the same time, we have seen a simplistic historicism (and/or vernacularism) promoted almost as a packaging solution to the problems of design and style. If content as well as form is valued, if we believe that form and image have to be sought through an understanding of their historical relationship rather than based on an easy pictorial reading, we can see in the best work of past years a true achievement in this direction. Today we can see new developments that are manifestly

creative, enriching and diversifying the language of architecture. It is this sense of contributing to development – not change for its own sake – that shows a continuing thread through Martin's thought and works.

In no way is this book another 'practice brochure'; rather it is a record of architectural endeavour that also, I believe, could be a source of new creativity in the underlying theme of continuity and ideas in development. Through varied presentation the genesis and essence of the buildings is made known, while the related texts and essays clarify the foundation of the work in general and specific thought about building and the Modern Movement and its intention towards an architecture that is responsive to changing requirements. Thus the emphasis is on context and the underlying order of each development and its relation to others of that type (and indeed, to other types). Yet underneath differing forms, forms that have sprung from the need of function – use, environment and structure – there is manifest the architect's concern with the primary qualities of architecture; the interdependence of these primaries is demonstrated but also the underlying integrity of the architectural idea.

I feel it appropriate to try to identify aspects of the architect's philosophy and approach to the order that is manifest in the buildings.

Firstly, at a broad level we might see in the designs or the buildings how needs have been analysed, digested and restated in total terms – the building is from early on seen as a whole rather than put together. The idea may often seem deceptively simple but behind it there is, among other things, a conceptual ordering that does not dismiss precedents but draws on and revitalises them. The university residential buildings restate the elements of the traditional college courts and then elaborate these in relation to different room clusters around staircases and differing sites. The auditorium buildings always coordinate planning requirements with a vision of movement – spatial flow and connection leading to central volumes. Or, to take a specific example at Oxford, we see three libraries of different size and volume brought into relationship around the central organising flights of the external staircase.

These examples illustrate a central theme of all the work, the sectional planning principle – not, of course, peculiar to Martin, but rarely found developed with such grace as an architectural generator rather than an intellectual exercise or ingenious device, whether in a modest house such as the one in Portugal, giving a fresh and spacious interior in a small space, or in a large development such as the Zoology/Psychology complex at Oxford, where it is tuned to circulation and the economic provision of varied spaces and future extension as well as spatial diversity.

Secondly, we may study with satisfaction how the conception has been brought into a total system, a consistent formal and structural language to which all parts respond. For example, in the Bristol competition design the 'post and beam' construction is part of the spatial and plastic system and orders the whole conception without strait-jacketing it. Or, at a more modest level, in the conversions, existing structures are respected and clarified and consonance between idea and means is attained in a most limpid manner.

Thirdly, the main body of work shows a sureness and fine sensibility in the handling of elements and materials that can be enjoyed almost for their own sake, conjunctions perhaps of brickwork and metal roofing, or brick, timber, glass and plaster, innately pleasing but enjoyed also because there is such a satisfying conjunction of whole and part. There is a sense of style that runs throughout from overall concept to, say, the way the doors are put into openings, in the quality of panelling and fittings, in the detail of a fireplace – all responding to the same aesthetic.

It is here finally that one touches on the question of other values and I would like to define the delight and satisfaction that comes from the perception of, say, one of the buildings as a total experience. Perhaps one can only make comparisons with other artists. If painters, then Nicholson comes to mind, for whether in two or three dimensions there is a common sense of serene spatial relationships, just scale and proportion, cool harmonies of colour. William Feaver used the word *gravitas* in connection with a Moore head and spoke of the same quality being achieved by elimination in Barbara Hepworth's 'Three Forms' and repeatedly in Ben Nicholson's carved reliefs.[3] With all these artists Martin has had long association and the same quality of *gravitas* seems evident in his architecture, showing a consistent threefold harmony that demonstrates a clear intellectual ordering, deep understanding of space and form and the craftsmanlike handling of materials. Behind it all there is the sense of structuring buildings about ideas of wholeness rather than the domination of, say, planning arrangements or preconceived expression or technical or sociological obsessions. A sense of consonance brings due importance to each and every part and structures the whole organically in relation to the greater whole.

In the catalogue of the 1930s Exhibition[4] the point is made that 'At the end of the war modernist architects found the means available to put their ideals into practice. The tragedy was that these ideals had been so narrowed and hardened in the ideological conflicts of the 1930s and so little tested or refined through the practical processes of building and development.' No doubt such testing would, but for the war, have occurred. However, in the case of Martin's own work we can see the steady development of an architecture and building mode that has its roots in those ideals of the thirties but has not become rootbound. For example, if we look at the nursery school at Northwich of 1938 we can, among other things, enjoy the structure for its clarity (as well as its material) and see that it is part of the grammar of the building rather than just a new way of building or, as now seems the case in so many thirties' buildings, merely a pictorial reference to 'functionalism'. Similarly, looking again at the Bristol proposals, the structure relates closely to planning needs but is also integral with the spatial idea. As in the earlier building it seems natural and inevitable.

When Martin received the Gold Medal in 1973 one perhaps thought his work complete. Gratifyingly, since then a decade has seen the design and often the realisation of a number of outstanding buildings, as well as some significant lectures and essays.

There has been a steady development of earlier and new ideas and their realisation in specific projects or buildings of varied scales. Especially one should mention the enrichment of Cambridge by the recently completed music school building group with its serenely lit concert hall and surrounding necklace of linked smaller spaces and courtyards. Then there is for the future the possibility at least that Glasgow may be enriched by the City Halls and shopping precinct which create a new nodal point within the city grid, and the new home for the Royal Scottish Academy of Music and Drama where a significant building is emphasised by its setting and its form. In this particular project again, a clear linear arrangement of the elements of the plan is enlivened by the development of the section which achieves a separation of the working levels of the Drama and Music Schools but provides also the flowing spaces that unite the main volumes of the auditoria.

Both these projects have evolved through a series of studies that have been subject to continuous development, both as a result of external changes of programme and also because of the review of designs as they have developed. Surely one of Martin's great strengths lies in this reflective re-appraisal of work in progress, as all who have worked in his studio will testify; the sense of not being satisfied with what was thought to be the right solution and the illuminating discovery that further development and new combinations are always possible.

Almost as an aside, at the private level, the Walston house or the Church Barns conversion renew the dialogue of spatial flow and natural lighting so evident in the earlier Kettle's Yard Gallery. There, through a poem of light and space we can relax, receive a sense of calmness that releases the spirit and enhances life – while in the more domestic works, through

material and colour a reassuring warm environment is achieved for human delight.

The Gulbenkian Gallery in Lisbon is likely to be one of his most eloquent works, for it unites spatial and structural concerns in a building type where the dialogue between plan and section, between form and light, is of primary consideration. There is particular revelation of the architect's method in the way the section of the building is 'brought forward', modified and given significance to become the 'portico' entrance. The total nature of the design is such that it reaches the point where it could be regarded as a paradigm of the architect's artistic philosophy. The architecture is serene and independent, yet entirely sympathetic to the subject. One feels how appropriate it is that this late work should be in a region where the architecture has been of such abiding interest to the architect and is also a building that is devoted to those arts with which he has had such a long and deep involvement.

The book gains wider significance for the inclusion of what Martin would deny was architectural history. It represents him as architectural essayist and teacher, notably with his recent reflections on the architectural ideas of the thirties, 'Notes on a Developing Architecture'. This, together with reflections on his own background (the Arts and Crafts movement, Lutyens and the end of Beaux Arts training), shows the varied influences on his development – the context of about fifty years' work of someone who was committed to the search for the principles inherent in the idea of CIAM and the MARS Group rather than the ideology and slogans that went with the fight for work and recogni-

tion in those heady days.

In the writings, there is a demonstration of the way ideas in architecture develop from analysis of tasks, from precedents and concepts, to realisations. The illuminating essay on some drawings of Leonardo is particularly relevant with respect to our understanding of the process of design, a process equally demonstrated by the selection of completed work or projects, showing how forms have been ordered round particular problems and then developed in a 'flux of mutation', and how parts can be brought together into a total solution – demonstrating that we are not concerned with either/or but with a whole range of factors that have to be brought into a harmony, art and science, and that this constitutes the theme of architecture in our time.

In writing these notes I have followed to some extent an address given at the RIBA in 1973 when Martin received the Royal Gold Medal. That touched on his wider contribution; here I have only attempted to define some aspects of his work and approach to design. Concluding now, as then, I draw on Martin's own words at a previous Gold Medal occasion: of Aalto he spoke of

distinctions between architecture of his kind, which is ordered, controlled, worked for and not just accidental; between the detail of his kind, which is the result of the completeness of a great idea and not just a trivial end in itself: between his kind of architecture, which cannot easily be drawn but rests in the building itself . . . and that which looks well only on the drawing board.[5]

Exterior and interior view of the extension to the studios at the King's Mill; the author.

Introduction

The book: structure and content

This book is not intended to be simply another set of illustrations of an architect's buildings. If its contents are worth assembling at all it seems to me that this will be mainly for several other reasons.

The first is that the work illustrated and described spans a period of around fifty years. It started during a period of change. Between 1933 and 1983 I have worked with a succession of younger colleagues, but in the main I think that we have shared a common view about architecture. It is therefore just possible that the work illustrated in this volume may demonstrate a developing attitude to architecture within all the changing shifts of opinion and fashion that have taken place from the thirties to the present day.

This leads to my second reason. During this period architecture has often been classified into different and apparently conflicting categories. Stress has been placed on rationalism, on technology, on the social relevance of architecture, on changes of taste and fashion or even, more recently, on revivals. In all this confusion it seems to me to be worth recording something far more relevant to an architect's activities: that is, how he and a particular group around him have thought about, composed and constructed buildings, and have tried to create out of all the disparate and conditioning elements some sense of harmony and formal order. This conception of what architecture is has always seemed to me to be so fundamental that I have never thought it necessary to stress the point. I do so now. It is central to the content of this book.

My third reason for publication is simply that the work illustrated shows the variety of problems that we have been asked to consider during a particular period of time. This in itself may be of interest. The range extends from larger projects which evolve within, and sometimes suggest, a possible urban pattern, to small-scaled and anonymous infilling. But in between these two extremes there is a main body of work which has allowed us to consider different classes or types of building developed in relation to changing conditions and different sites over a period of years. The work therefore demonstrates not only the range of problems in which one architect has been involved but within this, what may be equally important, both individual buildings and a series of buildings of different types in which some developing design ideas may become apparent.

My final reason is related to this and I have considered it important enough to try to develop the theme in the second section of this introduction. It is concerned with the continuity of architectural ideas as much as it is with the elements that change. The work illustrated in this book began when there was certainly a change in the way in which architects designed their buildings and in the emphasis that they gave to certain elements. But that is not to say that they ceased to organise and compose their work or that the forms that they created ceased to have any deeper meaning. I have in recent years valued very greatly the work of those scholars whose essays have concentrated on an examination of the ways in which architects in different and contrasting periods have organised the form of their buildings, and the changing intentions in this central process of architectural thought. This kind of assessment deepens our understanding of architecture itself and at the same time provides a more valid critical assessment of the process of change.

In contrast to this, the propaganda associated with the development of the early Modern Movement and the reactions against it seem to be both divisive and irrelevant. The work illustrated in this book was never intended to be propaganda for a particular style or fashion, and certainly not for any political attitude. It is rather the result of the way in which a particular architect and his associates have interpreted the developing art of architecture, and as such it has as much to do with an immediate past as with an emerging future.

These are some of the ideas that have influenced the form and the structure of this book. My work as an architect has itself been divided into three distinct phases. From 1933 to 1939 I taught and worked as a private architect. A central period after this was spent in public offices, and I returned to private practice and teaching in 1956. To attempt a chronological arrangement could have resulted in some confusion. I have chosen instead to preface the work with some introductory notes about my own background and my particular attitude of mind towards architecture: that clearly has some bearing on the work illustrated. The main body of the book then concentrates on the projects that have been developed since 1956 and which demonstrate some of the ideas that have been outlined in the introductory text. The general content is then divided into two main parts.

Part 1 deals with those buildings which, though built at different times over a period of years, can nevertheless be grouped into types or categories. The arrangement is thematic; the intention is to demonstrate within each category any continuity of thought or development of a vocabulary that exists. It has something to say about the form of buildings.

Part 2 deals with buildings in relation to their context in the urban environment and it concentrates on two aspects of the problem. The first is that in the changing patchwork of the city there are still buildings or areas which retain (or where it is possible to create) some emphasis of civic, cultural, religious or educational significance. The point that is stressed is not just one of preservation, it is rather the need to recognise and to create a sense of identity that is so vital to certain areas of a city. The second aspect of this problem of the urban environment starts from the point that by far the greatest mass of building in the city is neither significant nor symbolic: it consists of buildings or areas which make the existing fabric of our environment and where change, however small, may provide the opportunity to enhance or to destroy.

Finally there is an Appendix. In this I have included notes on the private and public work in which I was involved from 1933–56. It is a commentary in retrospect and it runs in parallel with a second general essay on that period which I have called 'Notes on a Developing Architecture'. In addition there are also some notes from lectures and papers which like the buildings themselves have been produced at different dates over a considerable period of time. Some of these have relevance to the illustrated buildings or, at least, they are part of the same developing process of thought about architecture. Other notes are included simply because I found the subject matter relevant to the overall theme. In general I have let them stand as they were written.

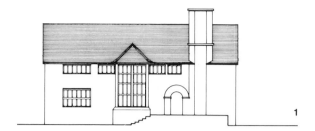

1

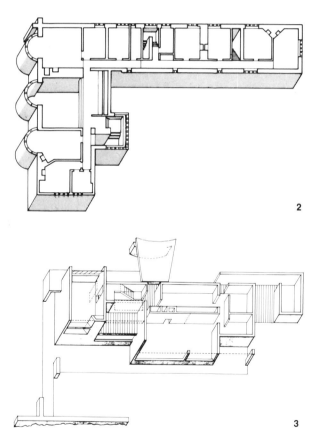

2

3

Background and belief

In this essay I have used the word 'compose' to describe what seems to me to be a central activity for the architect at any period. I am aware of the recent unpopularity of this word but I can think of no better description of the process by which an architect invents and organises the relationship of forms to produce a total coherence. In music 'composing' is clearly understood as a creative and developing process. I see no reason why this is not true also in architecture.

I do not think that it is easy, or even possible, for an architect to describe all the influences, the responses to a problem and its setting, the references to ideas and forms recollected somewhere in the mind, that cause him to arrange and compose the forms of his building in a particular way. Frank Lloyd Wright, who could certainly achieve a consistent result, could only speak generally about his effort to create an 'organic architecture: the growth in space and time of an idea'.[1] Alvar Aalto made a number of references to his own work as a kind of parallel to, and image of, nature itself.[2]

Nor do I think it possible to generalise about the responses of all the individuals who may see and use an architect's buildings. The question of how architecture communicates with the public and what is read into it is equally difficult. Lutyens clearly built into the strict composition of his architecture the added references to style or time. On the other hand Aalto, without a trace of overt symbolism, claimed that he worked with the 'little man' in mind and there is plenty of evidence from his own country to show that he made this contact and that his work received some popular support.

This question of the relationship between the initial impulse or motivation embedded in the way in which an architect works, and the meanings with which it may be charged, seems to me to be important enough to receive some consideration. I start from the simple and personal viewpoint that what I have most appreciated and admired in architecture is the sense of an effort to create an order and coherence of spaces and of forms. The question of how a building is put together, how it has been composed around a particular idea or problem, is at the root of architectural thought. It is the thread that connects the developing work of a period, no matter what differences of reference and communication it may contain.

In contrast to this as a starting point, it is equally clear that there has also existed the attempt, by deliberate and overt references, to stimulate a particular kind of public response. It was apparent forty years ago when 'futuristic' decoration was used as some kind of symbol of a new age. It is apparent now when forms are introduced into architecture at the design stage as a kind of quotation which is intended to evoke particular references or meanings.

There is of course no guarantee that any of these allusions will be understood, and the argument advanced here is that they form a doubtful starting point for architectural thought. The process of creating architecture around evolving principles of design and changing problems is far more central; and the process which is central to the creation of architecture is also central to any critical understanding of architectural thought.

During the last twenty years, one school of criticism at least has concentrated on this attempt to understand and clarify this central and evolving design process within which an architect works. In the light of that understanding, design can be seen as a continuing theme changing and re-emerging out of itself into new and developing forms. But these critical studies have added more than this. In the attempt to understand what it is that is being composed they have at the same time helped to clarify the place of meaning and allusion within that composition itself.

I am quite sure that I cannot argue this question of form and its meanings in any adequate way. I can simply illustrate, by descriptive reference, some aspects of this problem that are within my own experience.

I begin with my own background. I was encouraged from my youth to study traditional architecture and in particular the craft of building in stone or working in timber. If I have any sense of craft, that is to say of skill in the making and care about the way things are put together, it comes from this background. (To which I should add that any feeling that I have of form, volume, mass and hollowing out and interlocking composition was enriched and developed by long hours of drawing and rendering in a Beaux Arts tradition – and I still draw in similar terms with pleasure.[3])

But it was the creative use of the craft of building, for instance in the work of Edgar Wood (1860–1935) and J. H. Sellars (1861–1954), that was immediately available to me, and the master craftsman of my youth was Lutyens (1869–1944) whose work at that time I had never seen. The most important survey of Lutyens' work was to be found in Laurence Weaver's *Houses and Gardens of Edwin Lutyens* published in 1913, but his more recent work was readily available in the periodicals. Deanery Gardens (1901) was for me the supreme example of the master craftsman at work.

The attraction of Deanery Gardens was not just the craft. It was the organisation of forms that could produce the asymmetrical composition of its main elevation. This is Lutyens in his vernacular phase with some links at least with English Free School methods of design. It was that method with its informality, its planning arranged around use, site, and aspect that had done so much to produce a new open ended approach and which was to leave such a rich legacy for the future of English domestic architecture. For my generation it opened up the possibility of a continuing and developing process of design related to different needs and changing conditions.

It is of course well known that Lutyens in his later work moved steadily away from the principles of English Free School design towards a more formalised method of composition that reached its climax in the Viceroy's house at New Delhi.[4] These differences were recognised at the time but not clearly understood. Some of my acquaintances who had worked in Lutyens' office knew that he had his own private geometry. It was, I think, in the main a working geometry based on *T* square, set square and compasses. It established for him an ordering principle that left him entirely free to develop such ideas as the diagonal approach and plan of Greywalls (1901) or the brilliant linkage arrangements at Whalton Manor (1908).

But that is the drawing board technique. In order to understand the mental process through which he composed his buildings it is necessary to consider the frontal view of Heathcote (1906) and to appreciate to the full its symmetry and balance. Confronted by that, any student of the classical tradition might expect a

series of volumes opening out along a central axis with balancing compartments on either side. To make the point more clearly it might be worth examining the plan of a Palladian villa on which the cross axes have been drawn. The internal volumes are of course directly related to the axes and to the external form. But that is not at all what happens at Heathcote. Once inside the balanced mass of the exterior, the visitor's movement through the building is controlled by volumes and composition of a totally different kind.

Some time ago now, Allan Greenberg provided quite the most penetrating analysis that I have seen so far.[5] Greenberg studied five Lutyens houses built between 1902 and 1911 and brought out several common characteristics. Heathcote illustrates the principle. Within a square or *H*-shaped plan all have a central core: fireplace, stair or void. All have a symmetrical system in the external mass. The various cross axes and sub axes applied to this show a possible internal correspondence. But in place of this, the axes and external mass are contradicted by the internal spaces and in particular by the weaving movement of the circulation itself which is brilliantly and independently composed. It is a powerful and rich system at once personal and universally recognisable.

Leaving on one side the monumental buildings, I place this kind of composition at the centre of Lutyens' achievement. Greenberg maintains that the principle applies in some degree to all the Lutyens houses including the Viceroy's house at Delhi. He also provides some historical and critical perspective by relating the method used by Lutyens to the houses of Frank Lloyd Wright. Wright's houses too are often built around a core, usually the fireplace, but in contrast to the separate rooms and weaving circulation of the Lutyens houses, in the Wright house the space extends outwards from the core in a series of controlled sequences perfectly coordinated within the structural system. It is an architecture with a new and integrated formal system and it speaks for a future.

Critics of the calibre of Greenberg, Rowe, Colquhoun or Frampton[6] who have examined the systems within which architects compose their buildings have extended our understanding. When this formal aspect is examined it helps to explain what it was in the Lutyens buildings that Frank Lloyd Wright could admire and the qualities of composition that Le Corbusier could appreciate at New Delhi.

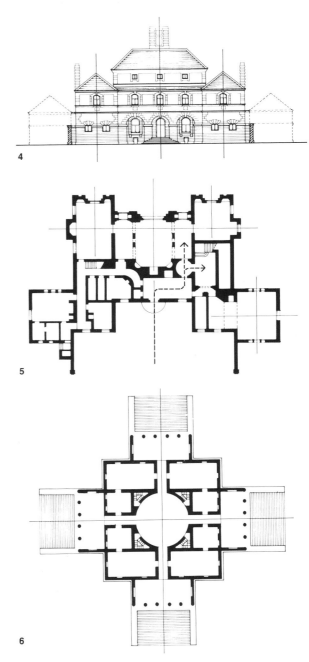

1. Deanery Gardens. 2. Free School planning, Voysey's Broadleys, 1898–9. 3. House in Cumberland 1937, planning around use, site and aspect (p. 203). 4. Heathcote, elevation. 5. Heathcote, plan. 6. Villa Rotonda, Palladio.

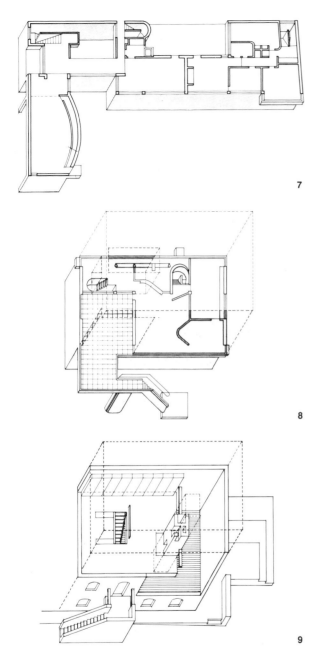

7. La Roche house. **8.** Villa at Garches. **9.** Interior space and cubic volume, the Mill, Shelford (pp. 177–81). **10, 11 & 12.** Forms and materials, Alvar Aalto.

Whatever the ultimate differences, there is a developing process of formal relationships within which architects compose their buildings. I now see that the sense of this developing continuity played an important part in my own background. The early admiration for the composition of a Lutyens building was widened by the experience of seeing work which was related to a different set of problems and composed in a totally different manner.

I was in Paris round about 1930 and met Oscar Stonorov, who had at that time just compiled (jointly with Boesiger) the first volume of Le Corbusier's collected work (1910–29), published by Dr Girsberger in 1930. For me at that time there was certainly no doubt about the organising principles behind Le Corbusier's work. Stonorov was not slow to contrast this with the 'modernistic' work which was then the popular fashion. Indeed the plan and the internal volumes of the La Roche house made the comparison obvious. But Le Corbusier himself was more specific. He had by that time completed the villa at Garches and the Villa Savoye was under construction. In the sketches which he made to illustrate some principles of design in the modern house, and which were published in the Girsberger volume, he defined different types of composition.[7] The first of these (La Roche) he describes as picturesque. This may be compared, with some profit, to the asymmetrical and loosely linked composition used by architects of the English Free School. But the remaining types were, when I first saw them, of a new and quite different order. They were generated within a cubic volume: they combined an external envelope, the pure prism, with an intricate internal plan arrangement which is called the 'organisation within'. The 'organisation within' is something more than a proportional system; though Le Corbusier, like Lutyens, has his own version of that. The organising principle behind the design of the villa at Garches with the interlocking volumetric effects illustrates a widening of architectural ideas. It opens up completely new solutions to the internal planning of buildings.

In the villa at Garches the structure produces a total cube: the cube itself is then divided into a sequence of interlocking volumes and spaces built up around different uses. Visually each space within the plan is seen and sensed in relation to the next; the view extends right across the entire cube; the subdividing walls form a series of screens defining individual areas but constantly exposing the spaces beyond.[8]

This kind of thoughtful analysis of composition looks beyond the surface of a building. It is concerned with the central ideas that govern the way in which an architect works when he designs a building. It emphasises a continuity of composition as a principle but it clarifies differences and recognises change. The changes that were being demonstrated in the early work of Le Corbusier had an application to an increasing range of new problems, and they offered immense scope for elaboration and development.

Such an analysis is not without its difficulties; however fundamental, it is in a sense too abstract. Quite apart from the problem of describing and defining the different principles that are at work and the different architectural effects that are presented by Lutyens' Heathcote or Le Corbusier's Villa Savoye, these buildings contain references to other values. In addition to the powerful system of composition that Lutyens employed, the Lutyens house is also consciously designed as an evocation of something else. Although it was built of brick, stone and timber in the twentieth century, the materials themselves had to give the impression of time that had passed. The reference to historical style was another aspect of this same idea. Lutyens, as Robert Lutyens said of his father, added in his buildings a considerable 'repertoire of colloquial allusion and quotation'.[9] Peter Inskip has explained this by the suggestion that Lutyens 'worked largely for clients who, following the nineteenth century pattern, sought historical styles for the security that they offered'.[10] These were buildings for what Robert Lutyens has called a *transient* generation and it can be argued that they introduced a transient element into the architecture itself.

It was, I think, this added element of reference and the changing allusions which were built up around the work of architects of another generation which in the thirties placed Lutyens in a kind of limbo, and I have not the slightest doubt that in recent years the more superficial critics have placed Le Corbusier in a similar category. In contrast to the historical references that Lutyens most certainly had in mind, a whole series of implied and often specific evocations was built up around the work of Le Corbusier and the Modern Movement by its propaganda.

In spite of the considerable range of new architectural problems that were identified in the thirties and the possibility of developing and elaborating a vocabulary around its formal innovations, this is not what is usually described. The early Modern Movement had built up its own set of references: the industrial product and the steel and concrete structure were the overt symbols of a new technology, and a new age of rational analysis and technical invention was written into the description of architecture as if they were essential to its creation.

These are the changing references that have divided the work of Lutyens and Le Corbusier and indeed many members of a more recent generation into separate camps and even into opposing factions. In view of all this it is of some interest to ask what it was that caused Frank Lloyd Wright to admire the Lutyens houses or encouraged Le Corbusier to pay his tribute to New Delhi. Certainly not, I think, the external allusions which Frank Lloyd Wright would have despised and Le Corbusier would not have understood. What they saw and valued in the Lutyens work was the originality with which he composed his buildings and the drama of the effects that this could produce. What they recognised was something of the essence of architecture that they introduced into their own work but developed and elaborated in their own very different ways.

The point that arises from this is the possibility of recognising and understanding the central medium through which architecture operates at different times and, within this, recognising distinctions and developments. Viewed thus, the formal composition used by Lutyens is something totally related to the problems and the culture of his time and it has left a rich legacy. The formal systems which are represented in the work of Le Corbusier and others are systems of a very different order and have their roots in a widely different range of problems and background; in my view they are part of a process which is still developing.

To recognise the character of such formal changes and to see the way in which they have been reassessed and redeveloped in relation to an increasing range of problems goes to the root of architecture and is the basis of all constructive criticism. This is something very different from the superficial assessment of appearances or the immediate classifications and 'isms' that have been used to describe contemporary work during my lifetime (rationalism, functionalism, modernism), all of which have seemed to me to be irrelevant and remarkably short-lived. They are also divisive and misleading in relation to the intentions of the architecture itself. As Edgar Wood once said in a different context, 'That is the language of the classifier. It never enters the mind of the artist.'[11]

And now the classifications are being extended into 'late modernism', 'post-modernism', etc. In that this latest manifestation re-emphasises the fact that architecture is an art, I can only applaud its intentions. But when architecture loses all sense of solving a problem and moves into a world of metaphor and decorative allusion, I find the result is closer to stage scenery in its intentions and as temporary in its effect.[12]

For me at least the cultivation of these superficial readings and references is no starting point for creative architecture. What has remained is something much deeper than that. It is to be seen in the developing process through which architects have taken problems of use and structure and have resolved these to create a new sense of order, coherence and harmony out of each new and changing problem. What I have observed and absorbed as part of my own experience is a constantly changing and developing process of architectural thought. And the strength of that lies, not in the pre-defined objectives and limits of a fashion or a popular style, but in the depth of formal meaning and the range, diversity and variety which architecture continuously explores.

The history of the development of the architecture of the last half century could now I think be written with a different emphasis. With the benefit of historical perspective it is possible to see that the narrow limits and classifications that have been used to describe modern architecture were wholly inadequate. We can now see the way in which the early assumptions and rationalisations were systematically overtaken and changed by what was being developed on the ground. We can see that numerous individuals whose early work was in some way linked with the initial propaganda have continuously widened the range of architectural ideas: how Breuer, for example, who did so much to pioneer the development of new materials and techniques in his metal and plywood furniture of the twenties, was saying in the thirties that the new ideas in architecture and design would have existed even without these innovations. In Holland the line of thought starting with Berlage develops its own set of ideas, whilst in

10

11

12

13

14

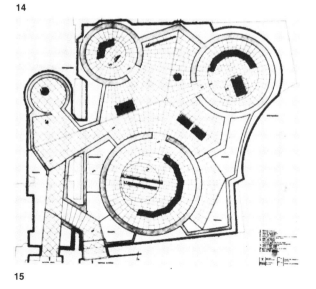

15

13. Natural materials. 14 & 15. The sense of space and the sense of enclosure, Franco Albini.

Germany Behrens' 'Fitness for Purpose', which had such an influence, is again broadened by the work of Haring and Scharoun. In France there is the Maison de Verre by Bijvoet and Chareau and all that this has meant to the transformation of technology into poetic expression. And of course there is Aalto.

What we see in fact is a highly complex pattern of developing and overlapping ideas. History is complex. And viewed from the point of view of history these extensions and elaborations of a variety of ideas do not represent oppositions. If any proof of that is needed it must rest in the fact that many of these varied aspects of development can be found embodied in the work of an individual architect. I could, I think, argue the case convincingly by reference to Le Corbusier himself: the ideas embodied in the Cité de Refuge or, in contrast, the chapel at Ronchamp, or the smaller houses designed in traditional materials illustrate quite different facets of his ranging thought.

But the retrospective exhibition of the work of the distinguished Italian architect Franco Albini (1905–77) brings out the point most clearly. Albini is in a sense typical of the second generation of modern architects and his work is now sufficiently well documented to take its place in any historical analysis.[13] His early work on low cost housing is of course rooted in the 'green city' and rationalised housing concepts of CIAM. But from this point on and in a series of brilliant exhibitions, the rational elements (the frame, the cage, the suspension system, the opaque or transparent planes) are transformed into an architecture of endless space and light. In contrast to this there is the volumetric enclosure of space, an architecture of the cave, in his remarkable Treasury of S. Lorenzo in Genoa. Each new problem has its own appropriate solution.

The Pirovani Hotel is another interesting example. It is built of stone and timber, but to regard this building as a kind of vernacular revival would, I know, be a complete misreading of the architect's intentions. It is indeed more likely to have its roots in Pagano and his rationalist interpretation of traditional housing. Stone and timber are materials that are well suited to the problem of building on a mountain, and what has been called this 'renewed interpretation'[14] is a method that Albini continued to explore with great skill in the typology of his later housing. And when the new technology is appropriate it is exploited with much formal invention in buildings like the Rinascente in

Rome in which structure and servicing elements are welded together in a highly creative formal achievement, unique, I think, for its time.

Historical studies which would outline in the work of an individual architect this opening up of ideas could demonstrate quite clearly the way in which the early tenets of the Modern Movement were elaborated. In the case of Albini, the development of its elements, like for instance the staircase, would in themselves form an interesting study. But it is the total range that is extensive and in itself an indication of widening areas of architectural thought. The range includes industrial design, furniture, housing and villas, stores and offices, the beautifully landscaped open air stadium in Genoa and the design and equipment of the underground stations in Milan. Add to this the restoration and adaptation of distinguished historical buildings like the Palazzo Rosso or the Palazzo Bianca in Genoa, the Bresa Painting Gallery in Milan, and finally, towards the end of a long career, the sensitive restorations and additions for the Civic Museums of the Cloister of the Hermits in Padua and St Augustine in Genoa, and the range, breadth and originality of the work is immensely impressive.

These brief references are intended simply as an indication of a line of thought that seems to me to have been overlooked. It is concerned with the fact that many architects whose work has been connected with some of the early ideas of the Modern Movement do not fit easily into its accepted classifications. They have on the contrary continuously challenged these and in doing so they have over a lifetime widened the architectural language by the buildings that they have created.

The range of formal innovation, even if it covered only the work of an early generation, would be extensive. But again with hindsight, we can now see that each successive generation has not only widened the range but has developed and deepened certain lines of thought within it. I have in mind three of these in particular. The first is that extra dimension which, over the years, has been given to the response to environment and setting, and nowhere has this been more clearly demonstrated than in the work of Giancarlo de Carlo in Urbino. It is a contribution that has lasted for more than twenty years.[15] It is a classic example of the way in which an ancient town can be 're-structured' (to use his word) around new needs, how old buildings can be given a new life and how new and completely contemporary buildings can take their place within the overall context.

The second dimension is the line of evolution around the applications of a new technology. It is high technology transformed by the imagination into the work of art and it has produced in the last few years a number of brilliant examples. And thirdly there is a development, linked with this, that reaches outside the boundaries of architecture itself: it is the extension of design into industrial production. During the twenties and thirties, Breuer, Aalto and the Italians were all designing furniture for mass production and the field was expanding into light fittings, radios and electrical appliances. By 1935, the *Architectural Review* could devote an entire number to the illustration of items of industrial design. A few of these were so good that they are still in production today. But all that, however important for my own generation, is small-scaled when compared to the range of well-designed industrial products that now exists.

I have called this kind of broadening of design ideas the development of a language. Somewhere within all this there is the possibility of trying to understand how a developing language communicates. Here again we might begin by making a closer examination of something that has happened: we might ask for example how it was that the work of a man like Aalto, for the greater part of his life at least, made so immediate an appeal to so many of his countrymen. In making that contact I am not aware of any stylistic or historical references in his work, at least after the studies for the Civic Guards building and the early entry for the Viipuri Library in 1927. From 1933 on the design of that library has been transformed into the language of forms that Aalto developed and used throughout his lifetime.

Aalto has on several occasions indicated or described some of the ideas in his mind that may have influenced the form of his buildings. In the case of Viipuri there was, behind the stepped levels and the carefully studied daylighting, a whole series of impressions of the light and the natural landscape in which he had grown up and by which he was surrounded.[16] Some aspect of this has certainly to be considered in relation to any question of communication. So too, has the fact that Aalto worked in materials and with a technology which were familiar to his countrymen. Above all, perhaps, there is the fact that

he worked on problems, like modest housing, small factories, and buildings for small-scaled civic communities (libraries, galleries, town halls) which were known and understood by the communities for whom he worked.

If the history of recent architecture were to be set out afresh along the lines that I have indicated, the range of ideas that have been explored and built might be given a different dimension. The early ideas may be seen in relation to a continuous series of re-evaluations that have widened and deepened architectural thought and which have still to be filled out into their potential. It will then also be possible to see this creative contribution against the background of the generalised and superficial form of building which has by now spread across the world and which in itself requires some historical explanation.

I include in this core of creative development all that kind of architecture that Breuer once described as having 'a mental surplus, an emotional plus, a conceptual generosity, a stance that is optimistic and creative'. I do not see the separate lines of advance that individuals may follow as oppositions. They are all aspects of that kind of architecture that does not rely on 'styling' the passing fashion, or the external allusion, but which is discovered in the imaginative solution of a known problem. And in that kind of architecture the meaning and the communication are built into the solution from that complex texture of formal values that lie deeply at the centre of each architect's experience. I have no doubt at all that when these are translated into creative architecture they can be appreciated and shared as part of a common experience.

Postscript

I am well aware that the interpretation of architecture that has been expressed in these notes, though it may be shared by others of my generation, may also be limited and prescribed by attitudes that have been developed in my own lifetime. Thanks to Professor Gombrich I now recognise this as the code within

which each architect works at a particular period in history.

The argument that I have advanced is that the code within which architects work does change and that the forms of architecture are part of a continuous process of development. But within this process, and throughout all such changes, what remains constant is the central medium of composition through which architecture operates. The kind of change that can occur within the limits of this general conception of the medium is, of course, a commonplace of history. One set of formal values is, in time, replaced by others of quite different formal intention.

But I have also drawn a distinction between this type of change, which is not a difference of kind, and the fashions and applied symbols that have been added at different times. This too has happened in history. The distinction is an important one: I have identified changes within the medium itself as those which have more lasting values, and I have associated the applied references with a passing appeal.

It is I think the first which is described by Gombrich when he says, 'a man can only be creative in relation to problems that he seeks to solve . . . working . . . within an established medium'.[17] The second seems to me to be again described by Gombrich in any work where the 'professed aim is to create an atmosphere . . . creating a mood rather than transmitting a meaning'.[18]

And there is no doubt that it is the second that has increased enormously since the nineteenth century and is being encouraged and promoted so widely at the present time. When the emphasis relies solely on eclectism and the applied form, whether it is a historic reference, or the technique of the commercial symbol, or the ephemeral effect of the stage set, it has in my terms ceased to have that deeper meaning that I have associated with architecture. It may be of course that these are the very aspects that a consumer society is more likely to encourage and accept. If this is so then the architects of a future generation will need to decide whether the medium that has so far been central to architectural thought can be continued or whether this is to be replaced by buildings of a more immediate appeal. There is indeed a 'glass of fashion'. But there is also, to be discovered, a 'mould of form', and it is that which has seemed to me to be deeper and more lasting.

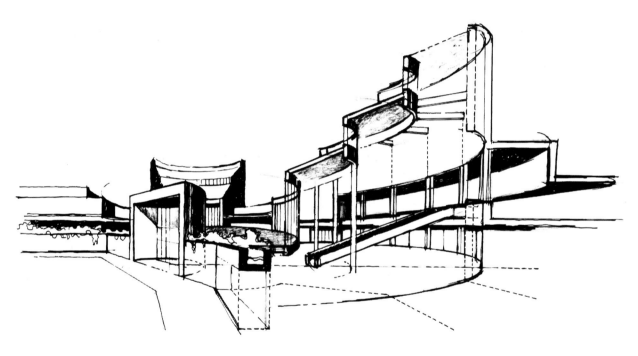

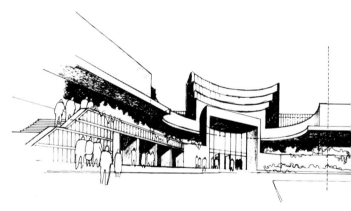

Buildings and form

Part 1 below illustrates the range of forms that has been built up around the exploration of the relationship between forms and different types of use. That in itself demands a continuous exercise of the imagination. It relies on formal invention.

It is this invention of formal relationships that remains constant and illustrations on this page are included here to underline the point. In this case the form evolved from a complex series of relationships between internal routes, junction points and a formal emphasis within the plan. In addition to these considerations the forms are intended to respond to the overall external conditions, for example the focal points that arise from placing an important building within a city plan. The building form in fact becomes a symbol rather than a type and this aspect of the architectural problem is discussed in Part 2, pp. 118 and 137–49.

1 BUILDINGS AND FORM 1956–1983

1

BUILDINGS AND FORM 1956–1983

It seems a suitable moment to remark first, that appropriate technical processes or constructional systems are rooted in and are inseparable from the needs of particular building types; second, that every building type (housing, offices, laboratories, etc.), can be developed to the point at which its own organization and therefore its characteristic forms emerge. These carry with them their own appropriate constructional systems.

The characteristics of the building 'type' are seldom studied except at the level of room relationship within a given envelope. Thus housing, for instance, the office block or the laboratory are repeatedly contained within a similar envelope – the slab. To apply industrialized techniques to these slabs is to mass-produce buildings which may be already obsolete as forms of housing, offices or laboratories. The characteristics of the type have first of all to be discovered and the development of the appropriate constructional system is essentially one of the parts of this process.

Architectural Design (Dec. 1964), p. 595

1. Roman theatre, after Vitruvius. **2.** Palladio's Teatro Olimpico, Vicenza.

1

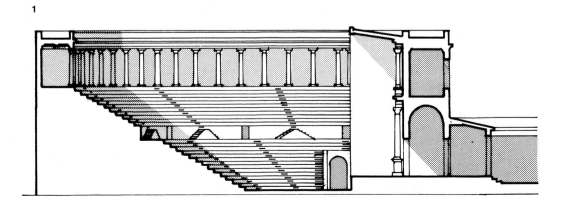

2

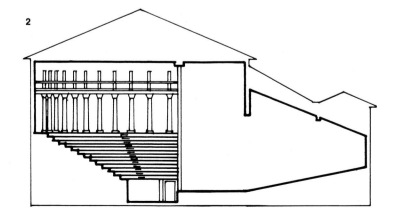

That note was written in 1964. To some extent, at least, it was intended as a protest against the kind of building in which the prevalent tendency seemed to be an over-emphasis of technical processes at the expense of form as a means of accommodating needs.

The reference to the 'type' form perhaps requires some clarification. The recognition of the existence of specific 'type' forms in building and their continuity has a long history. Indeed some nineteenth-century theorists, notably Durand,[1] made this kind of study one of the corner stones of teaching. Durand classified the building types, drawing for instance theatres, stadia, markets, halls of justice, etc., to a common scale, and this method most certainly illustrates the characteristic features of the type form. The system of ordering the spaces within these archetypal forms becomes the basis of his theory. It is a system of axes, hierarchies and balances within the component parts and it has had a lasting influence on many distinguished buildings.

What is not made explicit, however, is the evolutionary process by which the type form itself may develop.[2] On his page of theatre plans, for example, Palladio's theatre at Vicenza is illustrated; its debt to the Roman theatre of Vitruvius and its development beyond this can certainly be inferred, and the adaptation of the theatre plan for larger audiences or more elaborate scenery is explicit in the diagrams. The effect of change is certainly there. But it nevertheless remains true that the 'horseshoe' plan is the consistently adopted theatre form for at least two centuries, in much the same way as the parallel-sided hall remained the established 'type' for concert halls built as far apart as the St Andrew's Hall, Glasgow (1877), the Gewand-

haus, Leipzig (1886) or the Symphony Hall, Boston (1900).

The simple point is that for the difficult and differing acoustic problems of the theatre and the concert hall, these basic types were known to work. Their form depended on precedent. In this particular field at least the important elements that constitute what has been called the evolutionary process are part of a comparatively recent development. They have their roots in fundamental changes in the requirements of the auditorium itself, many of which depend increasingly on the development and improvement of the techniques of predicting acoustic effect.[3]

For me, at least, one of the contributions that has seemed important has been the increased interest in the range of formal solutions to the type form and the body of principles that can be built up from this. In the case of Aalto, for example, the whole corpus of his work can be seen as a series of elaborations of the type forms which he has explored for the concert hall, the library, the gallery and the office building.[4] The evolution of the type has been one of the generating principles of his work, and it is from this that any theoretical argument is most likely to be produced.

One example of this linkage is an article on 'Theory in Practice' published some years ago by Professor Robert Geddes, which describes five buildings from the office of Geddes, Brecher, Qualls and Cunningham and which illustrates very clearly the interactions of form and theory.[5] And it is of course not an accident that this work should emanate from Princeton where so much has been done in the field of historical and theoretical studies.

The five buildings illustrated are all teaching build-

ings for various campus sites: in the words of the author 'the buildings consciously set out to inform each other and thereby gain authority by continuing a line of thought about architecture'. What holds these solutions together as a series is not the technical solution of a common building task but the way in which they are coordinated and controlled into a formal system.

Geddes describes the elements of this system, the analysis of the spatial grids, the structural grids that can accommodate them, the fit between needs and form and the shared vocabulary of special spaces, movement paths and response to landscape and site. The buildings themselves seem to demonstrate a remarkable consistency and continuity in the architecture.

The buildings illustrated in Part 1 of this book were not designed with anything like the explicit theoretical basis that is described by Geddes. The buildings, worked out over a period of twenty-five years or so, can nevertheless be seen in retrospect as a series of groups or 'types'. Each building within the separate groups is in some degree an evolution from a basic type form that we have assumed or attempted to discover, and the process from this point has involved both continuity and innovation.

One stimulus at least was a basic opposition to the idea that fundamentally different needs can be accommodated in some universal envelope. Another was the predominance of blocks or slabs in so much building work. The work described here was in fact preceded by an effort to show that housing at high density did not require tall buildings, and that the mere figure of density is neither good nor bad in itself: we need to know first what kind of living is involved and

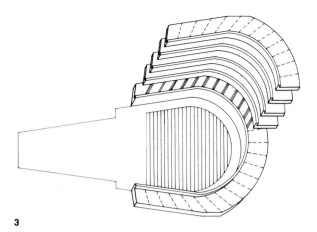

3

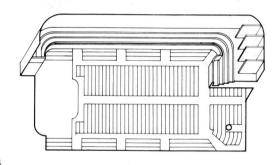

4

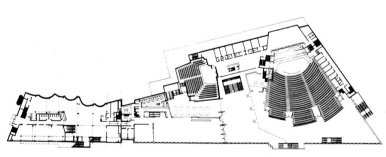

5

3. Theatre, type form. Royal Opera House, Covent Garden, London. 4. Concert hall, type form. Neues Gewandhaus, Leipzig. 5. New auditorium form, Alvar Aalto's Finlandia Concert Hall, Helsinki. This in turn has now been developed in later schemes (Berlin Philharmonic etc.) in which the orchestra is moved forward and is more closely integrated with the audience itself.

what kind of environment is created.

The argument was developed by showing that from a purely statistical point of view a density of one hundred people to the acre could be achieved by means of two storey houses arranged in terraces, three or four storey houses, four storey maisonettes, flats of varying height and of course many combinations of these. Clearly housing at high densities might assume many forms. Its success or failure will be assessed by other issues which would certainly include consideration of such things as the degree of urbanity; the balance of neighbourliness and privacy; the family groupings that can be accommodated and the range of choice offered; the provision of private open space and the way in which open space can be shared. With this interpretation of housing as a background, we were able to show the limitations of tall buildings and to demonstrate that these were not necessary even at quite high densities. We later extended these ideas by general theoretical studies which were taken to the point of geometrical or mathematical proof[6] and we designed a scheme in which low buildings around courts or squares included a wide range of dwellings.

Our studies of housing ended at that point. I am glad to say that the general concept of urban housing as a 'type' form has since that time been developed throughout the country with a degree of elaboration which no individual studies could have achieved. During this same period we also did some work on the design of laboratories and concentrated on spreading and interconnecting forms, but this problem itself was, for us, part of the larger problem of the form of university layout and is illustrated elsewhere.[7]

The work included in Part 1 consists of a number of individual buildings for four main types of use: university residential buildings, libraries, groups of lecture rooms which develop into studies of auditoria for varying uses, and finally an isolated building, a gallery for contemporary art which can nevertheless be regarded as a 'type' form. Although the individual buildings in each group have been built at intervals over a considerable period of time, they have allowed the possibility of some continuous process of design development. By presenting them here in this way it may become possible to see within each group such connecting threads as the buildings retain.

Between 1956 and 1970 our Studio produced a number of schemes for university residential accommodation. We started with the decision that we would use a way of housing a community that had been known to work: the court. We agreed that there might be many other valid assumptions, for example separate blocks or Le Corbusier's individual rooms and terraces entered from a common area below. But given the starting point of the court, we were concerned to follow the patterns of the clusters of rooms that could grow up within this and to test the tight fit that could be developed between the pattern of living and the pattern of the built form and its appropriate structure.[8]

It was from this, we argued, and not from any imposed symbolism that buildings derive their meaning. And I think that we would have added that architecture is not just a symbol of technology: it uses the appropriate technology. From a series of such buildings where the residential pattern is similar (College Hall, Leicester, Harvey Court, Cambridge, Royal Holloway College, Egham, and the postgraduate residence for Balliol and St Anne's Colleges, Oxford) and

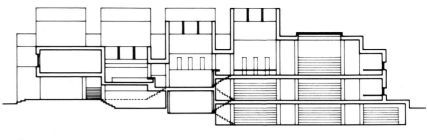

6

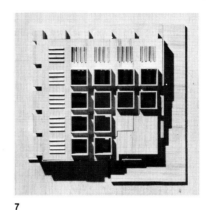

7

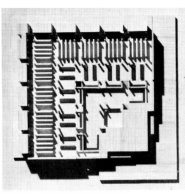

8

where the constructional system is the same (brick or block load bearing cross walls), it becomes possible to examine a range of built forms as the staircase arrangements and the room clusters change to adapt themselves to the orientation of a court, or to the linear forms that are required on the steep slopes of Royal Holloway College, or to the narrow south facing site of the postgraduate residence at Oxford.

We had the opportunity to follow this theme once again in another class of building, libraries. Clearly there are many libraries which, because of their special use or scale, work extremely well within the traditional buildings that house them. In other cases the special nature of the surroundings and the area of the site itself may set limitations; we built one such example at Pembroke College, Oxford and it is included in Part 2 because of this overriding consideration.

But in the case of the Manor Road Libraries at Oxford we had the problem of considering a possible basic form for the library plans. The advantage of this particular programme was that any proposal for a general form could be tested for three different libraries, each one with a different number of readers and books. In following up our general idea of what it is that gives meaning and significance to a building, Sandy Wilson, Patrick Hodgkinson and I worked through a considerable number of design ideas to try to discover a generating form. At Manor Road we were able to test this and apply it in relation to three types of library which were in turn related to each other within a total group.

At the heart of this library group and tightly related to it in plan, section and access points, there are two large lecture rooms and some seminar space. This

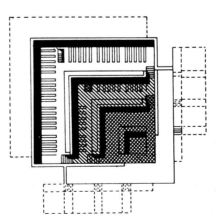

9

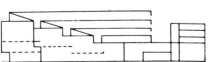

6, 7 & 8. Early studies of the library type form: corner entrance control and catalogue, L-shaped reading area, outside this L-shaped stack space, and around this again a band of carrels. The section introduced half levels which made it possible for a reading area to be associated with two levels of stack if desirable. The roof modelling is related to daylighting in the areas below. **9.** A development to suggest a possible plan for an expandable library.

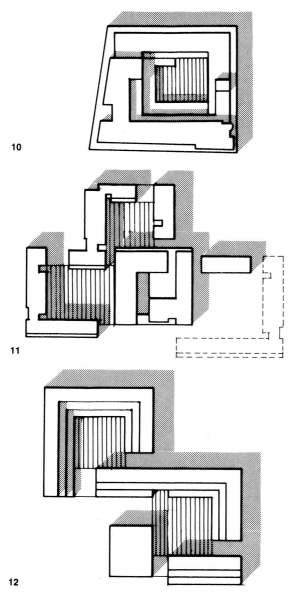

10

11

12

10, 11 & 12. Three developments of a type form: university residential building. 10. Scheme for King's College Hostel, Cambridge. The court of this building is hollowed out within a restricted urban site. 11. Leicester, College Hall women's hostel. The developed court plan built around the social building. The residential blocks have single banked south rooms and double banked rooms facing east–west. 12. Court development, Harvey Court, Cambridge. External staircase position; horizontal room clusters; south, east and west facing internal terraces.

now seen in retrospect was the start of another series of studies over the years built up aroud rooms for speech or the performance of music: auditoria. There are also groups of lecture rooms associated with the Arts building at Hull, but here the main auditorium itself (Middleton Hall), though linked to the lecture rooms, is virtually free-standing and is modelled within its surrounding base of promenades and special rooms; these include a small art gallery, a chapel and an enclosed garden court. The Cambridge Music School is again an auditorium surrounded by a belt of teaching rooms and foyers separated from the main central room by planted courtyards. Later variants include several schemes for the indoor–outdoor auditoria of a college group.

The clustering of auditoria in relation to attendant communal and circulation areas reaches its clearest expression in the competition scheme for the Arts Faculty at Bristol, in which the changing site levels produce a series of planes throughout the length of the building and an external arena links the faculty itself to the higher level of the central university buildings. And later at Glasgow, in the building for the Royal Scottish Academy of Music and Drama with its theatre, concert hall, laboratory theatre, recital rooms and teaching areas, the grouping of rooms is demonstrated in its most elaborate form and draws upon many of the earlier ideas, particularly those that come directly from the experience of building the Music School at Cambridge.

It becomes quite clear that in each building 'type' new work has in some sense been an elaboration of the earlier models. And throughout the work as a whole there are other unifying elements. Since the early work

at Harvey Court there has usually been an underlying grid which defines spatial arrangements and coordinates these with a structural system. In the case of Harvey Court the structural system is load bearing brickwork and it is this system (combined with frames where long spans are required) that has been used most frequently in subsequent buildings.

The grid, as used in these buildings, is not an attempt to find a system of numbers; it is a discipline or matrix within which forms can be organised. Square grids of 3·6 metres, or in the case of buildings of larger scale 4·8 metres, form the basic field, and simple subdivisions or multiples of these establish wall thicknesses and room sizes. The structure allows the enclosure and the identification of special areas (for instance the lecture room clusters at Bristol) or the opening out of circulation areas by brick pier supporting systems (as in the circulation routes and assembly areas at Bristol or the foyers of the Cambridge Music School or the Royal Scottish Academy building in Glasgow). The compositional system includes axes (Cambridge Music School or the Royal Scottish Academy, where the main alignment depends on these) or diagonals which can relate movement within the building to approach and access from outside. The brickwork system allows a solid modelling of the external forms; the capping and the superstructure are usually finished in metal.

Some interesting questions arise here. Are these buildings (which in each category use a limited range of structural techniques, mainly traditional) part of the same family? Do they in any way demonstrate, within a particular category, a whole range of solutions that can be built up from the same basic vocabulary? I would like to think so, for if they do, then they say something

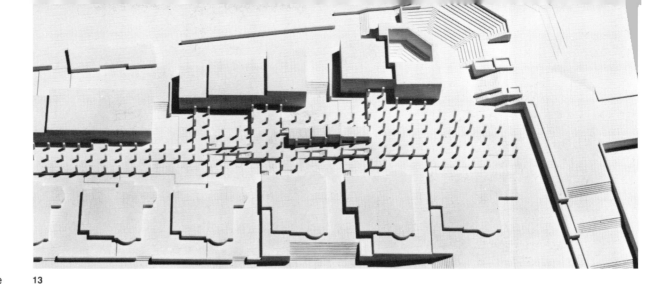

13

not merely about an individual building, but about the continuity of a theme and the variety of form that can be built up from it.

There is something more than this. The scheme proposed at Bristol is no longer simply a set of faculty rooms. It grows out of an existing urban fabric, establishes its own characteristic forms, and this in turn is related to its own focus: the centre of the university. There is consequently an extension of and a development within the texture of the urban fabric itself. The Royal Scottish Academy scheme makes an urban contribution of a different order. It is built within the grid of the city plan. It is related to its neighbours in height and scale, but with its wide surrounding pavement and with the special superstructure of its auditoria, it marks itself out from its neighbours and adds to the variety within the total pattern of the city. There are here two lines of thought which grow from these examples: these are the complementary questions of anonymity and significance and their appropriate place in the changing environment of a city. Work illustrating these things and the supporting discussion have been grouped together in Part 2 of this book.

There is, however, one building which stands on its own: the Gallery of Contemporary Art in Lisbon, and incidentally its children's pavilion. This gallery in its spatial arrangements contains all the special requirements of the 'type' but it responds also to its setting in a landscaped park. Its form is built up around these conditions and the necessity in Portugal to use a reinforced concrete structure. The accommodation for children is also a special building designed around an interpretation of their particular needs.

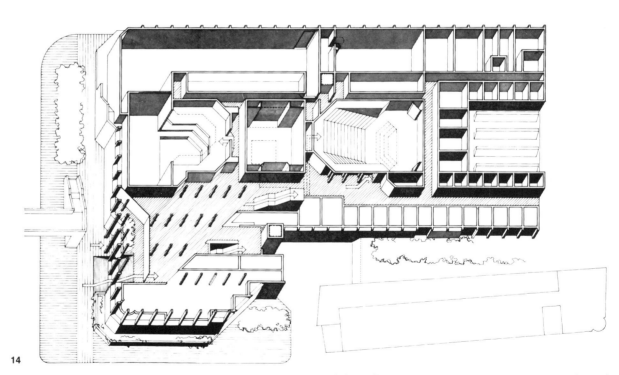

14

13 & 14. Grids, structural systems and movement. 13 shows the open circulation areas and pier system and the closed lecture room clusters in the Bristol competition scheme. 14. The Royal Scottish Academy building, Glasgow, illustrates planning along a main axis and diagonal movement routes. The grid relates both the pier system in the open areas and the general form of the enclosed spaces. The plan incidentally illustrates the contrasting type forms of the theatre, the laboratory theatre and the concert hall.

1 · University residential buildings: families of form

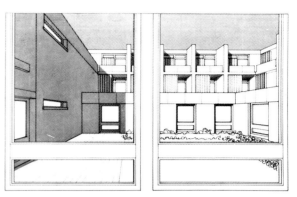

2

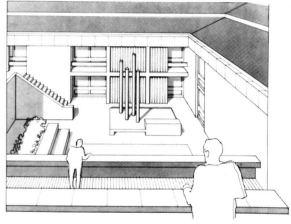

3

1. The traditional court: Loggan's view of St John's College, Cambridge. The powerful unifying form of the court is well illustrated. In the first court, buildings as dissimilar as the chapel, the hall and the residential accommodation are brought together. Though the style changes when new courts are added, the unifying form of the court remains and the pattern of the residential accommodation is constant. A central stair serving two sets on each floor forms the room cluster.

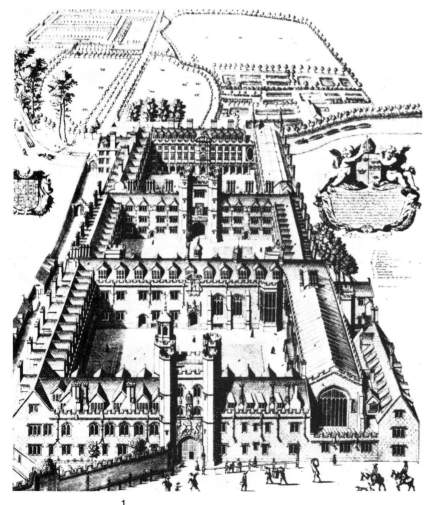

1

In July 1959 the *Architectural Review* published an essay called 'The Collegiate Plan', in which three of the schemes illustrated here were published for the first time and were linked to one central architectural idea – the idea of the court.

The essay made the point that this idea is fundamentally built up around the fit between a community and an architectural organisation. We had observed that in Cambridge from the thirteenth century on, the enclosing wall of buildings around a private space has identified the collegiate community. Courts of varying sizes added to each other have given a reasonable consistency and order to the buildings for the college society. The form of the court has persisted although the architectural style has changed.

The built form (the court) embodies a pattern of use. The individual is identified by the room; the group, by the clusters of rooms around each staircase; and the community, by the enclosed form of the court itself. Additional courts of varying sizes allow the community to grow and create the generic pattern.

Of course this pattern can be rejected in principle. Le Corbusier illustrated a totally different approach when he designed a 'mat' of individual rooms, each with its open terrace and all at first floor level over the common areas. He stressed in fact privacy rather than community, and other solutions may be equally valid. But if an organisational pattern has been known to work, we

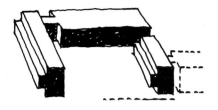

4

5

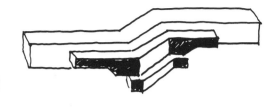

6

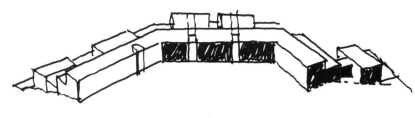

7

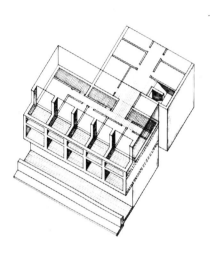

8

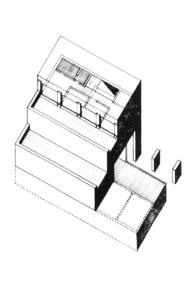

9

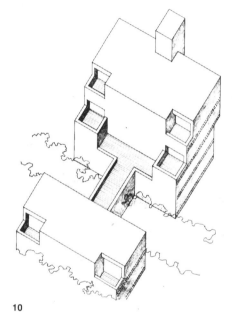

10

The variety of form within the type is the result of several considerations: grouping of rooms around points of access: the orientation of the rooms themselves and the possibility of the development of terraces in relation to this. **2 & 3** illustrate the descending south and west terraces in the central court of King's College Hostel.

The full range developed from these ideas includes the project for King's College Hostel (2 & 3). **4.** College Hall, Leicester, corridor access: preliminary scheme for Harvey Court with its stair and half level arrangement (see later). **5.** Harvey Court, external stair position and horizontal room cluster on each floor. **6.** Balliol and St Anne's, Oxford, an adaptation of 5 to suit a linear south facing site. **7.** Royal Holloway College, staircase and cross corridor to form clusters along a linear development for a steeply sloping site. **8, 9 & 10.** Brick load bearing structural system applied to 4, 5 and 7 above.

saw no reason for disturbing this. Given this as a starting point we were interested to follow through the patterns of the groups that could be developed.

In a series of buildings where the residential pattern is similar the examples in this chapter show a developing range. The buildings achieve a variety of form largely due to variations in the site conditions, in matters of aspect and in the grouping of rooms around points of access. The early project for King's Hostel was a special problem because the site is central and urban: the hostel is a building above another building. The central court is a means of gaining some open space. But with Knighton Hall, Leicester and Harvey Court in Cambridge the choice of the court plan on the

open site is deliberate. The buildings indicate the change from a corridor access form, through various intermediate design stages, to the fully developed staircase and room cluster plan of Harvey Court. In the scheme for the Balliol and St Anne's building the lateral staircase and room cluster remains, but it is now adapted to a linear and restricted site, and in the scheme for Royal Holloway College it is possible to observe the changing form that arises as the staircase access and room clusters adapt themselves to the contours of a steeply sloping site.

In one other residential building, for Peterhouse, Cambridge, the site influences predominate. The first design for this building followed the staircase and room

cluster pattern in two connected low blocks. Finally, in order to preserve as far as possible the sweep of the Deer Park and to remove any obstruction of view from the existing terrace building, these two blocks were superimposed. The resulting taller block still retains the load bearing brick construction and the grouping of rooms around each staircase remains constant.

In all these schemes there are also some basic conditioning elements. Quite apart from any continuity which might result from the organisational form, all these buildings are built in load bearing cross wall construction of brick or block. The capping to the roof is metal and the window frames are timber.

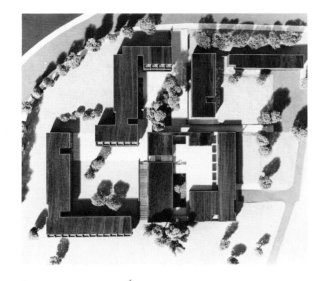

1

College Hall, Knighton, University of Leicester (1956–)

This scheme for a Women's Hall of Residence to house 170 has two related courts associated with a central block of buildings which contains common rooms, dining hall and recreation facilities. A third court, again different in size, forms a possible future extension. Courts in this case are built up around a central nucleus: three sides of each court form interconnecting groups of rooms which create a peripheral wall of residential accommodation, and the fourth side gives access to the central social block.

Again access and aspect vary the general form. In this case buildings running north and south have rooms facing east and west and a central corridor access. Buildings running east and west have south facing rooms only. Such an arrangement depends on corridor access. Staircases at the angles and ends of blocks limit corridor length. All south facing rooms have balconies.

These considerations have an interesting effect on the court itself. Within a single court no two sides are identical. South facing walls have their balconies; north facing walls are comparatively windowless. Long views through the courts pick up the repetition of wall treatment and convey the unity within the total scheme.

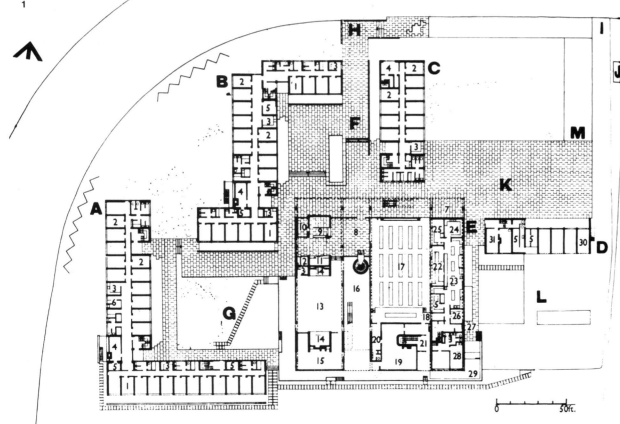

1. A block model of the scheme and below the general plan arrangement. The residential blocks form two courts associated with the main social block. Additional residential buildings could be added on the south east corner of the site to form a third court. The social block forms the central element of the total group. **2, 3 & 4** show three views of the preliminary model. They illustrate the effect of the corridor planning and the consideration of aspect. 2 is an eye-level view showing the south facing blocks and the social building on the right. 3 is a view from the north where the only windows required are for service rooms, lavatories, etc. 4 shows the repetitive south facing blocks and the wider double banked north–south blocks with east and west facing rooms accessible from a central corridor. The social building (illustration right) with its accommodation planned as a series of roof pavilions around a central terrace is also shown.

2

3

4

6

5

5. A view looking into the first court from the south. The windows in the block on the left face east. The social building is on the right. **6.** Looking out from the dining hall into the central patio shown below. **7.** The fireplace of the junior common room. **8.** View from the south with the social block on the right. **9.** Close-up of the balconies of a south facing residential block.

7

8

In contrast to the residential buildings (which are built in load bearing brickwork) the social block has a reinforced concrete frame to permit wider spans and to allow more freedom in planning. An overhanging first floor along the northern front provides a covered access to the entrance hall. This entrance hall leads to an open ended internal court. The social rooms are planned on either side of this patio and consist of a junior common room and library to the west and the main dining hall and senior common room to the east. The upper floor of this social building consists of a series of smaller self-contained units with separate access; this includes a warden's flat, rooms for the bursar and senior domestic staff, music rooms, games rooms, etc. These rooms are approached by public or private staircases and are planned as a series of roof pavilions separated from each other by terraces. A large terrace outside the music room can be used for outdoor concerts.

9

11

12

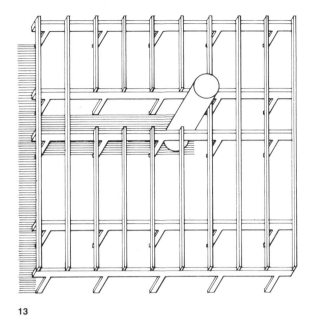

13

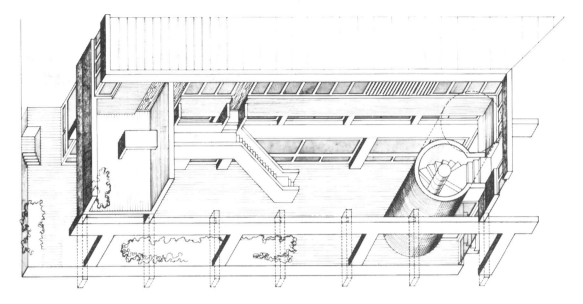

14

15

10. The south west corner of the social block; the library and senior common room are on the ground floor with the staff residential accommodation over. 11. The top of the spiral stair leading from the entrance hall to the first floor of the social block. 12. The patio of the social block. The stair on the left leads to senior members' residential accommodation: the brick drum contains the spiral stair. 13. Main concrete framing required by the larger spans of the social block and 14, the arrangement around the central patio. 15. The entrance hall with the access to the spiral stair on the left. The stair to the senior members' residential unit is seen beyond. Access to the junior common room is on the right.

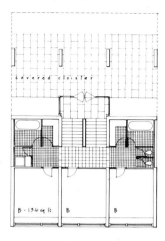

P L A N   O F   G R O U N D   F L O O R

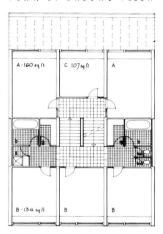

P L A N   O F   F I R S T   F L O O R

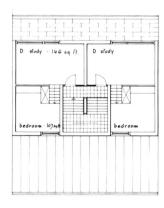

P L A N   O F   S E C O N D   F L O O R

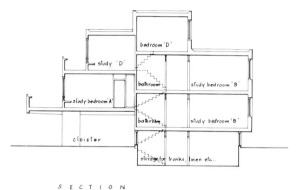

S E C T I O N

The plans on the left and the section above show an early study of possible room clusters around a central stair. The half levels used in the section produce a covered cloister, varying room sizes and east, south and west terraces in the court itself. **1.** Block plan of the final scheme. A south and outward facing block completes the fourth side and becomes the starting point for any future extension. In this final scheme the staircases are moved to the external wall and the room clusters on each floor have east, south or west facing terraces. **2 & 3** show the effect of this arrangement externally. **4 & 5** show the general form of the building.

Harvey Court, Cambridge (1958–)

The final design for this building of 100 rooms for undergraduates and fellows was preceded by studies of rooms related to traditional staircase access. In this early work each group of eleven rooms and service rooms formed a three bay unit with the staircase in the centre. The use of a stepped section and half level planning allowed considerable variety in the shape and size of rooms. Staircases were approached from a cloister and rooms around the court faced on to internal terraces. This form of layout was, however, open to several criticisms: one is the number of staircases, another is the orientation of the rooms themselves, which works well enough for blocks running north and south, but involves north facing rooms or a change of plan in the east–west blocks.

A court in which all rooms on its east, west and north flanks face inwards on to terraces seemed a sensible step. Such a court could be completed by a south facing block. To achieve this it is necessary to regroup the subdivisions of the community around the access points. Staircases placed on the peripheral walls at once achieve the greatest number of rooms facing the court itself. The number of staircase points can be reduced and each separate staircase serves a greater number of rooms, each group with its own private landing and a possibility of greater variety of size and shape.

The court itself is raised to first floor level on a plinth containing the communal rooms. The staircase points are approached from an enclosed peripheral corridor. The section of the building shows the stepped form of the terracing on the court side and the outward stepping forms of each staircase flight.

As a result of these ideas the general form of the court ceases to be a flat area of land surrounded by four continuous walls of building. It becomes one single unified and highly modelled structure in which the brick load bearing cross walls are clearly expressed.

The external materials and finishes have been carefully selected and limited to preserve the overall unity of the conception.

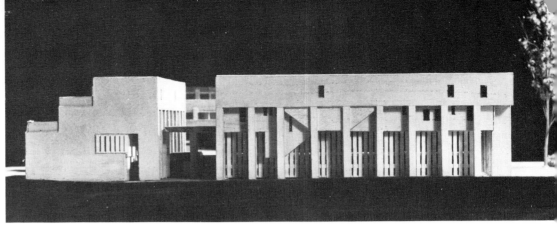

3

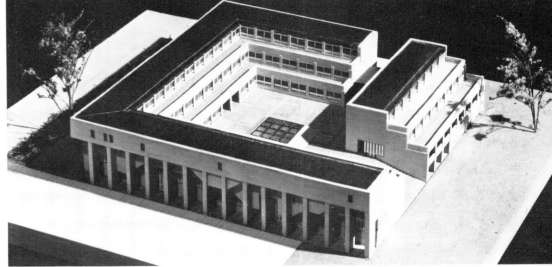

2

4

5

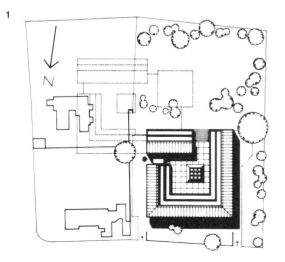

1

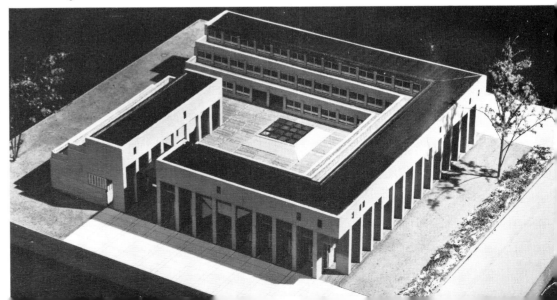

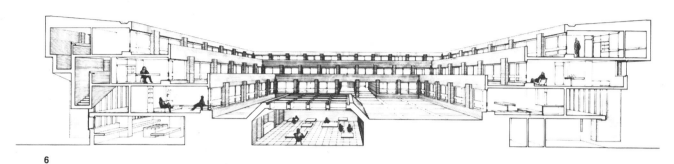

6

7

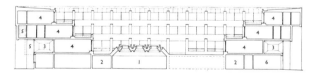

8

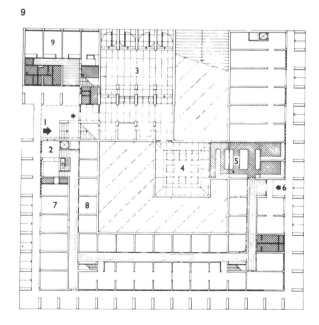

9

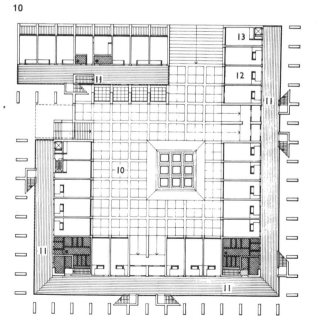

10

9, 10 & 11 illustrate the general plan arrangement. The basement provides a common room, breakfast room and kitchen: these rooms and the surrounding storage areas provide a plinth on which the residential accommodation stands. The central court is therefore at first floor level and is approached by flights of steps. From this court entrances lead to the main circulating gallery which runs around the external sides of the building. There are rooms at this level facing the court and from this corridor flights of stairs on the external walls serve the upper levels. Each staircase head serves a horizontal cluster of rooms. From each staircase head the flight to the level above steps outwards to serve another horizontal group of rooms on the level above (**13**). The arrangement produces a stepped section which allows variation in room size and grouping and external terraces. **6, 7, 8 & 14.** The external form (**12**) arises directly from the cross wall and pier construction, the circulating corridor with its slatted wood treatment, the stepped section and the staircase flights.

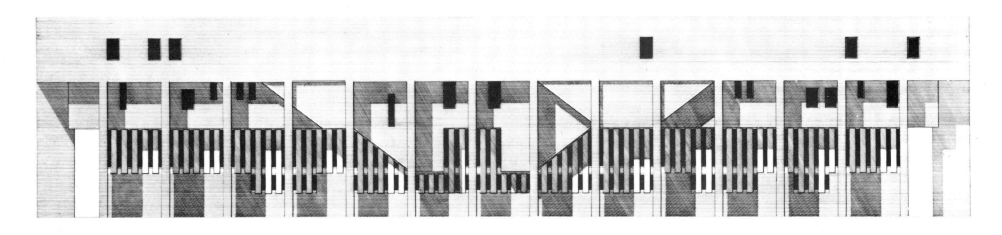

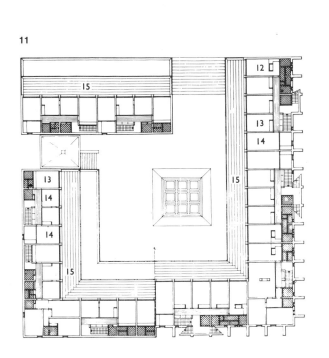

11

12
13
14
15
15
13
14
14
15

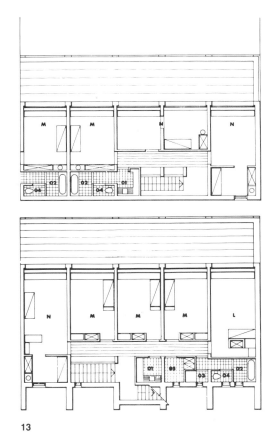

13

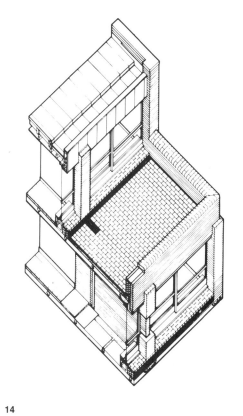

14

15

16

17

18

19

15. View of the main entrance staircase leading to the raised central courtyard. The entrance at ground level on the left leads to the common and dining rooms areas. The level of the first floor circulating gallery can be seen on the right. **16.** View along the external wall behind the pier system. **17.** Detail of the external brickwork and the alternating timber and glazing of the circulating gallery. **18.** Entrance from the courtyard, and **19** the stepped approach from the garden to the central court. The ramped rooflight to the breakfast room can be seen, also the way in which the internal terracing opens up the courtyard to the sky.

20. A general view of the building from the garden to the south. The courtyard and its flight of steps have been used for summer plays and the garden has been terraced to form a seating area. **21.** The eastern (and entrance) elevation from an adjoining garden. **22 & 23.** The central courtyard itself. The terraces of the east, south and west faces contrast with the rear elevation of the south facing block; the exterior forms are quite naturally introduced into the interior court. The top light of the breakfast room is on the right.

23

This accommodation takes the form of a graduate hostel on the St Cross Road frontage of the Balliol playing fields. The hostel is associated with Holywell Manor which stands on the diagonal and on the opposite side of the road junction. It is also related architecturally to St Cross church and the Manor Road Library Group.

The site runs east to west and is limited in depth. The southern frontage overlooks the playing fields, and the northern and entrance front faces the roadway. The first plans reflected the influences of the site. The complete building took the form of a single line of rooms overlooking the playing fields. This linear form brings together in a three storey building thirty rooms in the first stage; thirty-three rooms can then be added

and at this stage dining and communal facilities would be necessary. These are planned on the entrance frontage and are orientated towards Holywell Manor. On either side of this central group projecting staircases rise to the upper floors. The site also provides rooms for a third phase which can accommodate sixteen flats for married graduates.

The final design follows the same general principle of room layout and staircase access. The first stage only has been built and provision is made for future extensions.

Again the cross walls are load bearing and the general facing is brick with slatted timber on staircase and corridor areas.

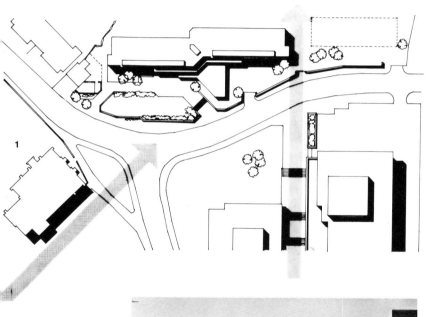

1

2

1. The site plan shows the linear form of the building. A break between the main block and the flats for married graduates provides a long view from the main stairway of the Manor Road Library Group across the Balliol playing fields and to the skyline of the town beyond. **2.** The diagonal line from Holywell Manor is picked up by the approach pathway and entrance to the new building. **3 & 4.** Preliminary scheme in which the plan is generated from two groups of south facing rooms served by staircases of the Harvey Court type: they illustrate the diagonal approach line into the common space and dining hall areas. **5 & 6.** The final plans; **7 & 8** the exterior form of the final scheme.

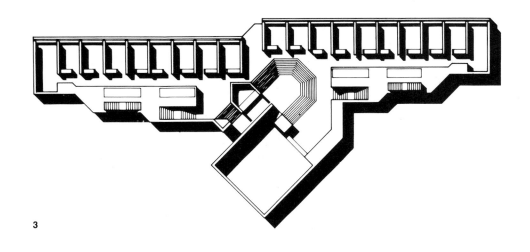

3

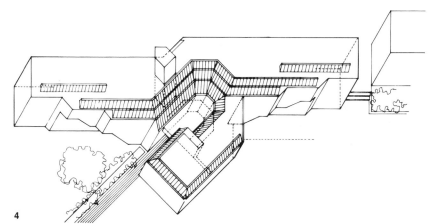

4

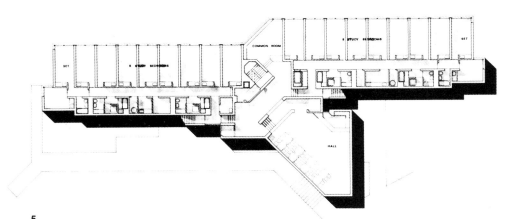

5

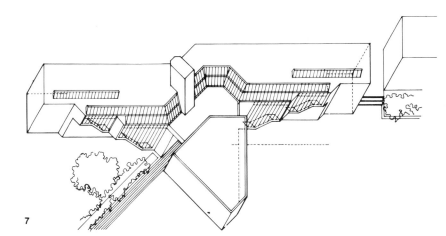

7

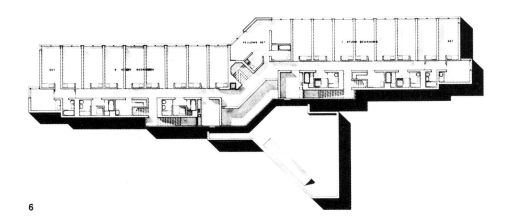

6

8

9

10

11

9. A photograph of the first stage of building extended to show the second stage. **10.** The first stage. **11.** View from the libraries.

The Stone Building, Peterhouse, Cambridge (1962–)

The first scheme for the Stone Building for Peterhouse, Cambridge was built up from two clusters of rooms and staircases arranged in linear form. Site considerations led to an effort to concentrate the building into a smaller area and the clusters were eventually superimposed, but the staircase and room arrangement remains (illustrations below).

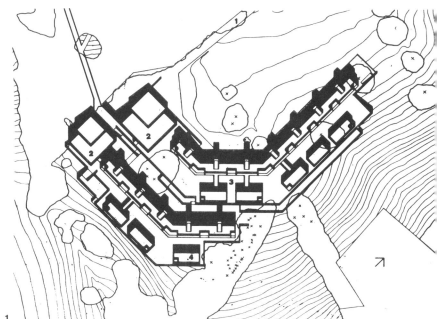

Royal Holloway College, Egham (1962–)

The form of this building again results from a consideration of staircase access and room grouping, but this has been powerfully influenced by the steeply sloping site on which the accommodation had to be placed.

The basic cluster is a five bay unit with a staircase or access corridor in the centre bay. These clusters are connected together to form continuous bands of building with gardens between. The section is developed to adjust the floor levels of these bands to the contours of the site. Again there is a stepped section with independent balconies. Communal rooms are grouped together and are accessible from the main linear corridor which connects all the room groupings.

In this case whilst the construction still uses load bearing cross walls the material internally and externally is concrete block.

1. Plan showing the contoured arrangement of the accommodation. 2. The early block model of the residential building related to a preliminary scheme for the development of the site.

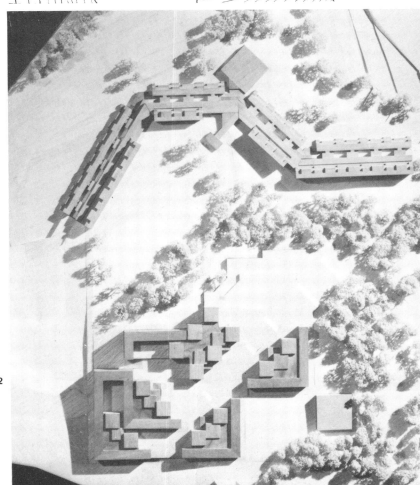

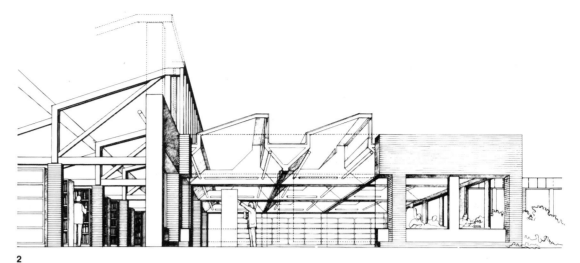

2

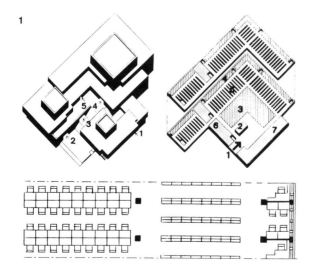

1

1. The Oxford Manor Road group. Three libraries of different size are related in a single group. The generating plan of each library includes a corner entrance and control, an L-shaped readers' area, associated with an L-shaped stack area and an enclosing band of study carrels on the external wall. The basic arrangement for readers' stacks and carrels establishes the structural grid. **2, 3 & 4** all derive from modifications of this basic plan during the development of the library for the Music School in Cambridge: **2 & 3** show a single-storey version and **4** an earlier split level scheme. **5** is a linear spine arrangement for the special case of the library for the Zoology/Psychology building in Oxford. In the small library for Pembroke College, Oxford (see p. 168), the restricted site area again controls the particular plan arrangement.

Alvar Aalto once described his experience whilst designing a Library.

> When I designed Viipuri City Library (and I had plenty of time – a whole five years) I spent a long time getting my range, as it were, through naive drawings. I drew all kinds of fantastic mountain landscapes, with slopes lit by many suns in different positions, which gradually gave birth to the main idea of the Library building. The architectural framework of the Library comprises various reading and lending areas stepped at different levels, whilst the administrative and supervisory centre is at its peak.[1]

That image of a landscape that Aalto had so much in mind is a reasonable and understandable equivalent to some of the ideas that he built into the interlocking levels and the beautifully controlled artificial and natural lighting of the Viipuri Library. We could leave it at that, and regard this building as a handsome series of

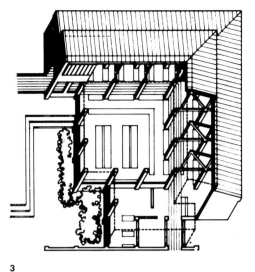

3

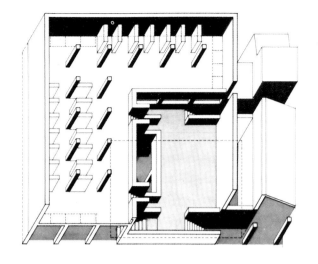

4

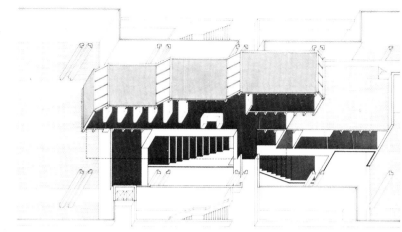

5

volumes and spaces perfectly adapted to their purpose, were it not for the fact that Aalto built a number of libraries in which he seems to make continuing use and development of the central ideas that originated at Viipuri.

The process has been studied with considerable insight by William C. Miller in his article 'From Viipuri to Mount Angel'. Quite apart from libraries which are subservient rooms in other types of building, Viipuri (1930–5) was followed by Seinajoki Library (1963–5), Rovaniemi (1965–8), the Library of the Technical Institute, Otaniemi (1965–9), and finally the Mount Angel Benedictine Library, Oregon, USA (1967–70). As Mr Miller makes very clear by his diagrams and general descriptions the thematic idea is continuous from one building to the next. All have the central point of control; the sunken level is an important element, so too is quality of light. These buildings are an example of the

development of a building type. 'Aalto has never been the least bit hesitant to re-use architectural elements as well as conceptual or organisational patterns from one design to the next. Instead of starting anew with each design project, Aalto based his design on the knowledge gained from past solutions to related problems and similar building types.'[2]

That note seems to me to be particularly relevant to some of the ideas that are illustrated here. When we began work on the Manor Road group of libraries for the University of Oxford we were faced, not with a continuous and developing theme from one building to the next, but with the immediate problem of bringing together into one single group three libraries of different size for three quite different faculties. We were forced to ask ourselves what these buildings had in common; what were in fact the characteristic elements of the library as a type. And it was from this kind of

study of the easy relationship between entrance, catalogue and control, reading desks, stacks and carrels that a pattern emerged that seemed to work well for each library – it became in fact a generic form. It is from this form that each library develops and it is from the link between these forms in plan and section that the total composition of the building is created.

We have built other libraries which because of a limited site (Pembroke Library, Oxford) or because they occupy a position within a larger building (Zoology/Psychology building, Oxford) have required variation from this generic type, but in principle the central ideas have remained and have shown themselves relevant again in the various plans that we have produced for the library for the Music School in Cambridge and in particular in the notion of a large library which is capable of growth and development over the years.

Library Group, Manor Road, University of Oxford
(1959–)

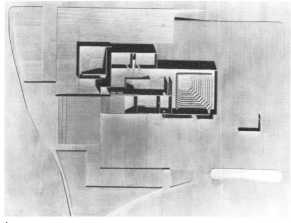

1

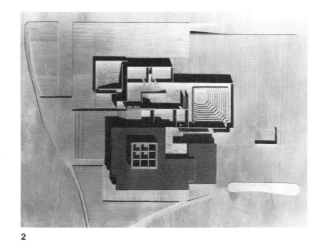

2

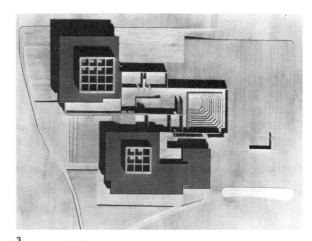

3

This building for the University of Oxford is a composite group for three separate faculties with some shared accommodation. The Bodleian Law Library is the main component of the group which includes the English Faculty Library and a building for the Institute of Statistics. The individual buildings differ in size and requirement. The Law Library, for example, provides accommodation for 450,000 books and 320 readers. The English Library is both a reference and a lending library, with 80,000 volumes and seats for 150 readers. The Institute of Statistics is principally a research organisation centred around a library of 50,000 books.

The planning of these buildings as one single group allows the maximum use of the site area available. It also allows certain accommodation, such as cloakrooms and entrance halls to lecture rooms, to be shared, and leads to a layout in which the three

buildings are planned at different levels (the accommodation for Statistics is planned on two levels, English on three and Law on four) around a main external stairway.

The general arrangement of interlinked but self-contained buildings is reflected in the external appearance of the group. The main approach stairway, which is seen at once from the approach road, leads to a series of terraces at various levels. The buildings are arranged around and enclose these terraces, but each building has its own separate entrance. That for the Institute of Statistics is at ground level on the Manor Road frontage; the ascending flight of steps leads to the entrance to English on the first landing, to the shared accommodation and lecture rooms at the next level, and to the Law Library at the level of the main terrace. The node around which each individual build-

ing is planned is its reading room, which is square on plan in each case. Externally the three reading rooms rise above the surrounding areas of stack and identify the centre of each faculty building within the general group.

The external identifying forms are, however, derived directly from the design of the libraries themselves and a description of the planning of the Law Library will indicate the generating principles. The basic requirements included the need to make all of the 450,000 volumes accessible and about half of this number closely related to readers. There are also different categories of reader, for example the undergraduate reader under visual supervision from the main control desk, and faculty members accommodated in carrels but also in close proximity to the stack.

The principal problem raised by such requirements

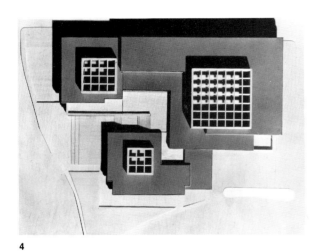

4

The generating plan form for each individual library is shown on the previous introductory pages. Here the block model shows how the libraries are arranged around the central core of lecture rooms, seminars, cloakrooms etc. They are entered at an intermediate level from the main external access stair around which the building is grouped. **1** shows this central core. **2** adds the smallest library for Statistics at ground level. **3** shows the position of the English Faculty Library and **4** the completion of the total group by the addition of the Law Library (the largest element in the group). The lecture rooms in this central area reflect the central form of the libraries over and this core forms an interconnecting link which locks the building together both in plan and section. **5.** The view of the main stairway shows the entrance to the English Library on the left and, half a level above this, the entrance to the core of cloakrooms, lecture rooms etc. These connect internally to the two main libraries. The main external entrance to the Law Library is shown at the head of the staircase. The Statistics Library is on the right. **6.** The site plan.

5

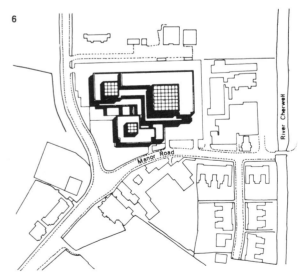

6

is one of sheer size, leading to the risk of confronting the reader with a forest of bookstacks in which he might literally become lost.

Preliminary studies established the principle followed in each library and this again can be illustrated by reference to the Law Library plan. The main reading room itself is seventy feet square and because of its size has a height of thirty feet; the effect of this is again increased by top lighting. The reading room is entered from one corner which contains the control desk and catalogue. The desks for the undergraduate readers are arranged in an *L*-shaped form in the remaining three-quarters of this square. The main section of the stack itself encloses this *L*-shaped form of the readers' tables in a single stack band. This is again enclosed by an *L*-shaped line of carrels or research readers' desks. The plan is therefore developed in a series of expand-

ing layers from the undergraduate readers through the stacks to the research readers and carrels around the perimeter. Books in the stack are equally accessible to different types of reader.

A study of bookstack spacing in relation to readers' desks and carrels establishes the structural grid. The plans of the three libraries are then related to this basic grid, the reading rooms being (Statistics) three bays, (English) four bays and (Law) seven bays square. The varying quantities of books in each library are accommodated by the development of the section; thus, whilst English has only two floors of stack, the Law Library has four. In this case 200,000 volumes of the more frequently used books are accommodated at reading room and gallery level and the remaining 250,000 volumes are in the closed stack below.

The same generating principles control the planning

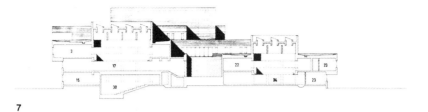

7

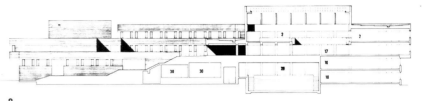

8

7. Section through the English and Statistics Libraries. 8. Section through the main approach stair and Law Library. 9. Ground floor plan. 10. First floor plan. 11. Second floor plan. 12. Third floor plan. 13. General view of the Library Group.

Key to plans: 1 Carrels. 2 Law Library gallery. 3 English gallery. 4 Wing stack. 5 Junior common room. 6 Kitchen. 7 Senior common room. 8 Workspace. 9 Microfilm. 10 Law Library stack. 11 Secretary. 12 Librarian. 13 Entrance hall. 14 Study. 15 Seminar. 16 Cataloguing. 17 Reading room. 18 WC. 19 Staff common room. 20 Binding. 21 Porter. 22 Statistics gallery. 23 Research room. 24 Courtyard. 25 Director. 26 Office. 27 Punched card. 28 Computing. 29 Lecture theatre. 30 Lecture room. 31 Plant room. 32 Receiving and packing. 33 Coffee. 34 Statistics Library reading room. 35 Janitor's flat.

9

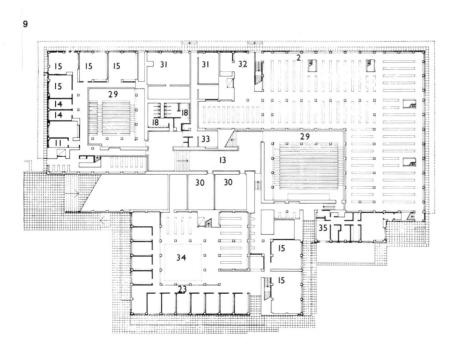

10

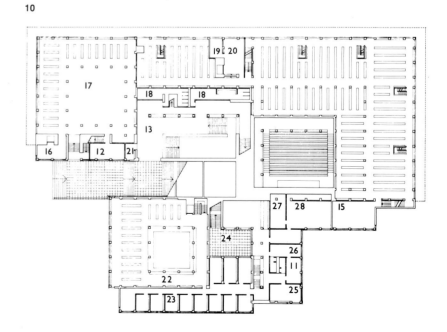

44

of each library which has as its centre a lofty galleried and top-lit reading room. The three libraries are then brought together into one single group which is arranged around an approach stairway leading to the various entrances and terraces and to the shared accommodation (lecture rooms, common rooms, etc.) which extends between the Law and English Libraries.

The external brickwork was selected to harmonise with the stone work used in the locality. The window frames are black anodised aluminium. The roofs generally are covered with copper sheeting. The interior is plastered and painted white but in the entrance hall and lecture theatres the external facing brick has been used internally in conjunction with hardwood strip ceilings and panelling. The bookstack fittings in the library are made of beech-faced laminboard: these and the reading room tables and their brass light fittings were specially designed by the architect.

The validity of the generating idea may be tested by an application to larger libraries, where the plan may have to take into account a number of specialised

13

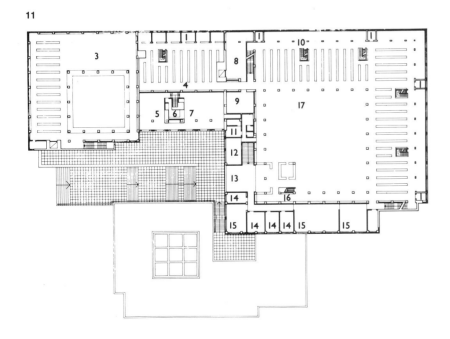

11

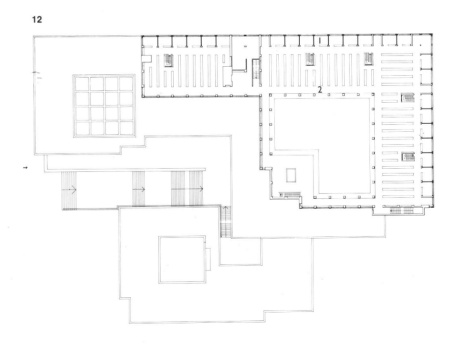

12

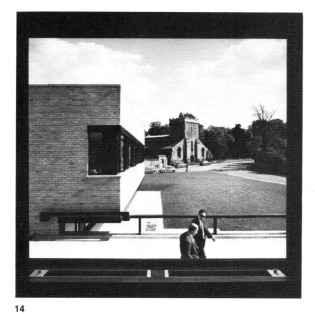

14

15

16

17

18

19

reading rooms. The expanding library in which additional space for books and readers can be added over a period of time seemed important for the newer universities where the library may in future have to contain over 1,000,000 books but where a building of this capacity, because of the rate at which books can be purchased, could not be used for library purposes for many years.

The expanding library would relate building need more closely to expenditure. It would remove temporary uses of unsuitable spaces. The problem is not one of flexibility; it is a question of the appropriate building form and the capacity of that form to expand.

14. View from the English Library looking across the approach stair to the Church of St Cross. **15.** The main approach stair. **16.** View looking towards the English Library entrance from the Statistics side of the group. **17.** The metal handrail on the approach stair. **18.** View showing the entrance to the English Library. The Statistics building is on the right. **19.** View of the Law Library entrance and the head of the main staircase, from the terrace.

47

20   **20.** Looking down into the Statistics reading room. **21 & 22.** The reading desk and light fittings designed by the architect. **23.** The reading room of the Law Library showing two levels of stack enclosing the reading space. The roof lighting is standard in all libraries: the square units define the size of each reading space (Statistics 9 squares, English 16 squares, Law 49 squares). These volumes are exposed externally and define the special character of the building. **24.** The catalogue area. **25.** One of the staircases between stack levels. **26.** The Law reading room from the upper stack level.

21   **22**

24   25   26

3 · Auditoria: variations on a theme

1. The auditorium for the University of Hull is hollowed out of a plinth of surrounding rooms within which the roof light of the art gallery, the rectangular chapel and its associated external court can be seen. **2.** In the Music School at Cambridge the belt of surrounding rooms is separated out from the main auditorium by small courts and a planted garden. **3.** This social building relates indoor and outdoor auditoria to a common stage area. **4.** Bristol competition. Open common spaces combined with clusters of auditoria. **5.** Royal Scottish Academy: first scheme. Theatre and concert hall and common foyer. **6.** A preliminary scheme for the concert hall in Cambridge from which 2 developed and which shows the cross wall and projecting pier system developed in 5.

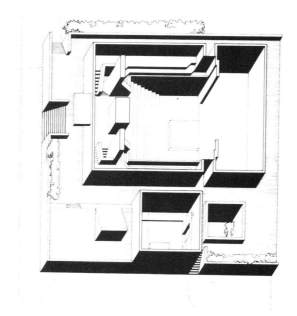

1

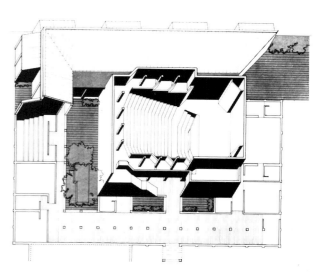

2

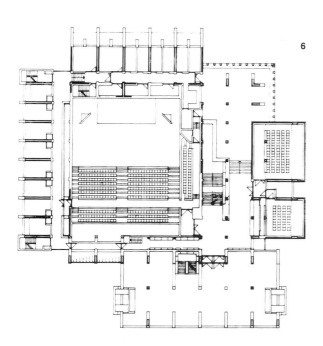

6

All the buildings illustrated in this chapter have to make provision for an audience and are concerned with hearing. The size ranges from small lecture rooms to independent clusters of rooms and finally to specialised halls. The range of sound varies from speech to music and with that variation the form and volume of the room itself will change. All these types of auditorium must accommodate groups of people and are thus in turn connected with their movement, places of entry and access spaces. The sites in which they are set are different and each site, because of approach or its scale and characteristic features, has a special influence on the final form.

The simplest form is the lecture room. In the case of the group of libraries at Oxford (1960–5) the two main lecture rooms and their associated seminars are embedded in the plan and their typical forms are locked into the total group and linked to it by their entrances and connecting routes. The lecture rooms

are designed specifically for speech with stepped seating and a direct sound path from the speaker to every auditor. The external brickwork is taken into the interior of the entrance hall and the rooms themselves; various forms of slatted timber are used for absorbent and reflecting surfaces.

The Arts building for the University of Hull (1958) also has a cluster of lecture rooms under the main teaching block, but the main auditorium (the Middleton Hall) is built to serve the needs of general assembly within the university and is used for special lectures. It is also used for drama and, by the use of a fore-stage to close off the stage itself, makes provision for certain types of musical performance. Associated with this auditorium there are other centralised uses: the foyers provide an exhibition area and connect together a chapel and quiet area and a small gallery for the university art collection.

In contrast to this general purpose hall, the auditor-

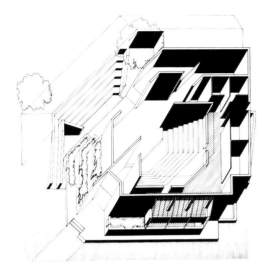

3

4

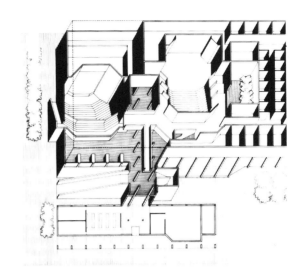

5

ium of the Cambridge Music School (1974) is designed specifically for the longer reverberation required for musical performances and for a high degree of sound insulation between the different areas of accommodation. The Hull auditorium is hollowed out from a base or podium which contains the surrounding rooms. At Cambridge the belt of surrounding rooms is isolated as much as possible from the auditorium itself by means of small planted courts and areas which also allow natural light and outlook.

The college social building again shows differences which arise from size and use. The auditorium is small (250 seats in contrast to the 500 seats provided in the Music School). The entry point on the diagonal relates to site and access and the outdoor–indoor auditoria divided by the stage itself provide a further opportunity to link the building to the surrounding site.

Each one of these buildings has a role to play in completing a part of a university development or adding to the existing buildings or layout of a particular site. They help to give definition and form, and when the requirements of a whole faculty are involved, as in the scheme for Bristol (1978), the total plan could make a major contribution to an area of the university. The elements are similar: movement and connecting areas in the main foyers and the clusters of special enclosed spaces.

The Royal Scottish Academy building (1980) is not only a larger building with different types of auditoria but it is also an urban building constructed within the Glasgow street grid. The building is intended to make a contribution to the architecture of the street. It is related in general height to the buildings of the surrounding area – one of these, housing the Scottish Opera, has a complementary use. The three storey building which results from these conditions has a *piano nobile* at the level of the first floor public entrance and the foyers of the various auditoria. The auditoria are in line and embedded within the total form; the approaching line of movement is diagonal through the central foyer space and leading to the interconnecting stairs placed in echelon.

Lessons from the earlier experience are built into this design, particularly the contrasting forms of auditoria for theatre and music and the laboratory theatre or opera rehearsal rooms. These are long-span rooms running down the central spine. The surrounding rooms requiring sound insulation have also been tested out and their effectiveness has been measured in the Cambridge building. As in this earlier building, the load bearing structure built up within a basic grid is expressed externally in the projecting piers which carry outwards the lines of the internal walls and act as sound baffles between the windows of the rooms themselves.

1

2

Lecture rooms, Oxford (1959–)

3

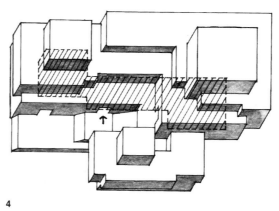

4

These lecture rooms form an integral part of the Manor Road group of library buildings. Together with their entrance and connecting halls, they interlock tightly both in plan and section with the Law Library and the English Library with which they are associated.

The levels of the main libraries within this building were described previously. From the main external staircase the English Library is entered at the first landing level. The second landing contains the entrance to the lecture room group and the third and highest landing leads directly into the Law Library.

The entrance to the lecture rooms at this interconnecting level leads to a common entrance hall with

1. The main approach stair. Oxford Library Group: the entrance to the lecture room area is from the half level on the left. **2.** The main internal stair. The floor is cork: the ceiling slatted timber. **3.** The entrance hall and internal stair between the lecture rooms for Law (right) and English (left). **4.** The position of the lecture rooms within the main group. **5.** Wood handrail to the stair. **6.** The Law lecture room with timber acoustic treatment. **7 & 8.** Interiors of the Law lecture room which incorporates a side and rear gallery area.

52

5

6

space for cloaks and lavatory accommodation. From this common hall, three flights of stairs lead down to the Law Lecture Room and two seminar rooms, and from this level a further short flight leads down to the English Lecture Room. The two lecture rooms being under their own library buildings are also separately interconnected with these libraries.

In both cases raked seating has been used; the external brick walling is carried through into the interior of the entrance hall and into the lecture rooms themselves. The acoustic treatment of the rooms is provided by wooden panelling.

7

8

Middleton Hall, University of Hull (1962–)

The new layout plan prepared for the university in 1958 is described in Part 2. It attempted to bring some coherence into the general form of the university buildings by arranging new buildings so that they formed interconnected courts and by creating a broad connecting pedestrian way through these.

This connecting pedestrian route became at that time the main thoroughfare giving access to all parts of the university. The auditorium group is associated with the Arts building. This takes the form of a ribbon of rooms, which from the rear becomes the enclosing wall to the new first court and from the main approach acts as a background to the auditorium group now known as Middleton Hall.

The auditorium, though associated with the Arts Faculty, is at the same time the central hall used by the university for its public lectures and various other functions. It holds 500 people and is associated with an exhibition gallery for the university art collection and a chapel. This group is also connected to the main cluster of seven lecture theatres associated with the Arts Faculty.

Seen from the road, the auditorium stands to the right of the main pedestrian route. Externally it is surrounded by a raised terrace which forms the main entrance level and which in suitable weather can be used as a promenade during intervals. Its surface is brick and it contains areas of planting. The auditorium floor is hollowed out within this surrounding terrace. The main entrance at terrace level leads to an entrance hall and connects directly to the back of the auditorium seating and to the side gallery. From this level the raked floor slopes down to the front of the stage which connects to surrounding galleries within the podium itself.

These surrounding galleries are used during the intervals and provide space for a promenade, refreshment area and exhibition display. They connect to a closed exhibition area in which the Hull University permanent art collection is housed. They are also associated with an inter-denominational chapel which is connected to a small patio and meeting room. Behind the stage there are changing rooms, green rooms etc.

The auditorium itself has an adaptable stage which may be used either for proscenium performance or, by closing sliding doors across the proscenium, for lectures on a small apron stage or for chamber music.

Structurally the buildings are a combination of con-

1 & 2. General view of the Middleton Hall and its surrounding plinth of rooms. **3.** The two earlier buildings are shown in the foreground on the left and right. The Middleton Hall occupies a central position and its background of Arts Faculty rooms establishes one wall of the new courtyard created by the overall layout. A pedestrian route passes from the main gate, along the side of Middleton Hall and through the court beyond. **4.** The terrace and Arts building beyond.

1

2

crete and load bearing brick. The brick used externally has been chosen to match that of the older buildings and to assist the overall unification which was one of the objects of the general layout. A permanent feature of the exterior is this overall use of brick in walls, paving, copings etc. in combination with the vertical lead cladding which is used to enclose the roof structure of the auditorium itself. Internally, the load bearing brickwork is painted white. Ceilings have been designed to introduce sound absorbents; floors are of wood block and all the joinery is in beech including panelling finishes to lecture rooms and the wall finishes to the auditorium.

The chapel, which externally forms a distinct element in the total group, depends for its effect internally on a carefully controlled reflection of natural light. Three plywood box beams form the main structural supports to the roof. The vertical roof lights stand over these and run round three sides of the plan, throwing their light on to the wall surfaces which are painted white. There is a direct toplight over the altar. The associated patio is intended to create a quiet area. It contains planting and has been used for the display of sculpture from time to time.

3   4

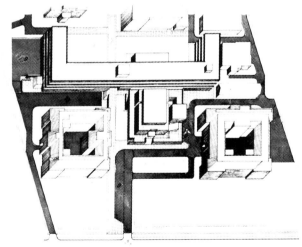

5. General view along the pedestrian route through into the court beyond. **6.** View along the face of the Arts building. Middleton Hall and its raised plinth. The brickwork matches the red rustic colour of the older buildings. The auditorium form is clad in lead. **7.** Model of the auditorium and plinth. Chapel on the right. **8.** Looking down onto the chapel roof and its private court. **9.** Plinth and auditorium. Brickwork and lead cladding.

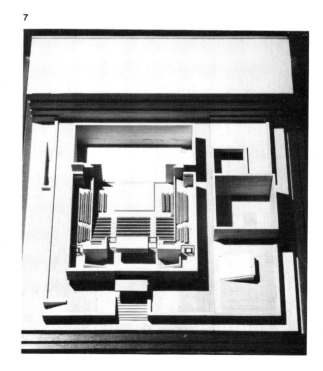

6

8

9

10

11

12

10. Plinth and auditorium. The chapel side. 11. View through the archway to the older building. 12. View from the Arts building. 13. One of the lecture rooms. 14. Diagram of the auditorium and connected lecture rooms within the Arts building. 15 & 16. Entrance to the auditorium and connecting stair to the surrounding rooms below.

13

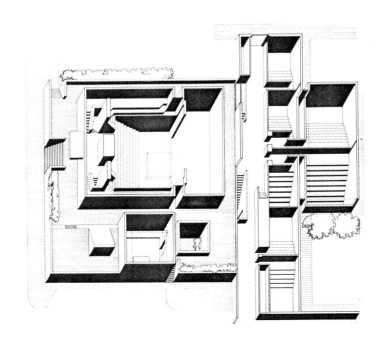

15

16

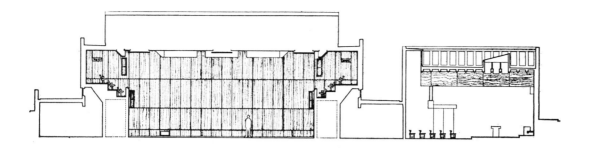

17

17. Cross section through the auditorium and the chapel. **18.** Interior of the auditorium. Stage screen closed. **19 & 20.** Interiors of the chapel. The roof is supported on plywood box beams. Timber cross beams support a clerestory which lights the wall surfaces on three sides of the room. A central roof light illuminates the altar. **21 & 22** are general views of the interior.

18

19

60

21

20

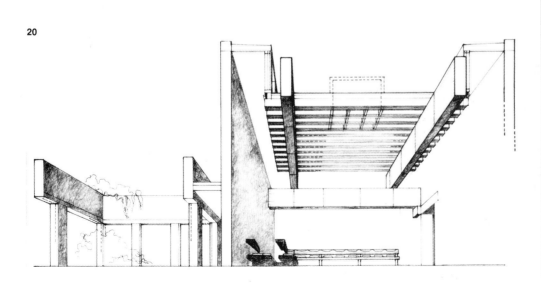

22

Music School, Cambridge
(1974 and later stages)

2

3

The preliminary scheme for the new buildings for the Faculty of Music in the University of Cambridge was designed in 1974. For many years the faculty had been working in cramped conditions in an old building in Downing Place adapted for their use before 1939 when the total number of students was about fifty. In the 1970s there were 150 members of the faculty. In addition to the Pendlebury Library, the faculty has always provided a centre for music in the university as a whole; the Cambridge University Music Society has traditionally used the faculty buildings. The new accommodation had therefore to include a main auditorium, primarily for music, to seat 500 people. Associated with this were lecture and seminar rooms (including a lecture room for seventy-five), practice rooms, display area for the historic collection of musical instruments, backstage accommodation and instrument store, rooms for faculty administration, foyers, student areas and common room space and, finally, a library. The site chosen is part of the Sidgwick Avenue development and is entered from the West Road frontage. It contained an existing house used by a university department and an unused stable building. The plans for the new building envisaged the auditorium as a central core with a band of supporting accommodation surrounding this.

With the limited funds available it was necessary to build in stages. The auditorium was completed in 1977; the faculty administration was accommodated in the existing house and provision for temporary teaching and backstage accommodation was made within the existing stables. The second stage consisted of rooms for teaching on the southern end of the auditorium and

1. Model of the complete scheme from the north. The library is on the left. 2. View from the east. Library forecourt and entrance in the foreground. 3. Temporary entrance to the first stage of building: auditorium only. 4. The stages of building illustrated. From left to right: stage 1 the auditorium; stage 2 teaching rooms and backstage accommodation; stage 3 completion of the surrounding belt of rooms to form entrance foyer and to complete the inner courts and finally the library. 5 & 6. The developed plans. The rooms surrounding the auditorium include: to the north (top), rehearsal room, changing rooms, etc.; to the east, main entrance and foyer; common room and bar to the north; students' area to the south. South band includes seminar and lecture rooms and on the south west corner the old music room with its collection of instruments. The west band accommodates seminar and practice rooms. The roof plan shows the planted court arrangement.

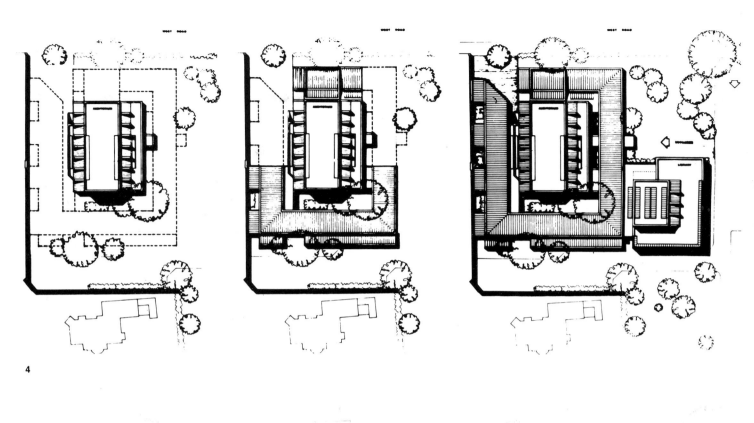

4

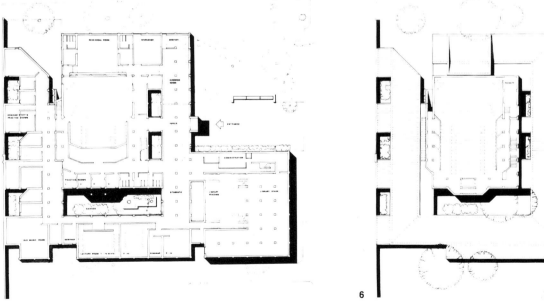

5

6

7

8

9

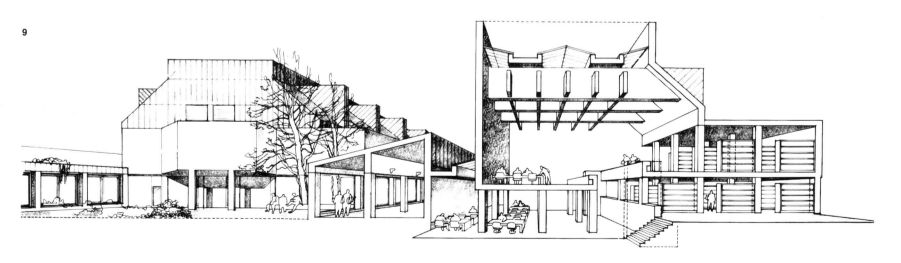

rehearsal and backstage accommodation has now been built to the north, and the library is being constructed. The band of accommodation surrounding the auditorium and including a main foyer will be completed as additional finance becomes available.

The fact that the building programme had to be staged and that only the auditorium was built in the first instance has added clarity in two ways. Firstly, the auditorium had to stand on its own as an isolated building, its structure and external finishes being clear-cut and separated as far as possible from the single-storey band of surrounding rooms. Secondly, this suggested the possibility of taking the idea of separation further by the introduction of small courts which offered several advantages. They provide an increased acoustic separation between the foyers, student areas and teaching rooms, and the auditorium itself. They allow practice and teaching rooms to be clustered in groups rather than arranged in serried ranks. They also preserve existing trees and provide a pleasant outlook from interior spaces.

The site plan, ground and first floor plans show these final proposals. The existing auditorium is surrounded by a single-storey building in which the width is increased where necessary by the use of a double pitch. The main entrance and future foyer is on the east side, approached directly from the West Road entrance to the Sidgwick Avenue site. The foyer extends along the

The auditorium only was built at the first stage. **7, 8 & 10** illustrate this. **11** shows the second stage addition of lecture rooms (compare with 7). Major trees outside the building and in the inner court were retained. **9** shows the inner court, the student foyer and the half level library as originally planned. The library has now been reduced in size and is being built as a single-storey building. Diagrams of this are shown on pp. 40–1.

10

11

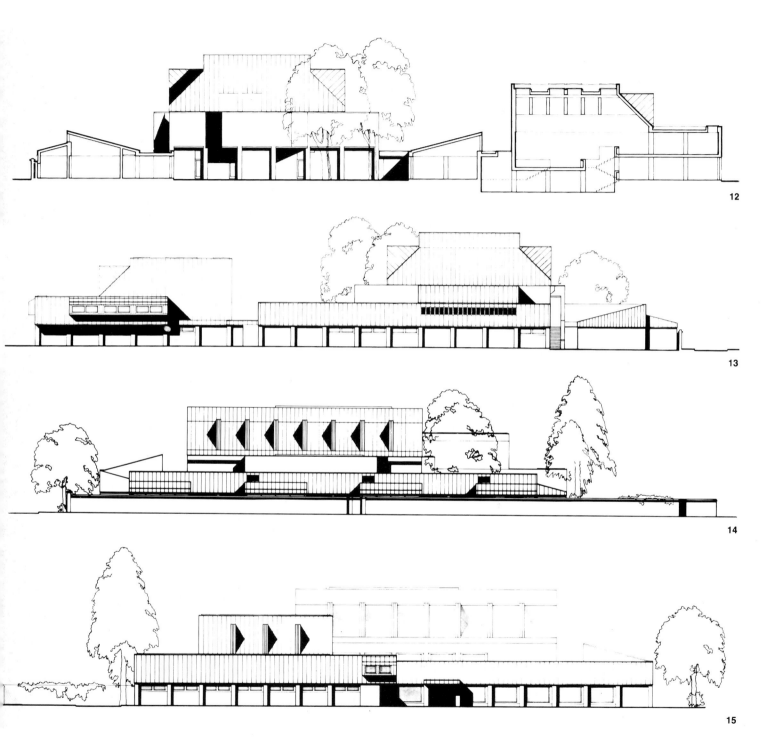

length of this east frontage, providing a common room and bar at the north end and a student area at the south end. This student area also gives access to the administration and library block. The main teaching areas are on the south front. They have easy access to the library and include a major lecture room (seventy-five seats), a smaller lecture room, several seminar rooms and a special room containing the historical collection of musical instruments used in teaching. On the west flank there are clusters formed by lecture and seminar or practice rooms, and to the north there is a rehearsal room which can also serve as backstage accommodation.

The completed auditorium is at present entered from an inner foyer. The interior itself needs some special description, as some specific requirements had to be met. It had to seat 500. The stepped floor for the main body of fixed seating is the result of considerations of sight lines and acoustics. On each side of this are stepped galleries with loose chairs. One entrance to the auditorium is at ground level at the front of the stage, and another is by means of a staircase from the entrance foyer, which leads to the rear of the seating.

The auditorium is designed for the performance of a wide range of music, but it is also used for teaching. This gives rise to a variable stage arrangement. Variability is provided in the first place by adjustment of the floor. A completely flat floor from the front of the stepped seating area to the back of the stage gives an arrangement which suits various teaching and faculty purposes. By the removal of a series of panels running across the front of this area a second arrangement can be made, which allows three more rows of loose seats to be provided and produces the effect of a platform for

12, 13, 14 & 15. Elevations of the total scheme; walls are buff brick. Fascias, roof, etc. are zinc. 12 Auditorium south face and section through seminar room, court and library. 13 The north elevation. 14 West elevation. 15 East and entrance elevation. 16. Stair from entrance hall to rear of auditorium.

performance and demonstration. The removal of an additional row of panels makes it possible to have an orchestra pit and straight-fronted stage for operatic performances.

All these arrangements at floor level have their counterparts above. Rotating panels over the stage area can be set to act as reflectors for musical performances. But they can also be used in a vertical position to allow lighting or the hanging of minimal scenery for operatic productions. A curtain track running along the rear wall and across the front of the stage allows some control of acoustic conditions and also provides a stage curtain. Two triangular vertical panels (periaktoi, movable by hand, can be arranged to give some background to individual performances, or they can be moved into position to form the sides of a proscenium opening when this is necessary.

These variable arrangements meet the needs of teaching, the rehearsal of orchestra or choir, solo performance, small groups, full orchestra, choir or operatic group with orchestra. One feature of the design that arises from these uses, particularly the teaching that takes place during the day, is the desirability of natural lighting; this has been achieved by top light. But the general form and finishes of the interior have obviously been affected by considerations of acoustics. A preliminary report from the acoustic consultant laid down some general considerations and specified a desirable total volume,[1] with the object of achieving a mid-frequency reverberation time of 1·4– 1·5 seconds when fully occupied and 1·8–2·1 empty. Some reduction of height seemed desirable over the platform for musical performances (the rotating panels provide this) and it was suggested that curtains that

16

17

could be bunched or drawn around the platform walls might be useful from the point of view of impressions of loudness and liveliness, particularly in the platform area. (Later consideration of this curtain use suggested a continuation of the track so that these background curtains could also be used as stage curtains in a proscenium condition.) The preliminary report was later developed by considering floor, wall and seating finishes, and standards were laid down for noise reduction within the ventilation system and in relation to room-to-room transmission.

The acoustic considerations required a section which could produce maximum volume. The interior is therefore opened up to the roof skin; trusses with their members cased for fire protection, drop ducts for ventilation, cat-walks and lighting are all exposed and placed where convenient. Below this, a partial screening and some visual definition is provided by an egg-crate ceiling formed in plywood. On entering the auditorium lower level the general impression is one of height; the top lights and artificial lighting emphasise this. The main bank of seating rises steeply and is upholstered in bright red fabric. The lower sections of wall alongside the seating are finished in birch ply and the main walls are buff brick. The reverberation time of the new auditorium was measured on completion – an exercise which demonstrated that very satisfactory values had been achieved. The whole building has been in continuous use for some years and its qualities have been proved by successful performances of many kinds.

17. The interior shows the opening up of the total internal volume for acoustic reasons. The ceiling is white plaster; the ceiling grid screening cat-walks, vent shafts, etc. is built in plywood. The buff brick of the external auditorium walls can be seen behind the galleries. Side walls have a birch ply finish. The platform is arranged for maximum seating with loose chairs on the first three rows. **18, 19 & 20** show three stage arrangements: 18 maximum, flat floor periaktoi in rear position, curtains bunched on rear wall. 19 Normal concert conditions, some floor panels removed and loose chairs added (see also **21**); for soloists or trio the periaktoi can be moved and used as a background. 20 Orchestra pit condition, periaktoi in forward position to form proscenium with stage curtain.

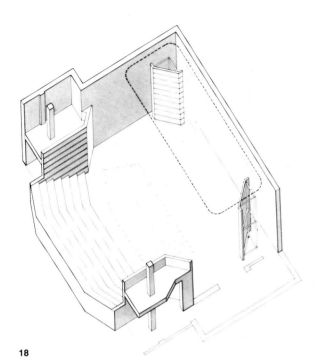

18

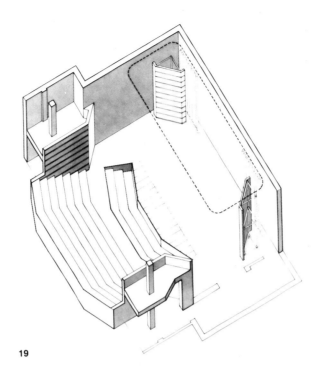

19

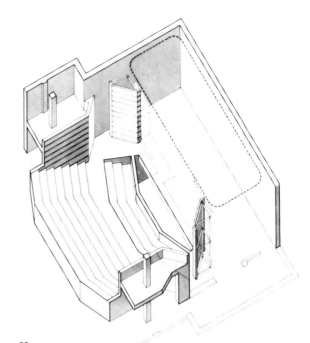

20

21

22

23

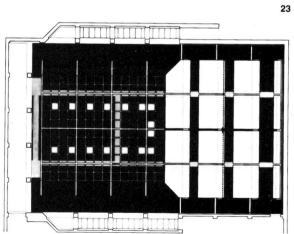

22. The ceiling treatment. The lines of the main trusses and the plaster ceiling can be seen screened by the plywood egg-crate which defines the level below ventilation shafts, cat-walks, etc. This open plywood form also allows special lighting, spotlights, etc. to be added if required. The two lines of plywood panelling on the right are shown in the normal position to provide a 45° angle of reflection (see also **23**). They can be rotated by a simple manual operation. The vertical position allows the curtains to run across the face of the stage, additional lighting for stage performance of opera, and the possibility of hanging some scenery or flats. There is no provision for flying scenery as the acoustic conditions for music are paramount. Opera has been performed very successfully when the limits of stage presentation are accepted and used imaginatively to create new forms of stage production. **24.** A view from one of the side galleries. These are stepped to improve vision and the loose seating arrangement allows flexibility of use. **25.** This long section through the main auditorium shows the total volume, lines of cat-walks, ventilation ducts, etc. The large door on to the platform itself leads to the main instrument store which houses piano, harpsichord, organ, etc. The orchestra pit and the stepped form of the side galleries are illustrated. The section shows on the left the rehearsal room where again considerable volume is desirable and on the right the enclosed courtyard with its existing tree. The corridor linking the surrounding rooms opens out on to this court; the main lecture room with its stepped floor and clerestory lighting is shown on the right.

24

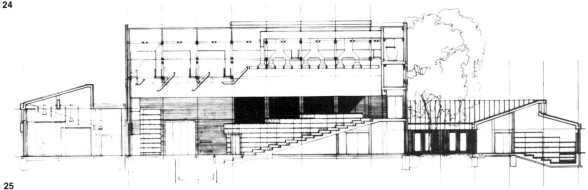

25

26

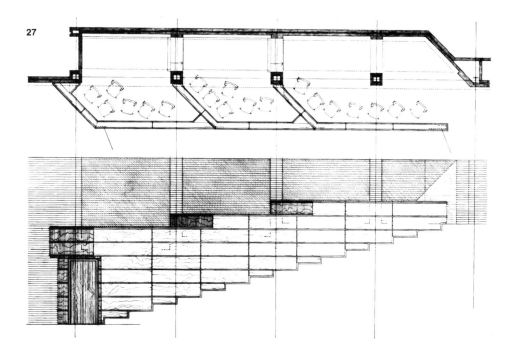

27

26. View across the auditorium and 27 the arrangement of the side galleries. These galleries have natural lighting from a roof light. The auditorium itself also has natural light so that in normal daytime use artificial lighting is required only over the stage and the lecturer or performers themselves. The roof lights have mechanically operated blinds. 28. View from the side gallery towards the rear of the hall. 29, 30 & 31. Views along the access corridors. In 29 the lecture rooms are on the left, the enclosed court with its major tree on the right. The access corridors have display cabinets (30). All the adjoining rooms require sound locks and double doors at their entrances and the display is usually arranged in the recesses between these. 31 shows the student foyer area with a display at the far end.

28

29

30

31

1

A college social building (scheme, 1979)

The older colleges of Oxford and Cambridge have traditionally consisted of rooms for members of the college arranged around courts with special rooms for the community: for example, the hall, the chapel, the college library. When new needs have developed these have often been accommodated by the conversion of some residential accommodation.

The newer colleges have, however, made special provision for these new needs, for example rooms for larger lectures or where plays and music and other activities associated with college interests can be accommodated. When this type of building has been provided it has also been borne in mind that colleges during vacations are frequently used for conferences, and buildings of this type can act as a social centre for conference purposes.

The proposal illustrated includes some ideas for a building which might be described as a social centre for one of the older colleges. The main element in the building is an auditorium for 250 which would be available for lectures, music, plays or conference purposes; the supporting accommodation for this auditorium might serve a number of needs. For instance, the backstage accommodation including scenery and workshop space might serve a double purpose as a studio for art or craft. The foyer and its supporting rooms might also serve as dressing rooms, seminar rooms, rooms for conferences, offices etc.

In the case of this building the stage serves both an indoor and an outdoor auditorium. A bar has been provided and a separate area has been included for a discotheque.

The building therefore serves a number of different but compatible uses and becomes a new centre for diverse college activities. One further point in providing this building is that when complete it can release some accommodation at present scattered at different points within the college, thus allowing areas of the college to revert to the residential uses for which they were originally intended.

The site is clearly important. The building requires a central position and the selection of the right site could allow it to have an external amphitheatre and to form a setting for such events as summer plays, reunions etc. which are traditionally held out of doors. The building had also to be sited so that there is reasonable road access for supplies and service deliveries to the bar and stage.

1. General view from the court. **2.** Ground floor plan: the diagonal entrance picks up two possible approaches and leads directly to the lower level of the auditorium. A mirror image repeats this pattern externally. The bar and disco are again accessible internally and externally from the outdoor seating. **3.** Plan at first floor level. The scenery room can be used as an art studio.

2

3

The plans (p. 76) illustrate changes in the arrangement of the basic elements within the building in relation to different sites. In each case the auditorium and the stage form the main volume of the building supported by two levels of accommodation. The height of this volume is related to the height of the older buildings of the college and is enclosed by the surrounding accommodation at a lower level. This accommodation merges with a raised grass bank which forms the amphitheatre for the open air seating, and in the final scheme the discotheque area is partially embedded in this bank. Existing trees are preserved in all proposals, and the surrounding foyers are faced in brick to match existing buildings. The upper part of the auditorium has a zinc facing.

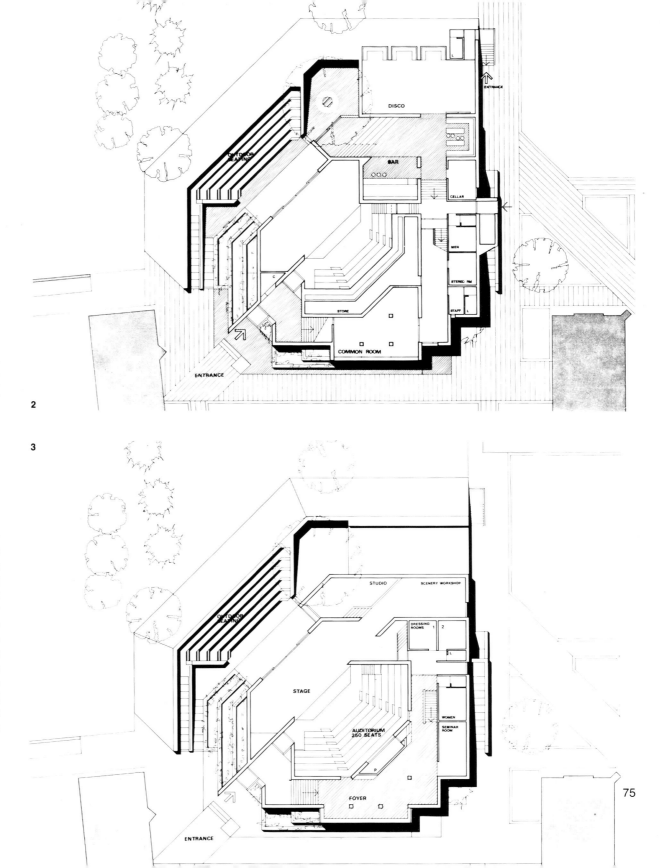

4

5

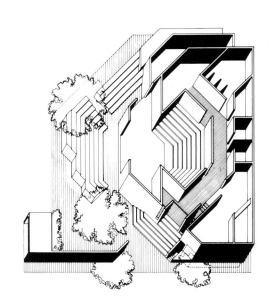

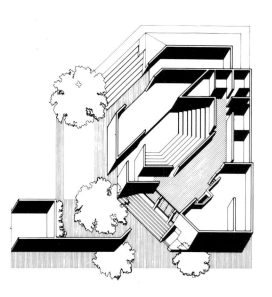

76

4. General view of the model: the glazed bay window to the foyer and common room areas overlooks the court. The walls were intended to be built in buff brickwork. The roof superstructure of the auditorium area is clad in zinc. **5** shows the form of the building for the site originally considered. The other two diagrams are variants on this plan as it is modulated to meet alternative site conditions. **6.** A general view. **7.** The stage and scenery entrances. The rear courtyard with its tree and the disco area are shown on the right.

6

7

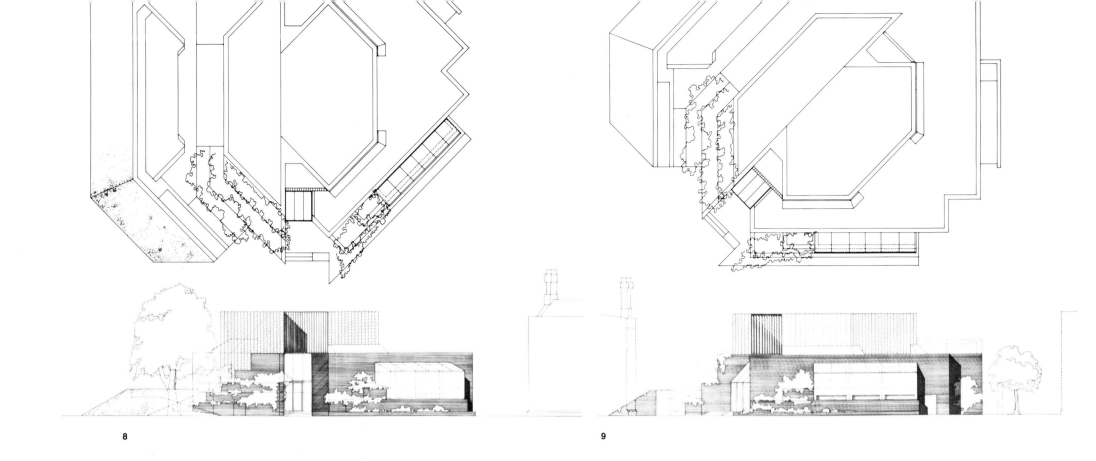

8

9

11

12

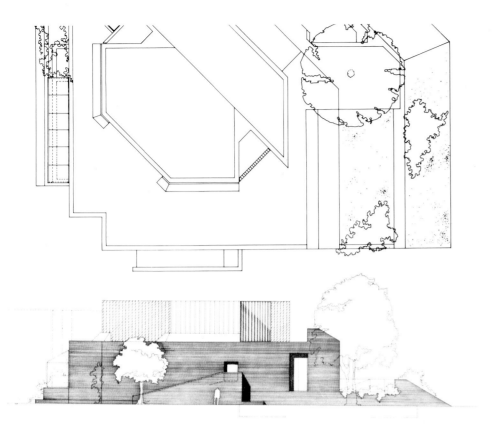

10

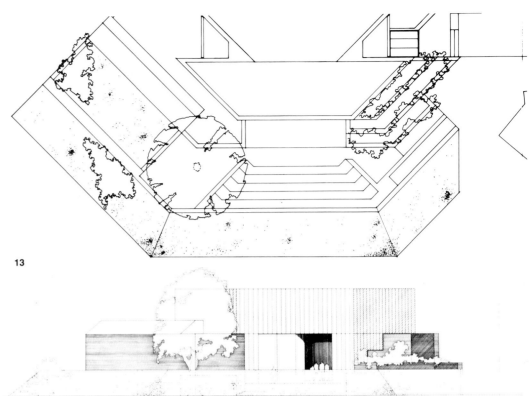

13

8, 9, 10 & 13. Studies of the general form. 11 & 12. Indoor and outdoor seating and common stage area. The model illustrates the use of external banking and planting to merge the building and the open landscape in this area. 14. The use of levels. The discotheque is sunk into the ground for sound-insulation purposes.

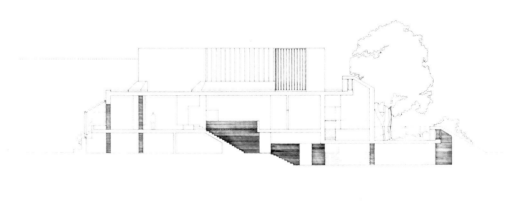

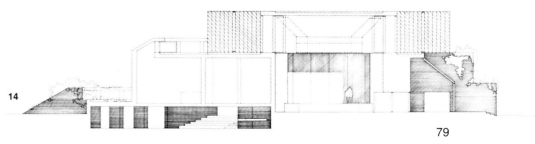

14

1 & 2. The models show the general distribution of uses within the faculty: houses on the right provide the base for individual faculties. The central area includes the circulation and communal areas. The enclosed lecture room groups are on the left. An outdoor arena connects this area of the site with the higher level of the central university buildings. **3.** General view of the ascending levels: enclosed lecture groups on the left. Open brick pier and slab construction in the circulation areas.

1

2

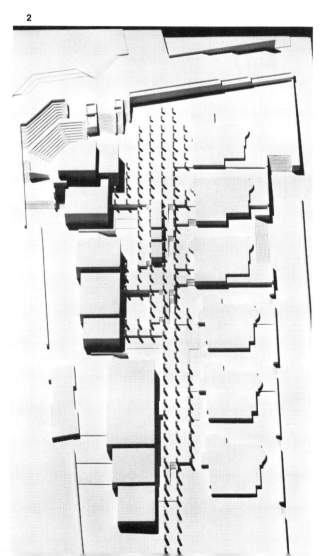

The proposals start from the fact that a series of houses along the main road frontage have to be preserved and converted for the use of departments of the faculty. One further overriding consideration is that the development will have to take place in a series of stages, each stage being related to the conversion of individual houses. The development clearly must allow the maximum flexibility of choice. The solution is not constrained by formal ideas but it nevertheless allows the step by step process to build up into an overall conception.

The converted houses will eventually form a linear arrangement of faculty accommodation. The gardens behind will give the opportunity for the linked and related layout of new buildings which by additive growth can provide pleasant accommodation at each stage. By this arrangement the departments in each house can feel that they are in some degree sharing the new accommodation and are not isolated from it.

The individual houses are intended to accommodate all the departmental offices, staff rooms and seminar rooms required by the departments. Each house or part of a house becomes a departmental base for staff, for individual tutorials or for seminar work. The larger rooms at ground floor level form the seminar rooms, and the other floors, which have rooms all comparatively small in size, will accommodate the staff rooms.

3

The houses require only a minimum conversion.

What the houses cannot accommodate are those areas which should be shared by all departments. The linear site formed by the gardens behind the houses provides the opportunity to form a second line of shared accommodation to which all houses can eventually be linked. This second line of building contains the linear connecting route which also provides cloakrooms, lavatories, the reading room and common room areas. This central area of shared accommodation is again connected at various points along its length to groups or clusters of lecture rooms, audio-visual rooms etc.

The whole plan can be thought of as three parallel belts of accommodation each linked to the others. The houses form the departmental and staff base; the central line of accommodation is the general meeting ground shared by all departments; the third line is formed by groups of lecture rooms and provides a linear dispersal of all lecture room accommodation.

The site increases in width as it develops from north to south. At the southern end and at a higher level there is the existing Senate House building adjacent to a site to be developed as a future refectory and Arts building. The chain of new buildings also increases in width as it approaches the Senate House and refectory end of the site, and the more important rooms used by

the greatest number of students (the large lecture rooms and common room) are closest to these central buildings.

The central spine of the building forms both a route and a meeting area. It contains all areas in common use by the faculty: waiting areas, lavatories, library, common room etc. The columnar structure allows a spreading form, with views extending outwards into the adjacent courts. The landscaping and floor levels respond to the changing levels of the ground. The roof has a stepped form relating to these changing levels and allowing south light to penetrate through the building. In contrast to this open form in the central construction, the lecture room clusters form a solid and enclosing wall.

The design works towards a solution in which buildings, landscaping and planting are integrated into a total layout. Car parking is kept to areas along the two long boundaries of the site where it is easily accessible from the adjoining roads. Students within the buildings will move from the domestic scale of the houses which form the base for their departments, into the open areas of the communal space and through these to the enclosed form of the lecture room groups. As they do this, views will be constantly extended into the planted gardens or the more private courts of the outdoor areas.

Whilst this layout of accommodation arising from the

programme of requirements forms a complete entity in itself, its most effective completion depends on the future development near the Senate House and the refectory site and the linking spaces between these.

The plans show that the proposed new buildings fan out at the Senate House end of the site to accommodate the larger lecture rooms and common rooms. Between these heavily used areas of the plan and the Senate House and proposed refectory site there is an effective change of level. There is also a need for a route to link these levels and to connect the new Arts Faculty buildings to the central buildings.

The design suggests that the existing Senate House and the new refectory might be developed not as two separate buildings but as one continuous group. Between this group and the common room areas and main lecture room areas of the new Arts buildings there might be some form of external arena or amphitheatre within the change of level. At the lower level the open areas outside the common room extend towards this. At the higher level the main rooms of the new refectory and its outdoor terrace could look out across it. The refectory forecourt and its amphitheatre could form a place for many summer activities in addition to providing a setting for plays and music. Spaces of this kind find their own uses and have a significant part to play in the life of a university.

STAGE 1   STAGE 2   STAGES 1 & 2   **4**

STAGE 4   STAGE 3   STAGES 3 & 4   **5**

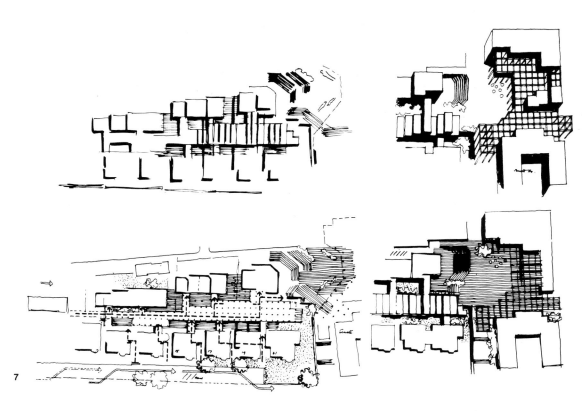

7

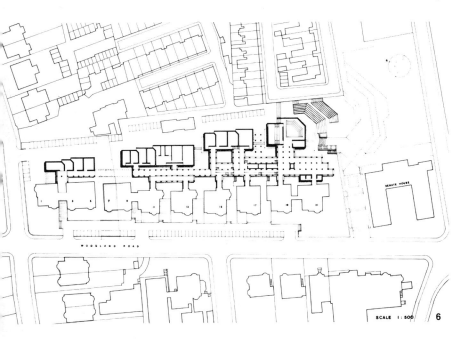

SENATE HOUSE

WOODLAND ROAD

SCALE 1 : 500   **6**

4, 5 & 6. The staged growth of development. **7.** The first sketches of the scheme and studies of the possible link with and treatment of the upper level including a new social building. **8.** General view. The broad flight of steps on the right leads to the main university pedestrian entrance marked by its entrance gateway. **9 & 10.** The lecture room groups.

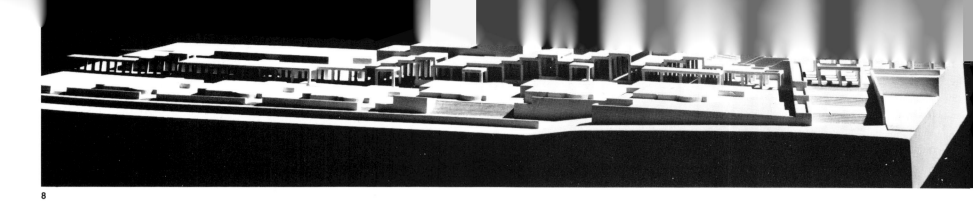

8

9

10

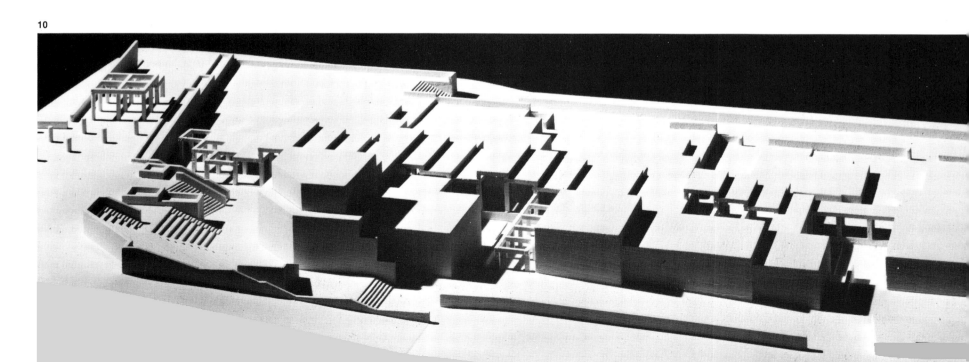

11

11. General view. 12. Top: elevation of the lecture room groups. Middle: section through the central circulation and communal area showing the descending levels and clerestory roof lighting. Bottom: elevation showing the connections from faculty houses and the courtyards formed by this.

13. The main lecture room and outdoor arena. 14. General plan. The central space is opened out by brick pier construction and externally overlooks planted courtyards. It includes cloaks and lavatory areas, reading rooms and main common room areas.

12

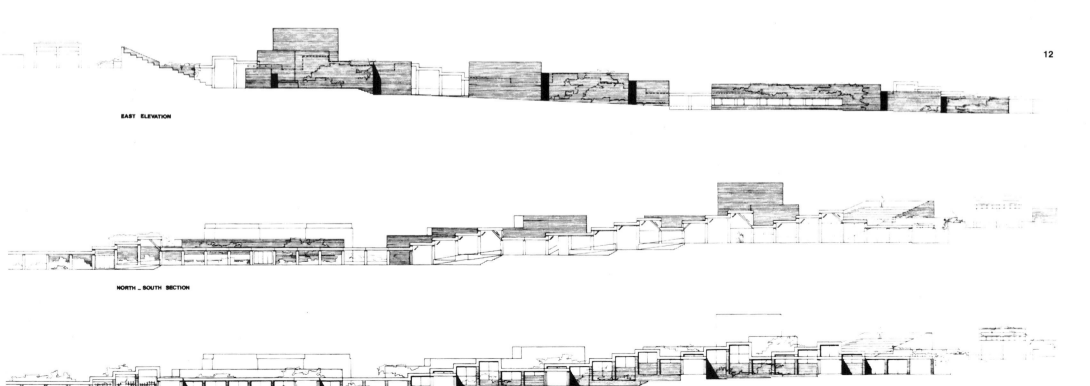

EAST ELEVATION

NORTH _ SOUTH SECTION

WEST ELEVATION

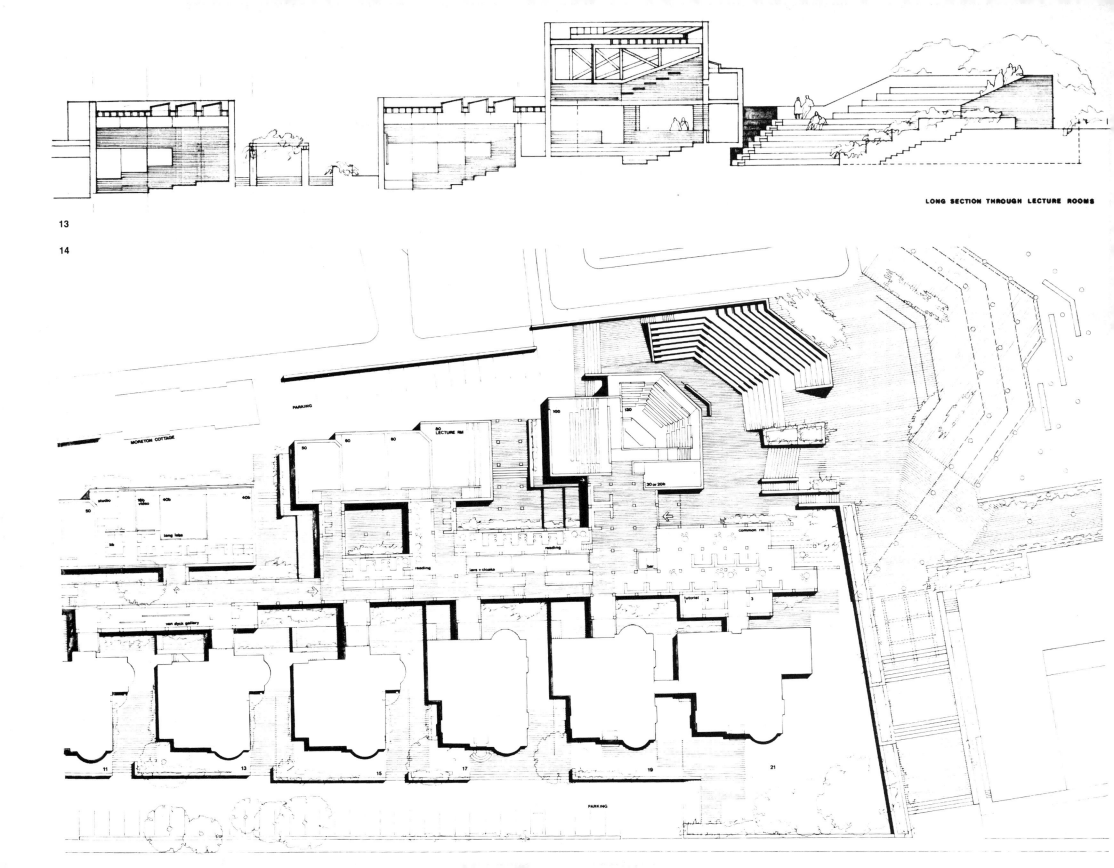

LONG SECTION THROUGH LECTURE ROOMS

13

14

Royal Scottish Academy of Music and Drama, Glasgow (1979–)

The Royal Scottish Academy of Music and Drama, founded in 1847, is one of the few conservatories in the United Kingdom and the only institution in Scotland which provides an education to prepare students for careers on the stage, in music and in opera.

The Academy is at present housed in an old building in the centre of the city and has spent some years developing plans for its new accommodation. From 1970 onwards various sites were considered: in the earlier proposals it was suggested that the building might form part of the larger civic group (see pp. 136–40) which included the new concert hall for Glasgow and its associated facilities. In 1979 further changes were made in the overall scheme and the Royal Scottish Academy decided, if possible, to build on its own self-contained site.

Various possibilities were considered and finally a site at the corner of Renfrew Street and Hope Street suggested by the Glasgow District Council was selected. The location is excellent. It is near to the city centre and to transport. It is also conveniently placed in relation to the headquarters of Scottish Opera already established in Hope Street and with which the Academy has close associations. The site, already cleared when selected, has sufficient area to allow a spreading form of plan which might avoid some of the problems of sound insulation that are unavoidable in any multi-storeyed structure on a more restricted site. The one adjoining block of housing and shops is the distinguished MacConnell building on part of the Hope Street frontage.

The accommodation required by the programme is complex. The School of Drama needs a working theatre to seat about 400 with full stage and backstage space and equipment. Associated with this main

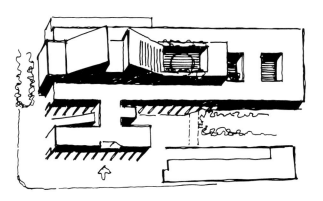

1

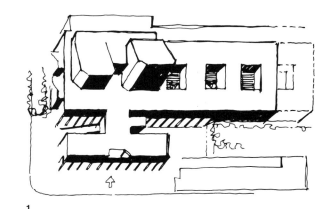

3

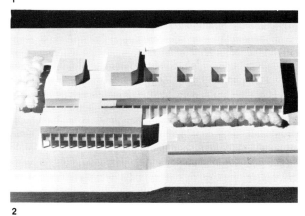

2

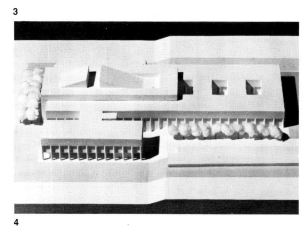

4

1, 2, 3 & 4. Diagrams and models of preliminary studies of two contrasting alignments of the auditoria. In 1 and 2 the theatre and concert hall run across the building, in 3 and 4 along its length. **5 & 6.** Illustration of these two early proposals in more developed form. The load bearing brick walls and the attempt to produce natural lighting in other parts of the building has remained constant. **7 & 8.** Other positions for the auditoria that have been examined.

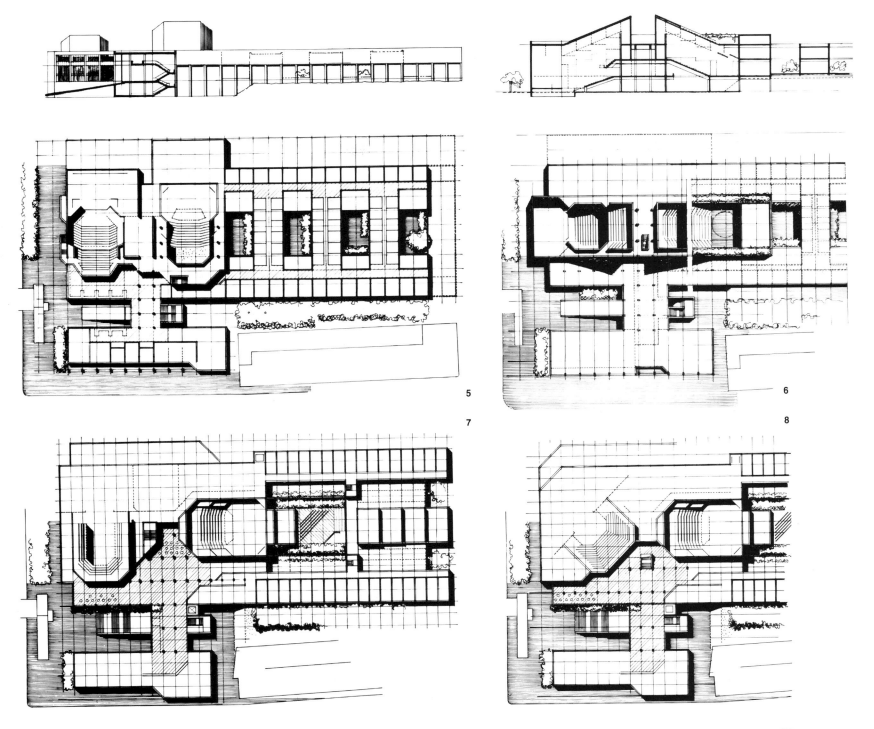

5

6

7

8

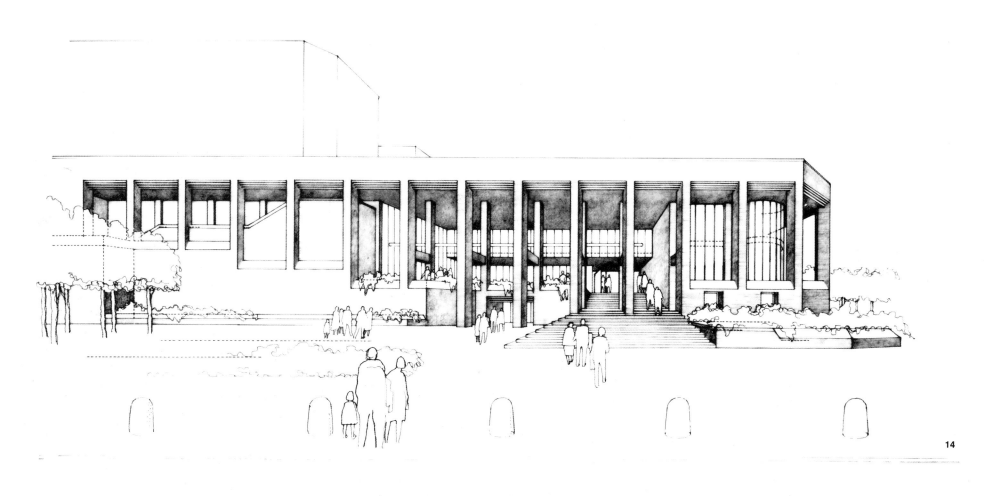

14

9

10

11

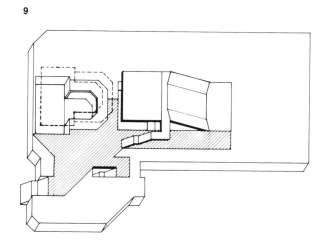

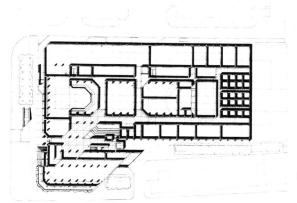

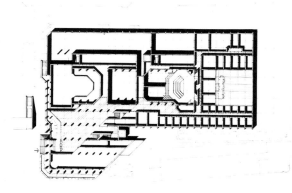

volume are dressing rooms and these in turn serve a 'laboratory' theatre and television studio. These major areas are supported by a number of teaching rooms for acting, voice, movement etc. There is also of course accommodation for staff. The main element in the School of Music is the concert hall, seating 500 with an adequate stage for orchestra and choir. There are forty-two staff and teaching rooms in the various departments of String, Piano, Wind, Brass, Music Theory etc., and class teaching rooms for group work. Rooms for electronic music and organ are provided and one major requirement is the provision of a large number of practice rooms of various sizes. In addition to this, opera requires special rehearsal facilities. The programme also includes accommodation for administration, communal and catering areas and a library.

One of the guiding principles behind the plan arrangement was the need to place the two main auditoria, the 'laboratory' theatre and the opera rehearsal room in positions which relate them to the various working areas but which also allow convenient access when performances are given. These rooms are in any case the major volumes within the building and their relationship is the key to its effective organisation. Various possibilities of grouping have been examined. The form finally selected places these auditoria in a linear arrangement which creates the spine running along the length of the building.

The remaining accommodation then takes its place

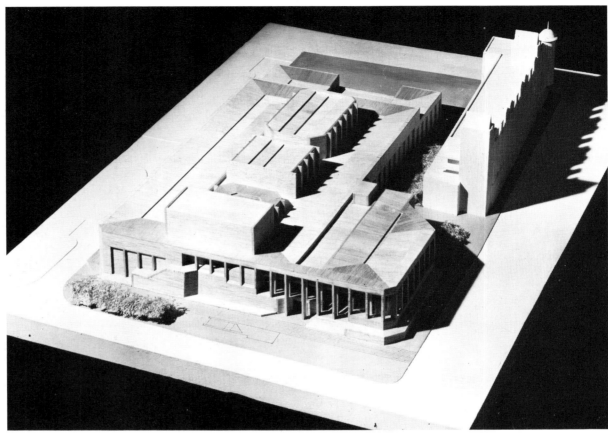

15

12

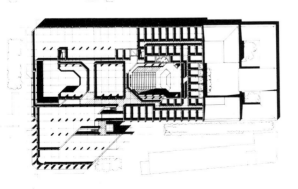

13

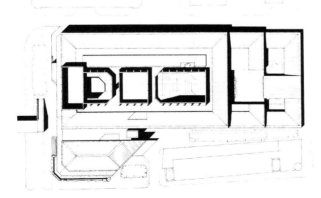

9. Final position and levels of the theatre and concert hall and the central opera rehearsal room in relation to the main foyer at first floor level. **10, 11, 12 & 13.** Plan at ground level (10) which contains the main student entrance and the main accommodation for drama. The common entrance hall gives access to a shared lecture room, the main dining facilities (bottom left) and the stair and lift to upper levels. Plan at first floor level (11) contains the main foyer, accessible externally. The Music School entrance is at this level. Plan 12 shows the library, common rooms and upper level of the Music School. The roof plan (13). **14.** General view, main frontage. The student entrance is at street level: the main public entrance and foyer is approached by the external stair. The library is over this. The drawing shows the wide pavement in front of the entrance. **15.** A general view.

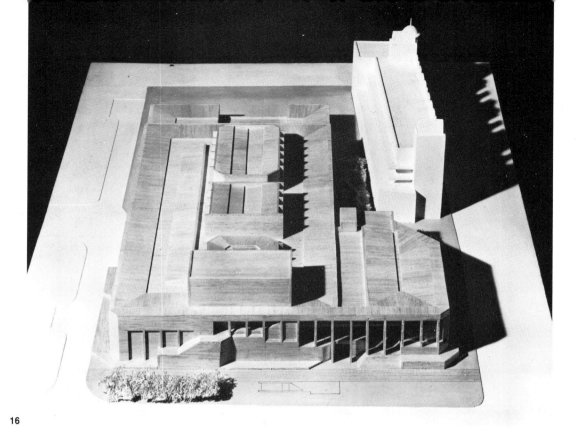

16

around these structuring elements. A common entrance for students at ground floor level gives direct access to the Department of Drama and the working areas for Drama students are at this level. The entrance to the Department of Music is at first floor level and this forms the principal floor level for the department.

A common foyer area at first floor level acts as a coffee area for students during breaks, but it also serves as the main public foyer for those attending performances in the theatre, concert hall, laboratory theatre or opera recital areas. The public enter this foyer at first floor level from an external staircase, an arrangement that allows effective control of entry either for internal students or external visitors.

This layout has several additional advantages. The ground level accommodation for Drama allows direct access to scenery stores, goods and workshops from the service road which runs along the length of the western boundary of the site. This band of scenery stores, workshops etc. provides a direct movement to the stage, laboratory theatre and television studio areas. A second band of rooms includes all the dressing rooms at ground and first floor levels. These again are linked to all the performance spaces, and whilst each department has its own allocation of rooms, they can be interchangeable between departments when

16. The entrance front and the central alignment of theatre, opera rehearsal room and concert hall. **17.** Plan at ground level: 1 Student entrance hall and lavatories. 2 Dining and staff common room area. 3 Kitchen. 4 Shared lecture room. 5 Drama School entrance. 6 Theatre. 7 Laboratory theatre. 8 Large acting rooms. 9 Movement room. 10 Dressing rooms. 11 Scenery and workshops. 12 TV studio. 13 Acting rooms. 14 Voice. 15 Music practice. The orchestra pit to the concert hall is at this level and there is also accommodation for music practice rooms.

17

special performances demand additional accommodation.

The dining and common room areas, the administrative accommodation and the student recreation rooms are housed in a self-contained block separated from the main working and performance areas of the School. One of the main problems throughout the whole building is that of providing sound insulation between room and room and this is particularly difficult when a large number of rooms, for music practice for example, have to be grouped. The experience at the Music School building in Cambridge proved very helpful, and the tests on that building led to the adoption of load bearing brick walls. Again the principle of providing daylight in as many rooms as possible and avoiding air conditioning has been adopted as a matter of policy.

The external appearance of this building is intended to make its contribution to the street architecture of the city. The main entrance front is set back to provide a wide pavement with some tree planting. The main foyer and public entrance level, which is also the principal entrance level of the auditoria, forms a *piano nobile* within which the main elements in the building can be seen or sensed. The external finish is buff brick chosen to harmonise with the colour of the adjoining MacConnell building.

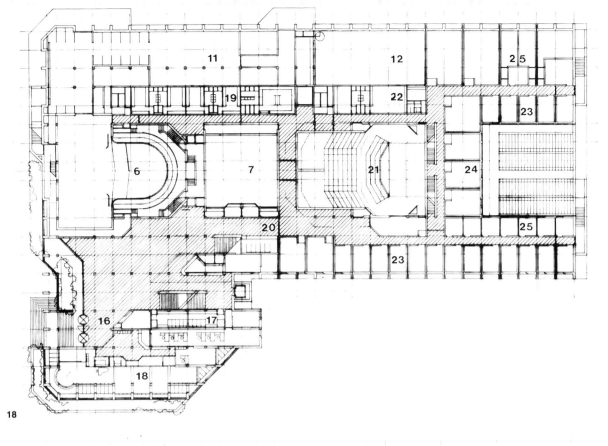

18

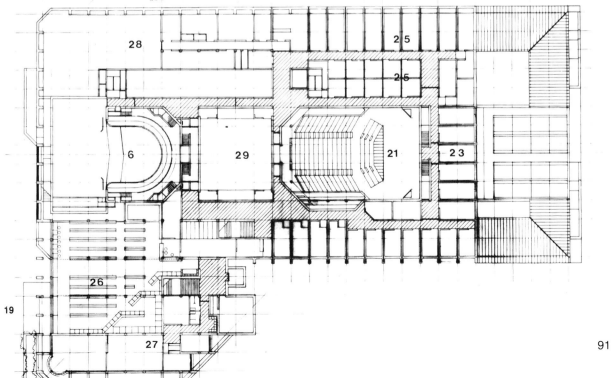

19

18. First floor level: 16 Public entrance and general foyer. 17 Lavatories. 18 Administration. 6 Upper part of theatre. 7 Upper part of laboratory theatre. 11 Upper part of workshops, etc. 12 Upper part of TV studio. 19 Second level of dressing rooms. 20 Entrance to the Music School. 21 Concert hall. 22 Dressing rooms. 23 Teaching. 24 Classrooms. 25 Practice. **19.** Second floor level: 26 Library. 27 Common rooms. 6 Upper level of theatre. 28 Wardrobe etc. Upper level of Music School includes 21 Concert hall. 23 Teaching. 25 Practice. 29 Opera rehearsal.

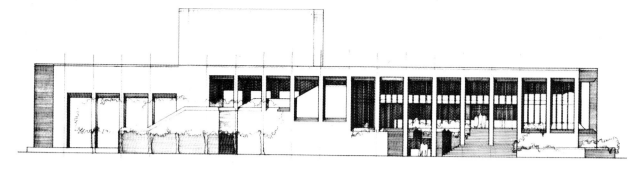

20

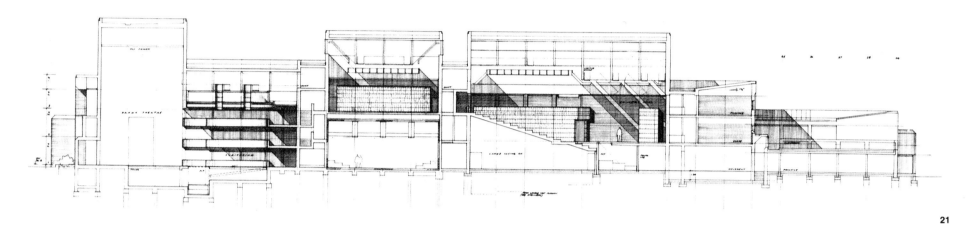

21

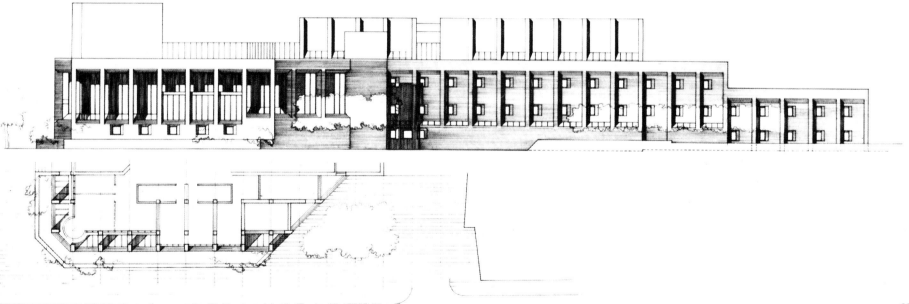

22

23

20. Elevation of the main entrance front. The accommodation for common rooms, administration etc. is on the right: scenery, workshops etc. on the left. **21** is a long section showing the main auditoria, theatre, opera rehearsal and concert hall. **22** shows the side elevation with the main administration block on the left. The building is built largely in load bearing brickwork with steel construction for the larger spans. This choice comes from the fact that good sound insulation between room and room is essential. The Music School in Cambridge proved the effectiveness of the brick load bearing system, which becomes particularly suitable as many of the rooms are small and the building itself is low in height. The structural method shows itself clearly in the elevations. The grid from which the plan and room sizes are generated produces a system of external piers. These projecting piers also act to some extent as sound baffles between windows of individual rooms. The windows themselves are small and double glazed. Experience at Cambridge seemed to show that the advantages of natural lighting in rooms outweighed any risk of external sound penetration from this source. **23 & 24.** The pier system over a plinth of varying height is used consistently throughout the external treatment. The infilling panels reflect the changes of internal need. The deeply recessed glazing of the foyers and library over and the double line of brick piers emphasises the point of entry.

24

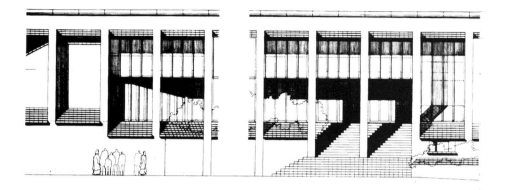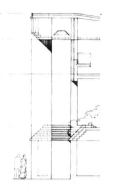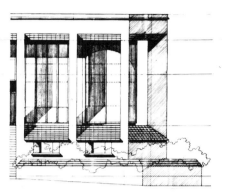

25

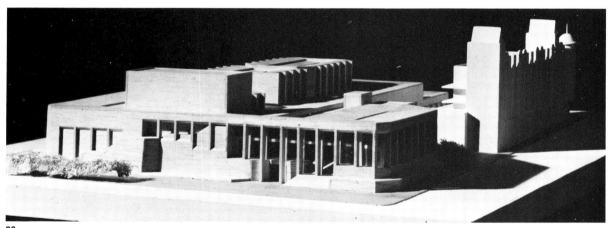

26

27

25 shows some of the variants within the external pier system. On the main frontage the piers become free standing and the entrance and foyer is deeply recessed to form a terrace overlooking the main street. The plan of the entrance and foyer area, **28**, illustrates this. It also demonstrates the grid pattern which guides the general proportions of the plan. In some areas the external piers are direct extensions of the sound-insulating internal walls. In this area the plan is opened out by an internal pier system which allows easy diagonal movement across the foyer area. Elsewhere the piers act as sound baffles between windows. The rhythm of the piers remains constant around the exterior of the building but the section between these piers is modulated in many ways to meet the special requirements of differing users within the parts of the general plan. The building is intended to mark itself out as one with a special purpose. It is not another commercial building. It is set back well behind the normal building line. Its pavement is broad to accommodate groups of people. It has a special pavement which is planted with trees. In its buff colour it is related to the stone of its distinguished neighbour, the MacConnell building. Its height is related to the reception suites of the new adjoining hotel and to the older building used by Scottish Opera across Hope Street. This new building for the Royal Scottish Academy together with the Scottish Opera activity and the residential and shop accommodation in the adjacent building will form a new enclave in this part of Glasgow.

26, 27 & 31. Views of the model. **29** shows the emphasis on the entrance created by the free standing pier system and the entrance steps. The depth and recession is again increased by the way in which the structural lines and materials of the exterior are carried through into the interior of the building itself. **30.** A study of the relationship of the forms of the theatre, the opera rehearsal room and the concert hall.

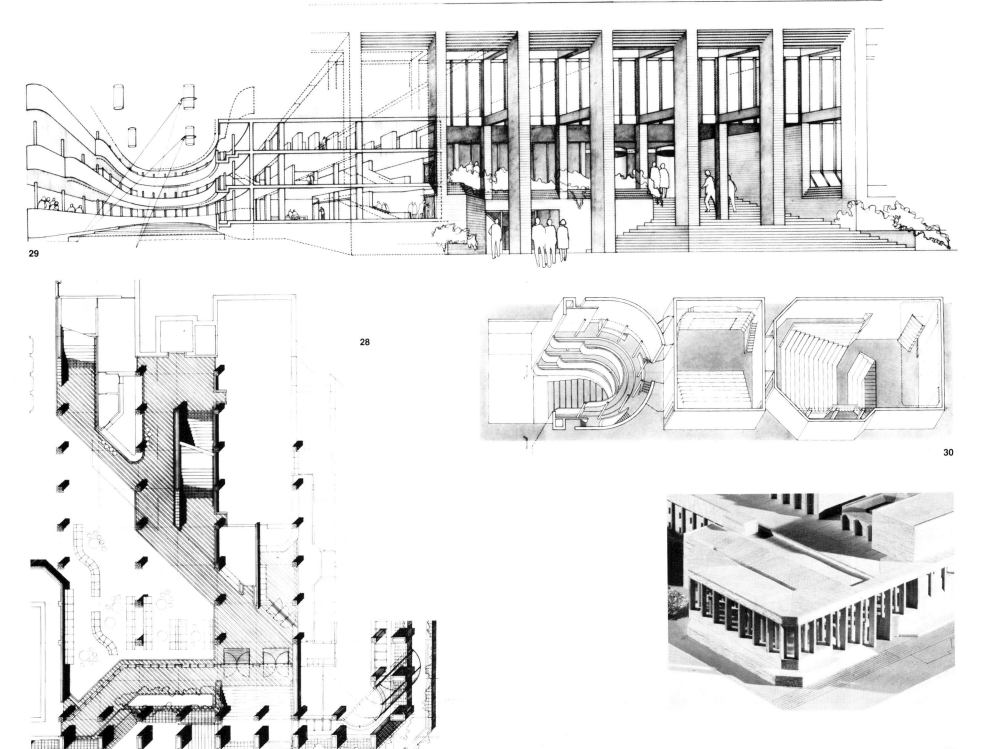

29

28

30

95

1

2

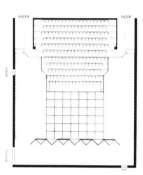

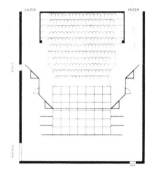

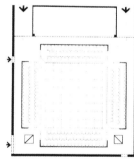

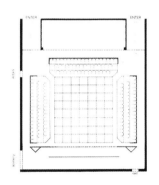

In the introductory note to Part 1 above a reference was made to the type forms of auditoria for the theatre and the concert hall, to the precedents which determined their form and to the continuity of that form over a considerable period of time in different parts of the world.

The differing acoustic qualities of the two type forms have long been recognised and in this country were brilliantly described and explained by Bagenal.[2] The acoustics of the theatre are, he once said, 'the acoustics of the open air, of sound reflected across a valley' or in the perfect valley of the Greek theatre where the direct sound is reinforced but is without reverberation. These are the acoustic conditions that are developed by Palladio's theatre at Vicenza and the later theatres and opera houses with their superimposed galleries all brought close to the source of sound. In contrast to this, there is what Bagenal called 'the acoustics of the cave' in which the enclosed volume continues the length of each sound, the sounds overlap into what is

Early work by Peter Moro in 1969 produced a drama studio for the University of Hull. This was in fact a teaching laboratory in which various forms of stage presentation could be studied. Since then the ten theatres that he has designed (as described in the *RIBA Journal*, Feb. 1979) show the range of flexibility that may be required by the modern theatre, not to mention the multi-purpose hall. The diagrams illustrate the various arrangements that are made possible by the use of mobile elements in the laboratory theatre at Hull. **1** shows a typical thrust stage arrangement and **2** the arena form; the variable auditorium at Moro's Bristol New Vic Theatre.

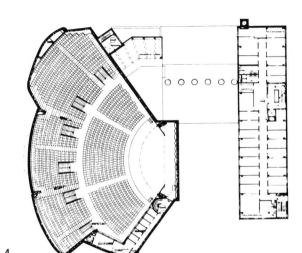

3

sometimes called richness or warmth and the reverberation time is increased; sometimes, as in the cathedral, to such a length that the speaker must intone.

It was from this kind of qualitative assessment that Bagenal continued to define the acoustic requirements of auditoria for various purposes. Meanwhile the method of predicting the forms that would produce these qualities remained uncertain. The recognition of the intrinsic relationship between acoustic need and desirable shape was made clear as early as 1835 when Dr D. B. Reid gave his evidence on debating chambers for the new Houses of Parliament.[3] In the first twenty years of this century, M. Gustave Lyon, in Paris, carried out a series of pioneering experiments to track down the reflection of sound in building and was subsequently responsible for the acoustics and the form in the Salle Pleyel. During the same period Professor Sabine of Harvard had made studies of the growth and decay of sound in enclosed spaces. His

definition of reverberation time and the possibility of calculating this in advance of construction opened a new field of influence on the shape of auditoria.

Thus with this new knowledge of reflection and reverberation the form changes: fan-shaped and sometimes asymmetrical plans and reflective ceilings are developed. Nevertheless even in 1948 when a serious effort was made to call on all the scientific evidence in relation to the design of the Royal Festival Hall, the question of prediction of the acoustic performance of the enclosed space (though not of sound transmission in the structure) remained uncertain.

A further complication resulted from the fact that the requirements of use within the field of auditoria were also changing. In the case of concert halls, fine halls for music like the Gewandhaus at Leipzig (1886) had a capacity of 1,500; the seating capacity of the Salle Pleyel (1925) showed an increase of seats to 3,000 as did the Royal Festival Hall (1951). As halls increased in size so too did the difficulties of maintaining the

4

5

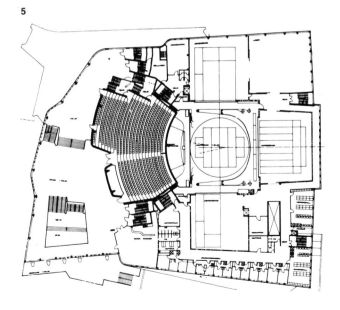

3. Acoustic form from Alvar Aalto's study for the Viipuri City Library, 1933–5. 4 & 5. Aalto's studies have added considerably to the range of auditoria forms. Aalto's House of Culture, Helsinki, and his Opera House at Essen.

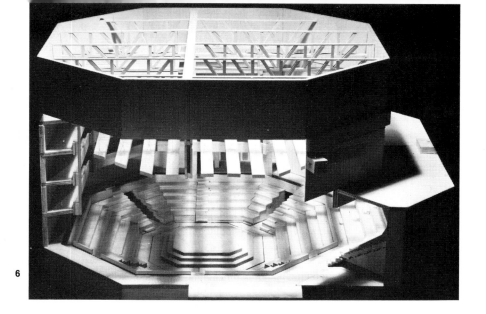

6

reverberation time. In addition it was becoming clear that the larger type of hall was unlikely to be used entirely for one particular purpose and it became necessary to consider either more specialised smaller halls or, where this is possible and when uses are reasonably compatible, the multi-purpose hall, and in these circumstances it is likely that new forms of auditoria may be developed.

Nor is the design of the theatre unaffected. New forms of presenting drama have produced the 'theatre in the round', pioneered in a number of centres in Britain and in which emphasis may be given to sophisticated lighting rather than scenery. At one stage in the development of the early schemes for the Cultural Centre in Glasgow an attempt was made to design a theatre which could be readily adaptable either in the form of an arena, a thrust stage, or the pure prosce-

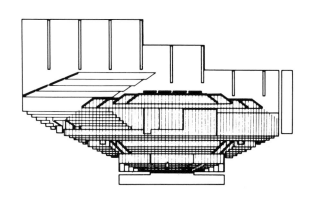

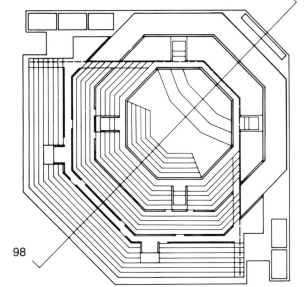

98

10

nium type. It is quite clear that the auditorium as a type form is in the process of adaptation and evolution. In these circumstances the value of testing and prediction in advance becomes obvious.[4]

In the last few years we have been involved in a number of these problems. The earlier designs for the Cultural Centre in Glasgow included a hall seating 2,500 and it was designed predominantly for music; the form of this hall, including the modified fan-shaped plan, the terraced seating and the reflecting ceiling, are the direct result of this influence. In later designs, whilst the use of the hall for music and adequate acoustic conditions for this remain unaffected, an attempt was made by the simple adjustment of seating and ceiling panels to adapt the hall speedily for the many other forms of presentation or display which are likely to be required.

The early designs for the Cultural Centre at Glasgow included both a concert hall for 2,500 and a theatre. The theatre element involved a number of studies in which an attempt was made to combine differing requirements. **6.** The general form that resulted. Within this form various adjustments were possible. **7.** The plan and interior form of a theatre in the round in which surrounding galleries were considered to be an important element. **8.** The dividing line of the proscenium and the provision of a thrust stage. With this arrangement, gallery seating is brought into use. **9.** A further modification of 8. **10.** A possible adjustment to the main concert hall form to make provision for other and quite different types of use requiring an arena form. The latest scheme for this project accepts the fact that planning for variable use is necessary and planning and acoustic studies demonstrate that the simplest and most effective arrangements are now being made.

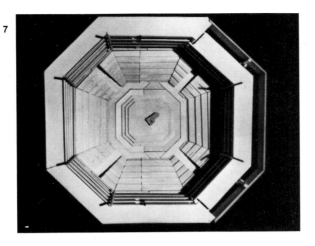

7

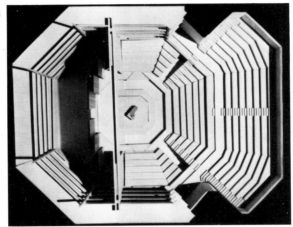

8

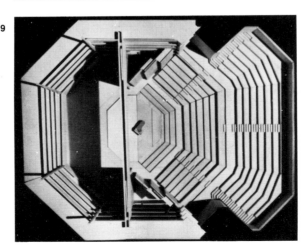

9

99

4 · The gallery:

buildings in a landscape

Gallery of Contemporary Art, Gulbenkian
Foundation, Lisbon (1979–)

The site plan of the park. **1** shows the main group of buildings which forms the headquarters of the Gulbenkian Foundation (bottom) and the new gallery (top). The gallery entrance is from the road on the right. The beautifully planted park rises from the level of the lake. The illustration at the head of the page shows the initial model for the new building. Its stepped form produced variety of height internally, good daylighting and the possibility of external planting so that the levels of roof form an extension of the landscape itself. **2** shows the actual building in the landscape during construction. From **3** it can be seen that the height of the frontage is modest and that the receding roof levels lend themselves to informal planting.

The buildings described in the preceding pages of this book fall into categories and within each category there are several developments of the same type of building. The Gallery for Contemporary Art in Lisbon is certainly a 'type' form, although so far as the work of our Studio is concerned it is unique. Earlier buildings designed for the exhibition of works of art like the small gallery at Hull or the Kettle's Yard group are small-scaled and highly specialised. They have similar problems of display and lighting but the Lisbon Gallery moves the problem on to a totally different level which has its counterparts in some of the large-scale galleries that have recently been built in other countries of the world. The Lisbon Gallery is also built in a special climate, on an exceptional site and with its own particular background of use.

The building has its origin in the history of the development of the Calouste Gulbenkian Foundation

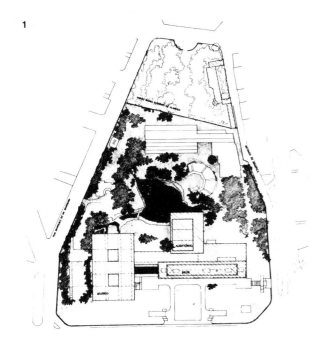

1

3

in Lisbon. In October 1969 the new headquarters building for the Calouste Gulbenkian Foundation was inaugurated in Lisbon. The building, in addition to providing the offices for the Foundation, included a main auditorium, suites of meeting rooms, a gallery for temporary exhibitions and in particular the gallery which forms the permanent home for the Gulbenkian collection.

This historic collection starts with Egyptian work and ranges through oriental and Islamic art; a European collection extending from the eleventh to the nineteenth century; French decorative art, furniture and artifacts of the eighteenth and nineteenth centuries; it ends with the work of Lalique. The building which houses this collection provides a changing background and setting for each varying period, and with the support of a library the collection forms an important centre for the enjoyment and study of the history of

art, and it attracts many visitors.

The Foundation has, however, continued to extend the artistic and educational interest of the founder by arranging, in a special gallery, temporary exhibitions of contemporary art and by building up a contemporary collection through purchases. In 1979 the Foundation took the first steps to extend its educational services into the future by building a new gallery for contemporary art.

The main Foundation building was built within an existing park. The park was redesigned and now includes a lake (seen from inside the auditorium) and an outdoor amphitheatre which is used during the summer months. The existing building and its approaches are at the northern end of the site. The land at the southern end is privately owned. The road along the eastern boundary is heavily used by traffic, but the road on the west boundary is a quiet street and

this seemed to be the most favourable point of access to the new building which is intended to be separate and self-contained. There is a service tunnel running north–south from the main building which can be used for the delivery of goods and works of art to the new gallery.

The elements in the programme for the building are a main exhibition area planned for flexibility; a linking route between this and the main entrance hall; a main entrance area connected with a restaurant and administration. The entrance hall and its adjacent accommodation will also serve a separate area to be developed for the art of animation. A large storage area is essential.

Two possible positions for the building were considered, both having the same point of entry. One of these, with its gallery running north–south, involved a difficult relationship with the existing building which

101

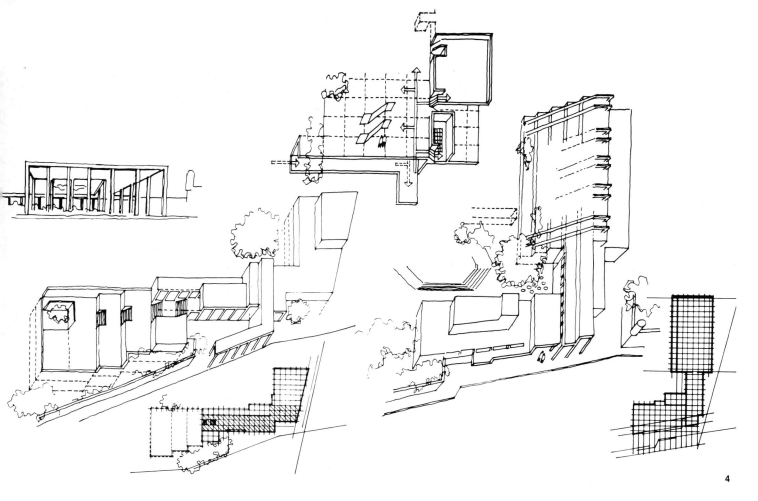

4

4. Diagrams of schemes to suit two possible sites. The scheme on the right forms the basis of the scheme now being built. Top centre shows the main gallery and its half level system of layout. **5.** Preliminary model. The main entrance. **6.** View along the building from the entry point. The roof levels of the entrance portico and hall continue into the roof levels of the main gallery beyond. The stepped form of the gallery allows northlighting for the interior. The building for animation is in the foreground on the left.

could only be avoided by placing the gallery partly underground and removing an important group of trees in this area.

The alternative position which was finally selected runs east–west along the southern boundary. There are several advantages in this location. The main entrance itself leads directly from the Estrada de Benfica, and takes the form of a lofty portico and covered area well set back from the line of the existing wall and marking in a distinctive way the entry point to the new gallery.

From this entrance portico it is possible to see through the glazed entrance enclosure into the interior of the entrance gallery. To the right of this there is the catalogue and book counter with the administration area over. To the left there is a waiting area, a restaurant overlooking a terrace with views across the amphitheatre and the park, and cloakrooms below. On

this left-hand side of the entrance hall there is also access to the animation building, which can be entirely self-contained if necessary.

The entrance hall is linked to the main exhibition space by a connecting gallery. This connecting link is used as an introductory area to the main gallery. It contains a special display of the six large tapestries already in the possession of the Foundation. It is accessible to the administration and has a small lecture room in which preparatory talks can be given to visitors to the main gallery.

A visitor passing from the entrance to the main gallery moves through this lofty connecting gallery space. The line of his route is extended into the main gallery and there is an impressive view from the entrance right through to the end of the gallery itself.

The main gallery opens up on either side of this linking route. To the left of the central route are the

main gallery areas opening out on to the park. To the right (at half levels up and down) are the display and drawing areas at the lower level and the linked gallery areas above.

The arrangement derives from the special character of the work to be shown. In the main gallery area there is to be a display of the work of several distinguished Portuguese artists and the British Collection. This main work will be associated with small audio-visual rooms and an area for drawings and archives at the lower half level. Above this half level is a continuous gallery in which international art connected with the work shown in the main gallery can be exhibited.

The entire volume of the gallery including the half levels can be appreciated as a single space subdivided by levels into the special areas described. The main beams of the roof have a clear span over the gallery itself; their slope allows a stepped roof which provides

5

6

vertical northlights to admit daylight over the whole of the area. This is supplemented by artificial lighting from the suspended lighting galleries so that the positioning of exhibits can be entirely free. Glazed lifts are provided to move objects from the store areas below the main galleries.

The gallery opens out on to the park and provides views across it. This arrangement suggests a natural extension for sculpture in the open air.

The area for the study and development of animation forms a separate but related group. Its planning, arranged around a central area, is left as open as possible for adaptation as the work develops.

The parkland and the lake in front of the building forms a distinguished setting. The new building is well related to the existing amphitheatre and fits naturally into the landscape. Its stepped roof areas will be planted.

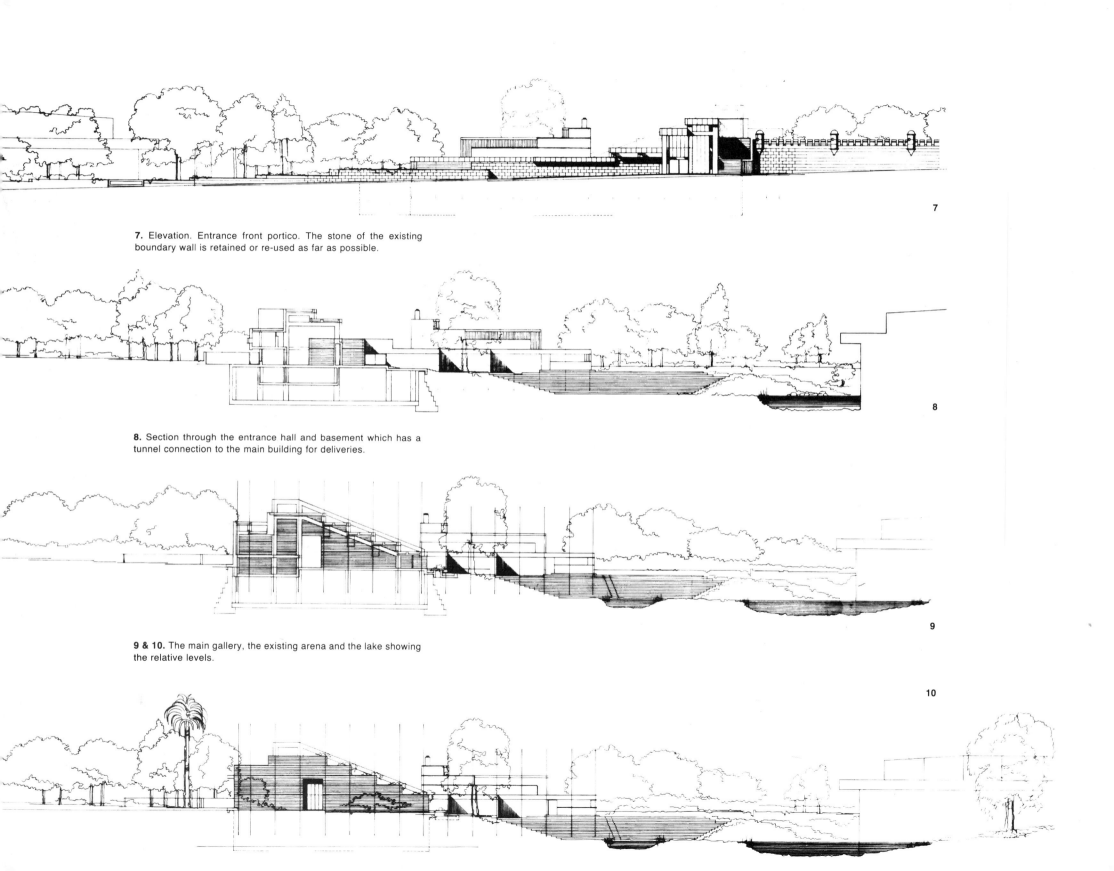

7. Elevation. Entrance front portico. The stone of the existing boundary wall is retained or re-used as far as possible.

8. Section through the entrance hall and basement which has a tunnel connection to the main building for deliveries.

9 & 10. The main gallery, the existing arena and the lake showing the relative levels.

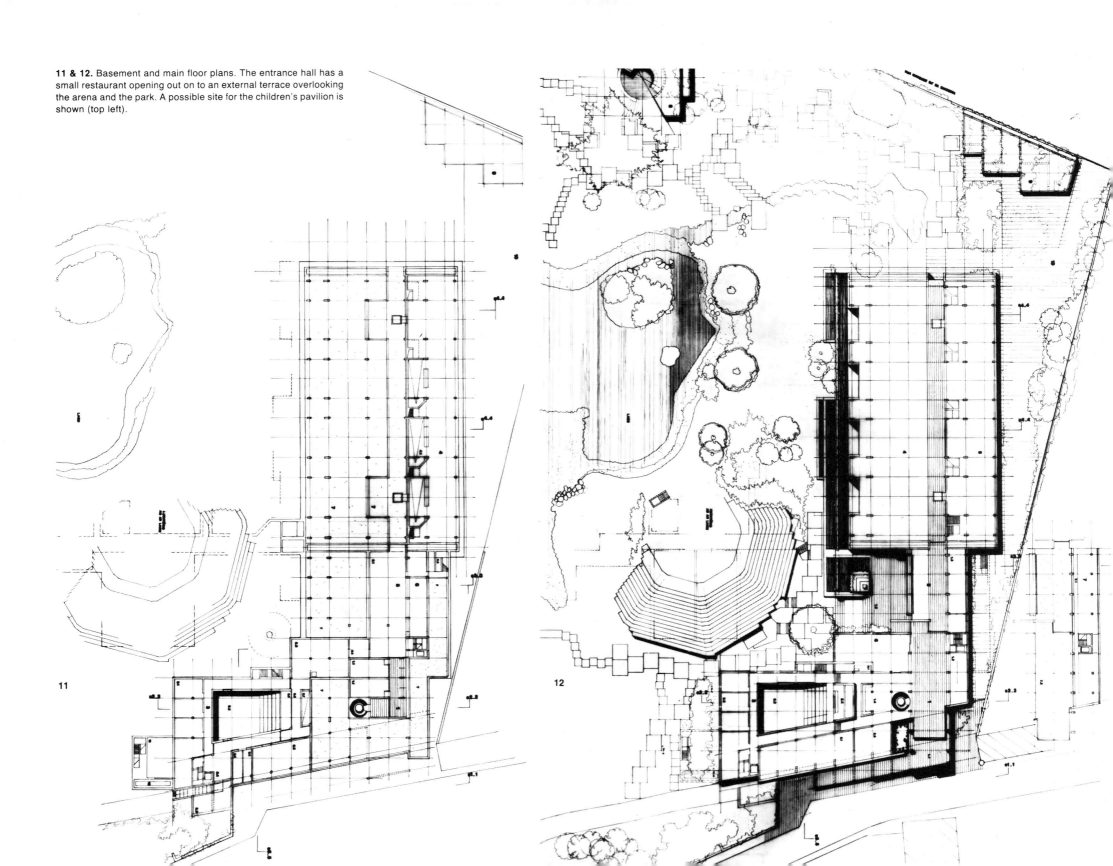

11 & 12. Basement and main floor plans. The entrance hall has a small restaurant opening out on to an external terrace overlooking the arena and the park. A possible site for the children's pavilion is shown (top left).

11

12

13

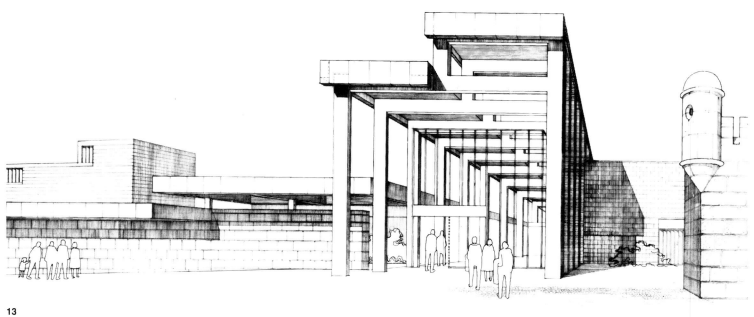

15   16

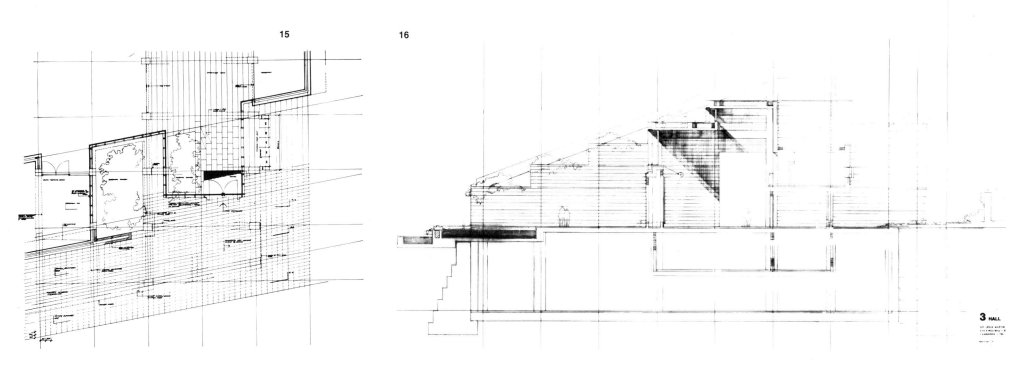

14

13 & 17. The main entrance. One of the turrets of the old stone surrounding wall is on the right. The portico itself is in concrete with a light finish. The fascia is metal and has a bronze colour treatment. Aluminium window frames have the same finish. All the walls of the building have a stone veneer. 14. General view from the south west. 15. Plan of the entrance portico. Indoor and outdoor planting. The pavement has a traditional black and white tessellated pattern. 16. Section through the inner hall specially designed to take three large tapestries, and the outdoor restaurant terrace. Photographs show work in progress.

17

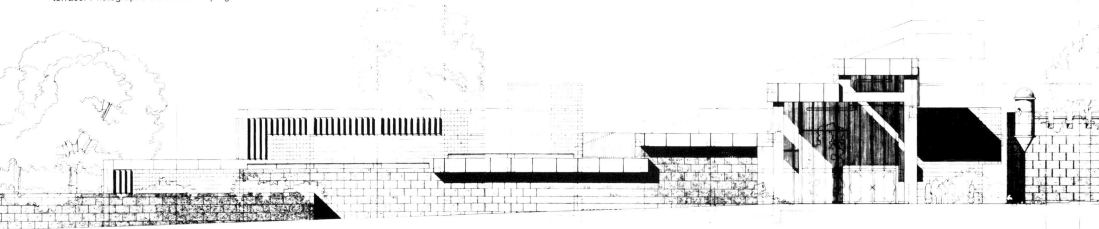

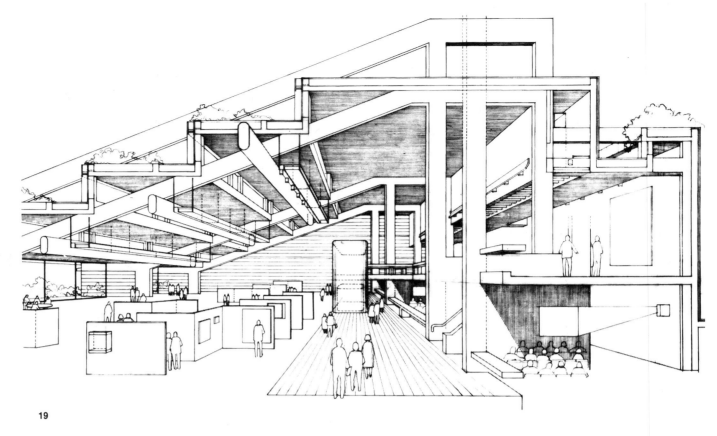

18

19

18 & 19. Interior in construction, and perspective of the interior of the gallery. This shows the northlighting, roof planting and ceiling levels increasing in height from the park frontage on the left. The gallery contains the main collection: the half levels on the right will provide a special gallery (upper level) and areas for display and audio-visual presentation (lower level). Short flights of stairs (faced in stone) and lifts (with a glazed enclosure) connect the levels and the reserve area below. **20 & 22.** Cross section and long section through the main working area in the animation building. **21.** View from the south.

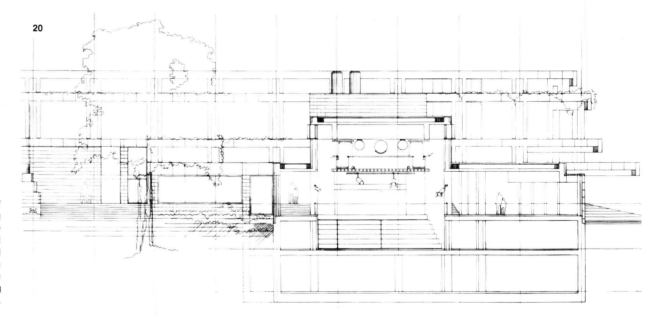

20

21

22

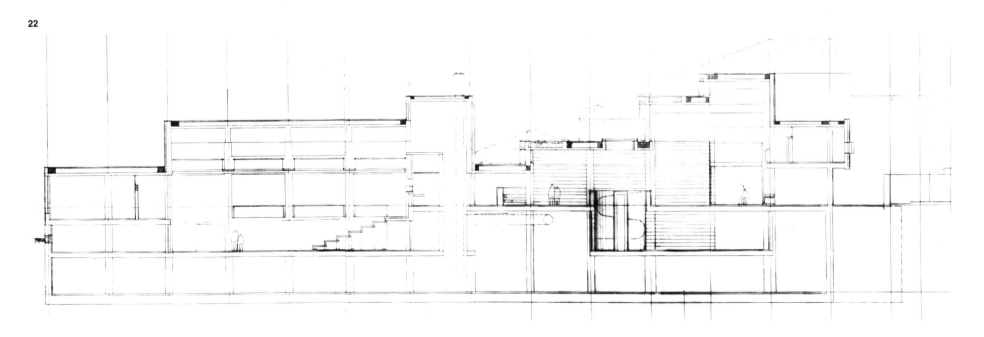

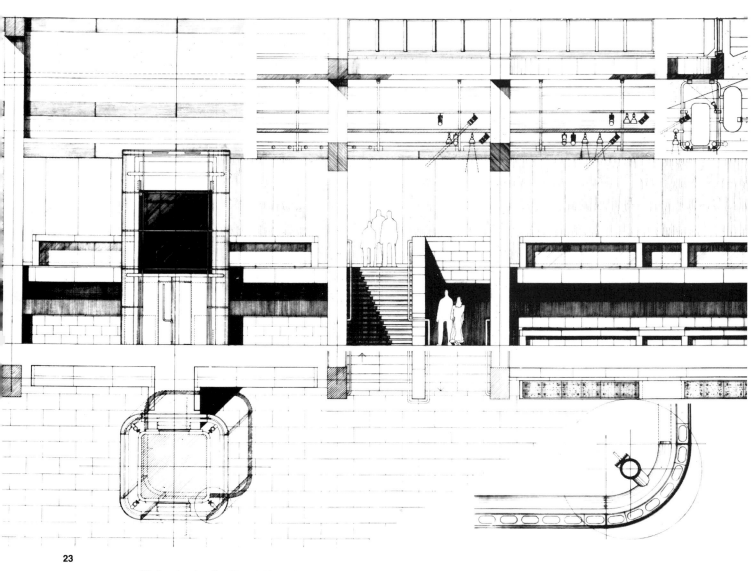

23

24

23. Interior details. Glazed lift shaft; connecting stair and balustrade infilling between the concrete frames. The rear wall of the upper gallery is panelled in timber. Main walls and floor are finished in stone. All artificial lighting to screens etc. is adjustable from the cat-walks which also support the main ventilation ducts. **24** illustrates one of these cat-walks during construction and not yet fitted with its lighting system. **25** shows the arrangement of clerestory windows (right) and gutters and downspouts (left). All this metal work has a bronze coloured finish. **26.** Gutter and downspout (section). **27.** Elevations. **28.** The metal gargoyles at the lowest level. **29.** The building in construction and before the metal cladding is added to the fascias.

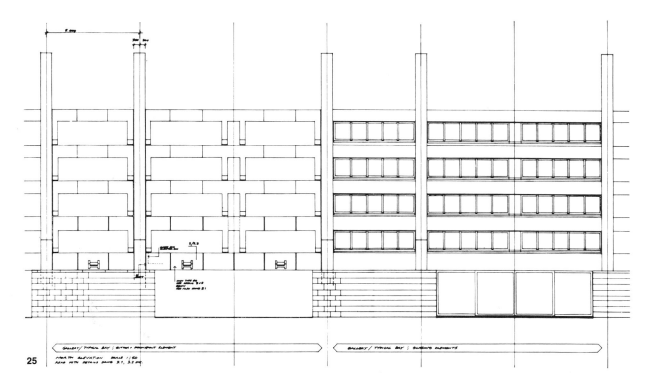

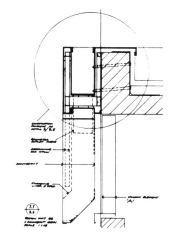

26

25

29

27

28

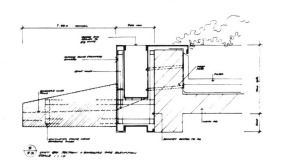

30. The site and work in progress (1982–3).

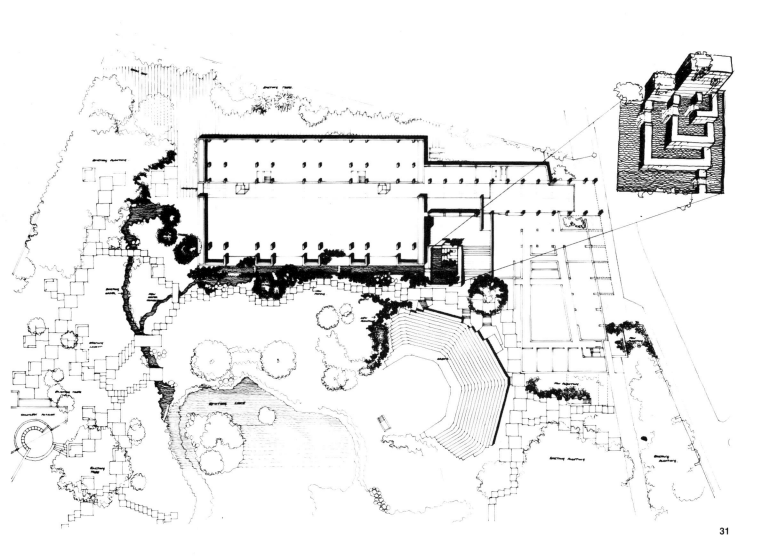

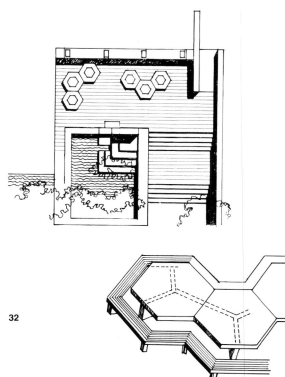

32

31

31. Building and garden. Water and planting protects the face of the building and relates it to its setting. The fountain (right) is the source from which water flows to connect to an existing water course and to the lake. **32.** Outdoor tables and below view across the lake.

114

The childrens' pavilion

One additional building element in the park is a small and informal children's pavilion which will form a working area for children from schools in the area who visit the main collections. Provision will be made for small groups to work on painting, drawing and model making. There is an audio-visual area, staffroom, cloakrooms, and a space in which parents can wait to collect their children.

33. Preliminary ideas for the children's pavilion. This was first designed as an isolated building standing in the park. (The site has now been changed and a new design prepared.) The original scheme centred around a protected outdoor space. Internal rooms are freely arranged for multiple uses. The diagonal approach is related to access points. **34 & 35.** Two views of the first model. The building has a stone veneered finish. Windows and fascia are metal finished with a bronze coloured treatment.

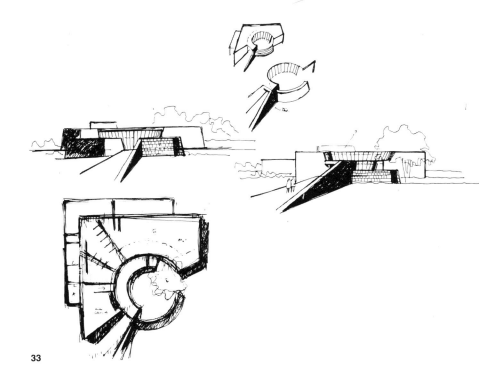

33

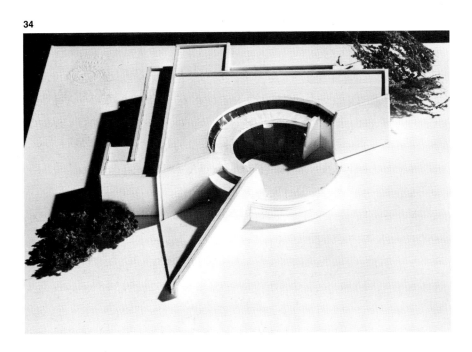

34

35

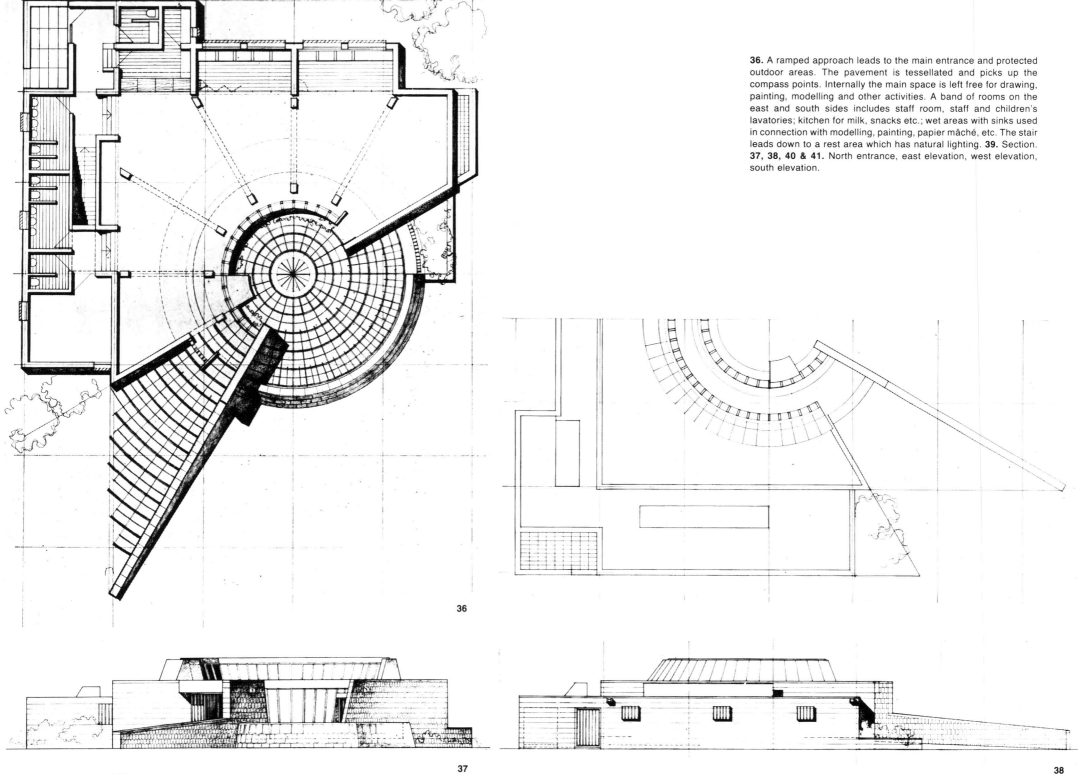

36. A ramped approach leads to the main entrance and protected outdoor areas. The pavement is tessellated and picks up the compass points. Internally the main space is left free for drawing, painting, modelling and other activities. A band of rooms on the east and south sides includes staff room, staff and children's lavatories; kitchen for milk, snacks etc.; wet areas with sinks used in connection with modelling, painting, papier mâché, etc. The stair leads down to a rest area which has natural lighting. **39.** Section. **37, 38, 40 & 41.** North entrance, east elevation, west elevation, south elevation.

36

37

38

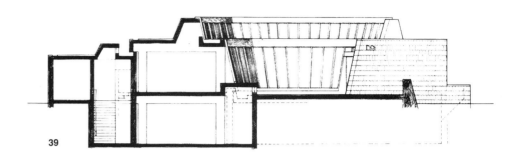

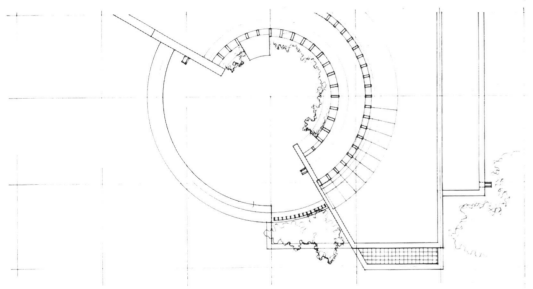

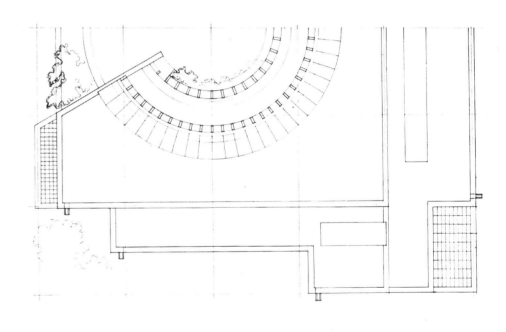

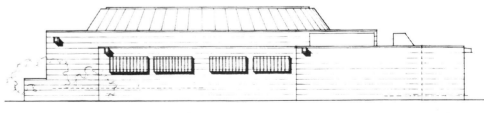

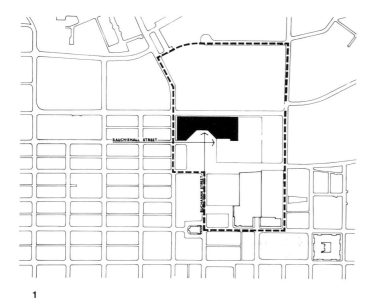

The symbol within the grid

Part 2 below deals with the question of symbol and anonymity within a city. The central area of the city of Glasgow retains its original grid of streets lined by buildings. But at certain points within this general pattern the grid has been opened out around important and significant buildings (for example the buildings in Royal Exchange Square, 1827–9, or St George's Tron Church, 1807), which are given additional emphasis by their setting. The drawings on this page illustrate an attempt to continue this tradition. They show how on the same site three schemes for the civic halls and commercial development, produced between 1968 and 1982, have all retained this central idea: the attempt to provide a special setting, a new point of emphasis within the city grid. This occurs at a deliberately created junction point between two important and established streets (Buchanan and Sauchiehall). Between 1968 and 1982 the component parts within the building group have changed or developed and as the buildings change the form of the junction point itself has moved from octagon to elongated square and to circle. But the central purpose remains. A special building is given a special setting. A new public place is generated by the building form and the public space is itself extended by the creation of pedestrian streets.

1. The site selected for the city halls. The emphasis within the grid.
2. The 1968 plan, developed 1971–9. 3. The 1979 proposal. 4. The 1982 proposal.

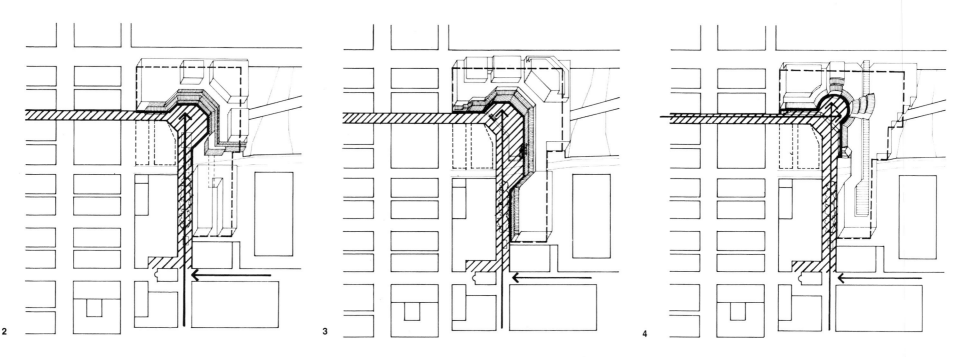

118

2 BUILDINGS AND ENVIRONMENT: SYMBOL AND ANONYMITY

2

BUILDINGS AND ENVIRONMENT: SYMBOL AND ANONYMITY

The second part of this book, like the first, is concerned with buildings. But it has a different emphasis. In the work that has been illustrated in Part 1, buildings have been grouped into families in order to show any continuity of ideas and thought that might exist. Here, in this second part, the schemes or buildings illustrated can be seen to relate to a larger question. They raise two aspects of the problem of building in a city. At one end of the spectrum there is the question of significance, symbol or sense of place; at the other there is the critical issue of fitting in, of infill and anonymity.

Part 2 is not concerned with planning. Nor is it concerned with any idealised notion of the effect that architecture might have on a possible future or with any nostalgia for the merit of an immediate past.[1] The argument starts from the fact that every living city inherits a past, some of which is of great significance. Often it grew up organically and by accretion. But the notion that this was all and that towns and cities were never built within a framework for development has been shown to be untrue.[2]

Planned or planted towns were quite usual in medieval England. What is true is that every city with any history has some kind of imprint from the past, and each succeeding century has overlaid in part at least an earlier form. The city, to use Giancarlo de Carlo's phrase, is in a constant process of 'restructuring' itself around new uses (see p. 228 n. 15).

It is also a commonplace that several towns in the past laid down a pattern for their future development and worked within this. Many cities of the world have been built within an existing grid and many European cities are an impressive illustration of the fact that a pre-ordained city form does not prevent the creation of a distinguished architecture and environment. One such example, and perhaps the best documented demonstration of the argument, comes from Barcelona where Ildofonso de Cerda's competition plan of 1859

1. Change and adaptation: the Roman amphitheatre at Arles, like others, was adapted to different uses during the Middle Ages. In this case it became a fortified town with towers, gates and a concentric street pattern and an open square at the centre (cf. Christopher Hohlers essay, 'Court Life in Peace and War' in *The Flowering of the Middle Ages*, ed. Joan Evans). **2, 3 & 4.** The city of Barcelona as planned by Ildefonso de Cerda. 2 The road system; 3 the railways routes; 4 zones of use: service areas, green spaces, areas for state and industrial use, markets etc.

remained substantially the framework for the city's subsequent development of its *Gran Vias* and *Ramblas*, its public squares, its city blocks and its transport system.[3] Within the overall unification of that framework the scale of building has remained constant, the planning within each individual block has great variety, and buildings as different as those with completely glazed frontages or the plastic modelling of Gaudi's Casa Batllo (1905–6) have been held together by the overall consistency of the plan.

Another city which is directly relevant to the work illustrated here is Glasgow. In 1783 the City of Glasgow was little more than a small town built up around two principal thoroughfares. The plan of 1831 shows the new shape of Glasgow: the pattern is a grid, a new framework for the future. But of course the future takes care of itself. Over the years the framework has been filled in, often by distinguished city buildings. Churches and public buildings have developed special points of emphasis, often taking advantage of the changing levels in the surrounding roads. Squares and pedestrian areas have been opened up within the grid, notably around the Royal Exchange. The grid created George Square, the natural site later for the City Chambers (1883–8) and now with its commemorative statues and memorials the obvious centre and symbol of the city. And when the railways came the grid was developed and restructured around their terminal points.

The process is continuous. And one thing is certain, the city will change. It is not and never can be a static entity. It is an evolving organism in which elements may be introduced around new uses which can add to the quality and character of the city, or indeed the change can be so ruthless and inconsiderate that many may now believe that change is best when its scale is small and when its objectives can be clearly visualised.

This historical process has been described because Part 2 of this book is concerned with some of these issues. The building for the Royal Scottish Academy of Music and Drama has already been illustrated. It is an infilling within the existing grid. Its broad pavement and planting open up the rigid street pattern. It is a building which speaks for a new use or a special interest within the community. In association with its neighbour, the home of Scottish Opera, it may give a special quality and character to an area.

But Part 2 is concerned also with a wider question. At one end of the scale it is intended to say something about the contribution that the form of buildings might make towards what has been called a 'sense of place'. It touches on such things as some of the forgotten symbols of a city: its entry points or gates, its ceremonial ways or public squares and the opportunity that exists of recreating these by the process of building. These are the elements that might recreate a recognisable form at certain points in a city. And at the other end of the scale it has something to say about modest attempts to create a small-scale improvement in the general environment.

In August 1962, Colin St J. Wilson and I had an opportunity to study the larger scale problem when we were appointed to prepare a report on the proposed new library for the British Museum. The site, bounded by Great Russell Street, Bloomsbury Square, New Oxford Street and Bloomsbury Street, had been designated for library use in the County of London Plan of 1951 and was discussed at length at the public enquiry in 1952. The main objections voiced at that enquiry centred around the ideas that the new library buildings would displace the publishers and shopkeepers and that people resident on the site would have to be rehoused elsewhere. The Minister approved the County of London Development Plan in 1955 and therefore the designation of the site. At subsequent meetings,

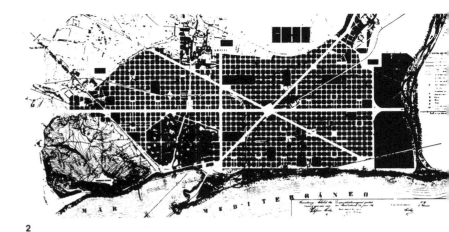

2

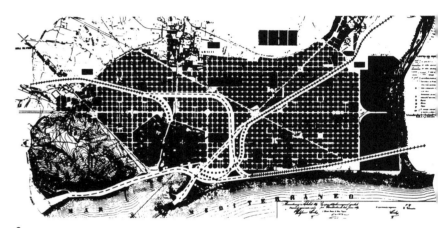

3

4

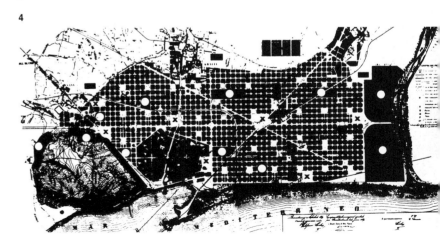

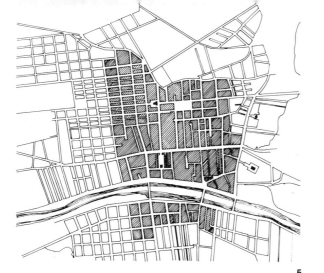

6

5

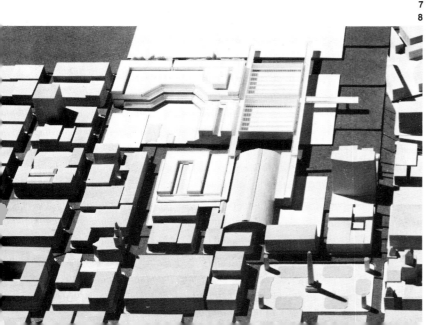

7
8

however, it was agreed that any scheme should make provision for the replacement of specialised bookshops and so on and as much housing as possible, and the brief to the architects included this requirement.

The Report and the Plan,[4] which was in outline only, made it clear that in addition to the accommodation required for the library and associated working areas, an exhibition gallery and a public lecture hall and restaurant were included in the scheme. The buildings were arranged so that they enclosed a new 'place' or public square which provided a frontal view of the Museum from New Oxford Street and created a proper setting for St George's Church, at present completely hemmed in by buildings. Under this pedestrian square there was accommodation for buses and cars; the scheme provided shopping frontages on to Great Russell Street, Bloomsbury Street and New Oxford Street. These shops were associated with one floor of offices over the shops themselves and housing accommodation was provided for 350 people in flats and maisonnettes. Altogether it was clear that a lively combination of uses could be achieved, a new public square created and two historic buildings could be given a more adequate and distinguished setting. The plan offered a choice.

The Report on Whitehall was produced some years later and was wider in its range of study and its implications.[5] I was asked in 1964 to examine various proposals which the Government had under consideration for the redevelopment of the Whitehall area. The brief extended to the study of traffic in the area and Sir Colin Buchanan produced an accompanying report on this subject.

The Government at this time had under consideration the redevelopment of the entire Richmond Terrace–Bridge Street site for Government and Parliamentary offices and also the rebuilding of the Foreign Office block. The consultant was asked to look ahead to the

possibility of the eventual redevelopment of other buildings in the area such as the King Charles Street–George Street block. The Government had under consideration a proposal for a conference centre on the Broad Sanctuary site and on the same site there was also a scheme for a new building for the Royal Institute of Chartered Surveyors. Other development proposals might well have affected the western and northern approaches to Parliament Square.

All these schemes taken together would have meant a considerable change in the area. Any one of the building proposals might have gone ahead independently. The object of the study was to outline a series of related factors so that the Government could take related decisions. For instance, the development of any separate site could be considered in relation to its effect on traffic and road proposals. Within this total view each separate part can be seen, and decisions can be made in relation to a whole. The plan produced some ideas related to the significance of the area as a national and Government centre, and illustrated these in a possible building form. It was by no means the first to draw attention to such matters. Its lineage includes Sir Charles Barry's plan and building proposals,[6] the Abercrombie–Forshaw London Plan, and various schemes for developing a Government precinct.

The proposals started from the point outlined in the County of London Plan of 1943 that the area around Parliament Square should be seen to be the centre of Government. It is also a centre for ceremony, international meetings and a place for visitors who themselves need facilities. One first step might be to remove from Parliament Square traffic which need not be there. The London Plan and other proposals had suggested the removal of through traffic from this area. At that time 50,000 vehicles a day moved along the Victoria Embankment, and along the Chelsea Embankment 30,000 a day, many of these making the connection through Parliament Square. The Martin–Buchanan Report proposed as a first step a riverside tunnel to remove this traffic.

The main Government building proposals were obviously generated by the Bridge Street–Richmond Terrace site, but behind the studies was an attempt to assess the possibility of accommodating, nearer to Parliament itself, those departments that by the nature of their work ought to be in this vicinity. Out of a total of 5,000,000 square feet of Government office space 3,000,000 square feet was scattered throughout London in commercial accommodation.

The plan demonstrated that Government buildings might have their own characteristic forms designed around the special groupings built up within the structure of the civil service. It demonstrated diagrammatically a possible form very different from the standard office block. It showed incidentally the completely illogical measures of plot ratio used in town planning, and demonstrated that quite a high floor space use could be secured without the usual cliché, the tall building. In the Whitehall proposals, any new buildings could have a low, spreading form which took into account the special needs of the Ministers' access, car parking and interconnecting service arrangements.

The Broad Sanctuary site, where separate developments were proposed, was considered suitable for an enlarged conference centre, public rooms, public restaurants and amenities. The Bridge Street site was suggested as suitable for Parliamentary offices, but these were linked in their form to Government offices to allow flexibility and interchange. The Scotland Yard main block was preserved and the site also contained shopping facilities.

Within an interrelated plan of this kind, any site may be redeveloped or a building added, without losing sight of other factors which could improve the amenities of the area and add to its significance as a centre

9

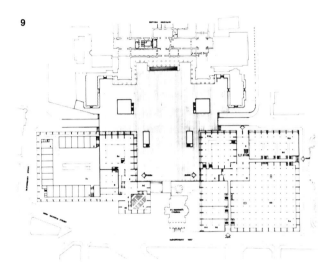

10
11

5. By the 1830s the Glasgow grid was already established. 6 & 7. George Square, the Royal Exchange and its environment had been created and the square itself became a central symbol which continued to attract the monuments, significant buildings and finally the City Chambers. 8. The grid extended the site for a new group of civic buildings to be established, a new square created, the bus centre replaced and the traffic routes rationalised in a plan for the new cultural centre (see later). 9. The British Museum and St George's Church related. Traffic and parking moved underground. View from the south. 10. The new library, exhibition area, shops and housing combined around the new square. 11. View from the museum to St George's Church.

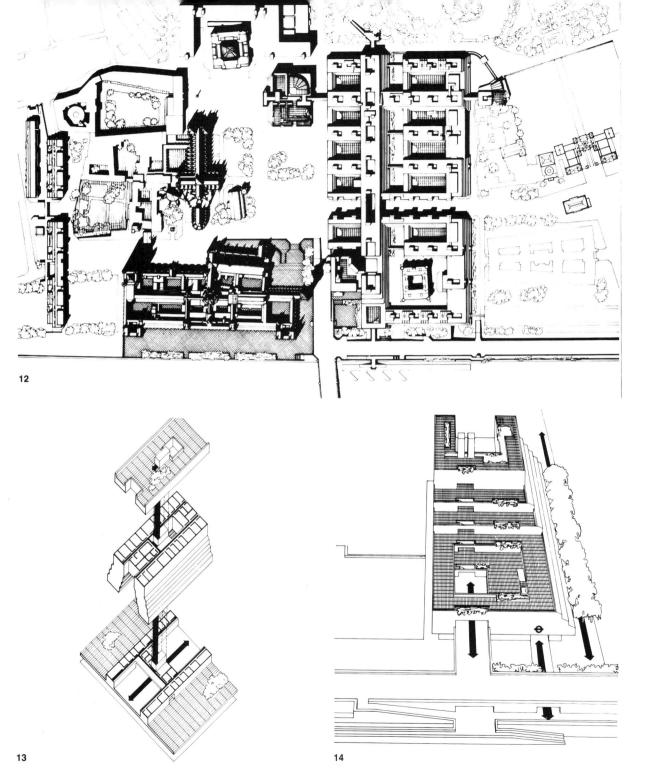

12

13

14

of Government. The plan left or was intended to leave certain images. Amongst these was the idea that the boundaries of the area or precinct could be more clearly defined by the building form. This in turn produced the idea of gateways from the Whitehall, Millbank and Victoria Street approaches. The ceremonial aspect associated with the area was recognised by the way in which buildings along Whitehall responded in their form to the need for viewing terraces. A public 'Galleria' formed a connecting pedestrian link from St James's Park to the river, acting both as a pedestrian way (well recognised in history) and as a public front to the various Ministries that flanked its length. Above all the plan attempted to leave a total image of Government buildings of modest height built up around internal gardens centred on an area of ceremony, public enjoyment and accessibility.

When Barry's plan for the same area was produced just over a hundred years ago he hoped that it would 'set men's minds to work . . . and stimulate and guide the free conceptions of the future'. The plan for Whitehall had the same ambitions. It did not present designs for building but ideas around which future buildings could be structured.

Some years later at Glasgow, when we were asked to consider the siting of an important group of civic buildings including a concert hall, we started with the question of existing uses: what were the areas of the city which could be seen to work and to bring people together? Here it was a question of trying to add a new and significant point within an existing pattern. We examined many sites and finally moved away from the isolated site that had first been considered. We extended the grid of the city to bring into connection two established and popular streets in order to create a new and important site at the junction, properly related to access and transport, on which a city development might take place with some sense of pride.[7]

We had a similar problem when considering the form of Government buildings in the very different cultural

and climatic background of the Middle East. Government buildings are being built in many cities in this area. The question raised is what impact do these buildings make on the cities in which they are built? What kind of buildings should they be? They are not commercial offices. They have their own generating activities which might also generate their form and they might evolve within particular conditions of culture and climate. Exemplars now exist in the National Assembly building by Utzon and the Foreign Office building by Pietila, both in Kuwait. Another is the scheme for Government and Municipal buildings produced by the Albini Studio for Riyadh. Our own Government Centre at Taif had a defined site which marked its special position within the city; the gates, and their response in the entrances to the building itself, gave definition to its component parts, and the shade-creating and spreading plan evolved within the communicating internal routes. That building provides a symbol within the city and the housing that we have worked on in the same country is its anonymous counterpart.

Other schemes, like Wellington Square, Oxford, have been concerned with definition of open space, and our university plans have had as a starting point the central problem of establishing an identity, usually in the form of enclosing walls of buildings, internal routes, gardens or courts.

The university development plans, for example at Leicester and Hull,[8] were directly related to building proposals which were by and large achieved within the following decade. They started from something that existed, and they attempted to bring this into relationship with a new and expanded programme of development, having as a central idea the simple notion of an overall form which can provide some sense of wholeness and community and yet be achieved in stages by different architects. They outline a strategy for growth: at Leicester by a centripetal development around two central levels which are directly connected to the main campus, and at Hull by a

12. The plan brought together: a total assessment of site capacity in terms of low buildings and open courts; possible siting of a new building for Government and the public; pedestrian and visitors amenities including a public 'Galleria' from the park to the river; riverside restaurants and underground station; a traffic system to remove through traffic from Parliament Square. Within this overall plan it might be possible to take decisions about the development of individual sites without prejudice to some overall ideas that may be important. The plan shows the riverside tunnel which was part of the system developed by Professor Buchanan to remove through traffic from Parliament Square. 13 shows central ministerial meeting rooms and offices planned in relation to a main public gallery with low office buildings and courts on either side. 14. The terraced riverside end to the gallery with its public restaurants, riverside route and underground station below. 15. The general view shows the Whitehall gateway (top) and the housing which creates a wall and gateway (bottom). 16. is a section through the main public gallery and 17 shows the relation of this to the ministerial offices and planted courtyards. These offices are spreading in form and low in height. Along Whitehall itself the section in 18 shows how the external form of the offices creates a public viewing platform along this route to Parliament Square.

15

16

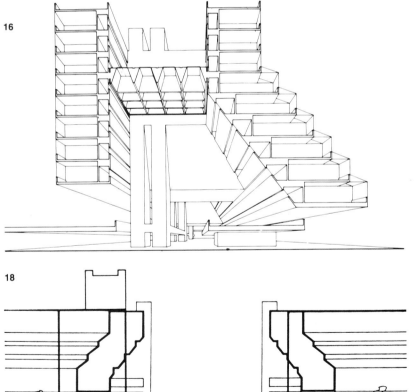

17

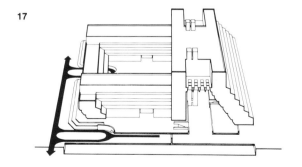

18

125

19

20

series of courts joined by a central promenade.

At this same scale we have also worked on projects which might form a framework for the future. The science buildings at Oxford are one example; the buildings for Zoology/Psychology were starting points for a large Science area.[9] Our proposals were worked out in terms of overall grids, with linkages, routes, lines of circulation and the variety of packages of building space that are formed by this procedure. Within such a system, we hoped that it might be possible to build what is immediately required and to leave open the options for future development; that we could start at a particular point, and that over a period of time an area could be transformed into a new and more flexible building pattern. Ultimately it is a matter of opening up more choices. These are not fixed development plans. They show the related factors that have to be considered at any stage, and from these we can build what is possible.

In the very process of making studies of this kind, we are forced to ask ourselves some deeper questions. What are the limitations of our assumptions about building and planning? And more important, what is the range of building form that is open to us, and at what scale does it begin to open up new choices in the pattern of living and in the pattern of cities?

When Lionel March and I first began to think about these issues, we called our work 'speculations'.[10] I have never been able to understand why this simple extension of the questioning process, which is so much a part of the creative architectural process, has led to misunderstanding. Clearly research can become a specialisation. For me it is always a necessary extension of architectural thought.

The concept of a spectrum of forms which puts the same floor space on the same site, starting with a tower and then, with a continuously changing envelope, gradually transforming itself into a court, is a beautiful way of thinking about the range of forms that is possible on a site. But when supported by an elegant mathematical proof, that concept is given tremendous power. It becomes a way of thinking about concentration or dispersal in housing or in regional development. The thought has been lifted from the particular to the level of principles which have general application. That is the purpose of research. It can emanate from design ideas but it is separate from them. It does not make or mould design decisions; it explains the effect of certain choices.

In contrast to this larger work we have continued to build at a small scale. The Kettle's Yard Gallery in Cambridge (1969) is an extension to a house standing next to a church and seen across a green foreground. Externally we tried to make this building as anonymous as possible. The extension with its long brick wall is still an appendage to the house and the church above it which dominates the group. Internally of course it is quite another matter: the visitor moves through a series of descending levels and top-lit spaces within which the collection can be creatively arranged.

The small library for Pembroke College, Oxford (1972) is again infilling, and added to this there are conversions to existing buildings. I am delighted to have worked at this scale because it is perhaps at this level that architects can make one of their most effective contributions to the enrichment of living and to our general surroundings.

These are schemes that start within the existing environment; they build into it a new use and they are in this sense part of a developing process, as we realised when we were studying housing in 1959. We considered not just the strict rules of density but such things as neighbourliness and privacy, the provision of private space and space that could be shared, but above all the extensions of choice and variety that can be made available through invention and design.[11]

At a more personal level the question of range of options and the opportunities for widening the choice of dwellings has been brought home to me most forcibly by the conversion of older buildings. Each one of these existing buildings, because of its limits or its opportunities, requires an entirely fresh approach. To convert a mill or the village granary into a place in which I could live has seemed to me to be as natural an activity as it is to design a new building. And I have learned a great deal in the process. In designing a new home, for example, it might not have occurred to me to start with a cube of space forty feet by twenty-five feet in plan and forty feet high. Yet it served as a home for my family and the Studio for over twenty years. Nor would I have thought of starting a plan with a rectangular area seventy-five feet long by fifteen feet wide, but that has produced the linear arrangement of spaces in which I now live. And as a result I have appreciated more and more the rich potential of space and form as a background for living. These conversions start from a past; they have a reference back, but the spaces for living that have been created turn the thought forward into possible increases in the range and choice both now and in the future.

The work illustrated here includes significant buildings of various types; it involves small-scale infilling; it illustrates work at the city scale, and when the knowledge of how to work at this scale has been inadequate it has included an extension of the architect's activities into investigation and research.

This is all within the province and the range of architecture. I cannot see this total range as a series of bits and pieces divided one from another. For me it is all part of the same process of architectural thought, rooted in the attempt to create some sense of coherence and form, seeing through chaos towards some perception of a possible unity. That is my personal conception of what an architect should try to achieve.

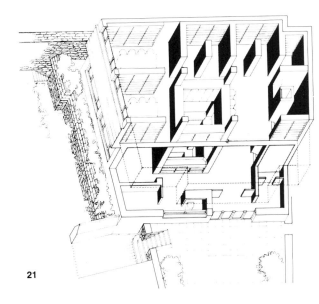

21

22

23

19. The creation of enclosure. New faculty buildings for the University of Hull planned to create courts and unite existing buildings. **20.** Plan for a development around Wellington Square, Oxford, including university offices. **21.** The McGowan Library, Pembroke College, Oxford. Infilling on a restricted site (see later). **22 & 23.** Views of 21.

127

5 · Structure and growth: university plans

Various sites (1956–62)

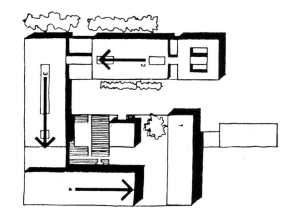

1

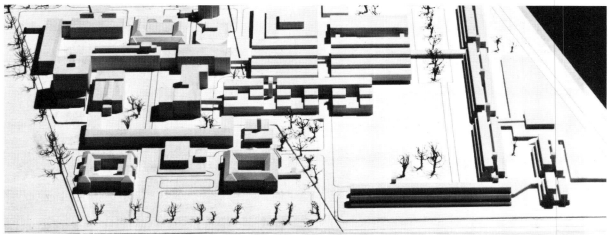

2

A series of studies made during the late fifties and early sixties were all concerned with building for university expansion. Proposals for the Universities of Leicester and Hull were large enough to provide a new structure for the layout of the university and at that time the programme of building was certain enough to give some guarantee that the buildings could actually be built. In these cases the conception visualised in the preliminary layout was carried through to the completion of buildings and garden layout and different firms of architects were responsible for individual buildings within the total group.

Both schemes started from an existing nucleus. In the case of Leicester a central approach road led to an elevated level on which (to the right-hand side of the road) the old University College buildings were grouped. The new development created a series of science buildings on the vacant land on the left of the

entrance drive. The layout of the old and the new buildings is held together by a broad terrace which runs at right angles across the top of the entrance drive. The new buildings are built around a square court; the linking terrace forms the upper level of that court, below this is a second and lower level with pools and planting. The main lecture hall and the connecting stairway to the lower court form the pivot around which the various science buildings were built. The building work followed the rotating pattern indicated on the plan.

At Hull a distinguished symmetrical layout of buildings had been planned in the pre-war era. Two of the forecourt buildings had been built but the rapid expansion of accommodation had produced changes of form and height which departed from the original conception. The layout appeared to be scattered. The main effort behind the new layout was to try to achieve some

3

4

sense of coherence in a plan that had to be developed rapidly. The proposal made was simply to move cars to a perimeter road and to create pedestrian courts by the form of the new buildings. The pedestrian walk through the centre of the plan connects the main forecourt buildings to the principal recreational and dining area. The buildings form the enclosure and provide a traditional overall form.

The Hull layout demonstrates three distinct stages: first the individual buildings of the pre-war period, second the attempt to bring these into relationship by the use of linking buildings to meet the needs of various faculties, and third a new development on the adjoining site to cater for a second wave of increase in the student population, in this case largely on the science side. A development on this scale has many repercussions. Increased student numbers required increases in the central social, recreational and cater-

ing facilities. The new science buildings might need a form which could allow for internal changes of use. At the same time student movement should be as direct as possible and the university should still be recognised as a single whole.

These considerations were met by the creation of a new 'Mall' running east to west and linking the old and the new areas. A second Mall running north–south forms a spine for the new development. The new catering and social buildings are placed at the crossing of these two 'Malls'. The science buildings developed along this spine use certain planning and structural ideas which were at the same time being built into the new buildings for the Oxford science area illustrated here and described on the following pages.

1. Layout for the University of Leicester. Four stages of development form a central court with two levels and a general lecture room. **2.** University of Hull: the first courtyard development is shown on the left and on the right the extension of the university to form a new science area; two main pedestrian malls unite the scheme internally. **3.** The new science area, Oxford, designed for easy extension and flexibility of use. The part on the right is now built: the building on the left shows one possible grouping of new buildings using the same structural and servicing system (see pp. 130–1). **4.** Royal Holloway College, Egham, science buildings on a sloping site.

1

Some of the ideas which have affected the structure and form of this building were first considered in 1963–4. A planning enquiry in Cambridge at about that time made it desirable to consider the question of student numbers and the possible floor space that might be developed for science departments on the central university sites. This raised two questions: the first related to floor space and the various ways in which it could be disposed on the land available; the second was concerned with a system of building designed to meet the general needs of various departments and organised in such a way that uses might change or new departments might be set up within the whole.[1]

The proposals for the Zoology/Psychology building in Oxford provided the opportunity to test some of these ideas in practice. Since these were a part of a

Zoology/Psychology building, Oxford (1963–)

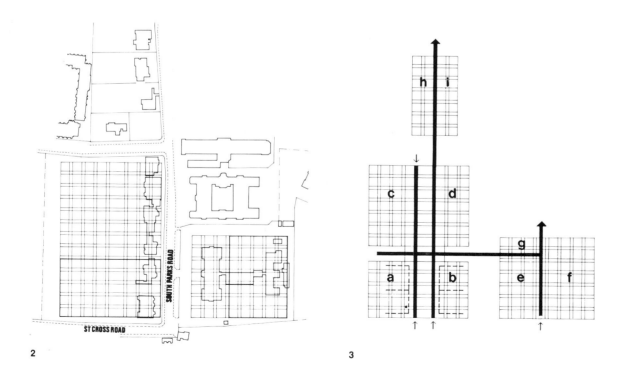

2

3

1. View along the spine which contains lecture rooms and library. Zoology is on the right, Psychology on the left. Two bridges connect the departments. 2. Application of the grid to the new science area site and the adjoining area. The grid is regular apart from the wider bay to accommodate the central access spine. The location of the site for the Zoology/Psychology building is

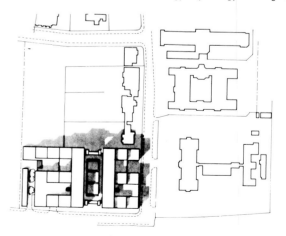

4

development for science buildings on a new site adjoining the existing science area, the brief clearly called for some consideration of a system of layout. The other part of the brief that dealt with particular buildings gave the possibility of testing a system against actual requirements. Both the system and the building form have certain implications which have since been the subject of more theoretical study and the following notes may serve as a commentary.

The first question raised is the way in which a particular built form uses the available land. In the Cambridge study the total layout is governed by a grid of squares and servicing spaces between these, and it is from this that the built form is derived. The prototype may be thought of as a flat slab of three or four storey buildings which receive their daylighting by means of courts sunk into the slab. In the Oxford building this prototype remains as a principle, but the floors have been stepped externally to provide outdoor roof space. The flat slab lit by courts and with spreading form has its exact opposite or inverse in a series of island buildings which replace the courts and are surrounded by free space from which they receive their daylight.

This contrast of pattern is important. Most urban university sites are examples of this island type of building development: it grows naturally from the needs of separate departments accommodated on a plot-by-plot basis. It is from this form that tall slabs or towers develop through rebuilding and greater intensification of land use. But if larger areas of land are considered then other forms of building arrangement become possible, for instance the spreading court form described above.

outlined. **3.** Diagrammatic illustration of possible routes and grouping of accommodation. **4.** The site plan of the Zoology/Psychology building. **5 & 6.** Studies to indicate different groupings of teaching and research accommodation within the grid. **7.** General view of the preliminary model. **8.** Elevation of buildings on either side of the central spine. The stepped form allows outdoor space adjoining laboratory areas. **9.** Central spine with libraries, lecture rooms, etc., departmental access corridors and lifts. Zoology (left) and Psychology (right). This plan at first floor level shows the spreading form of the large teaching areas which is possible within the system. **10.** The areas at upper levels are sub-divided as necessary to form research laboratories.

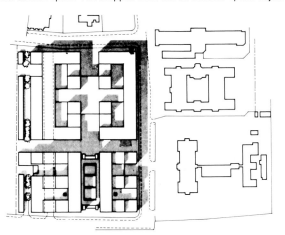

5

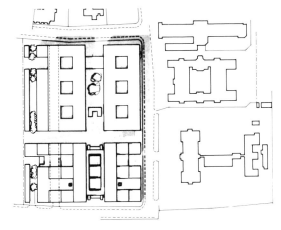

6

11

12

These two types of development are in fact extremes within a total spectrum of built forms in relation to land available. In 1966 an initial attempt was made at a theoretical and mathematical level to contrast the performances of these two built forms in relation to land use[2] and this work has subsequently been refined and extended.[3] One aspect of this theoretical study is that with identical conditions and larger sites the spreading court form will place the same amount of floor space on the same site area in precisely one-third the height required for the island form.

This is not an argument for a particular type of building development; it is knowledge which can guide a choice. The Oxford example initiates a spreading pattern of building in place of the existing island pattern. It opens up the possibility of a gradual replacing of buildings in a manner which can extend this new pattern.

The second question that arises from any proposal to use this spreading form is a consideration of the means by which it is structured. There seem to be two interlocking considerations: one is the overall grid, the other is the routing system which links the component parts.

An overall grid can be applied to any site. At Oxford it was used to give rough estimates of possible floor space. Within such a grid the main linkages or lines of circulation through the site can be laid down. When this is done the total grid is divided up into packages of building space defined by the routes and controlled by the grid and the site boundaries. If the approximate floor space requirements were known for the component units to be housed within a science area, and if some guidance could be given on the hierarchy of relationships within groups, it would now be possible to

14

13

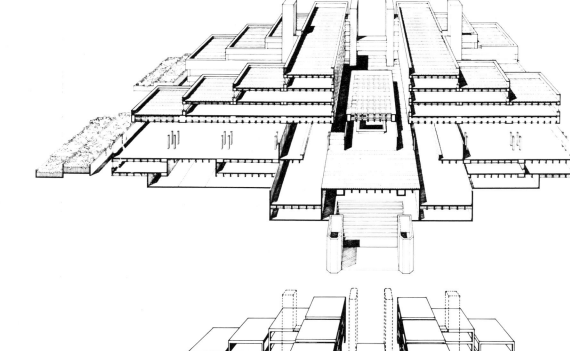

allocate related floor space accurately within these building packages.[4] Space could be reserved in each package for expansion. With such guidelines it becomes possible to start building at any point on the site without losing the opportunity of interconnections later.

In the case of the Oxford building the initial grid and the first stage of a route simply established two building areas. These were then fully developed by building to what appeared to be the right total capacity of the site. The building form was controlled by the grid, in this case thirty-five foot squares arranged in the form of tables with five foot servicing strips between. The size of the grid was selected primarily because of its capacity to meet the needs of both teaching and research with the same structural system. The accommodation itself is layered; the stacking of the 'tables' is arranged in stepped form so that research areas can have adjacent outdoor space. The other controlling factor in the stacking arrangement is the requirement to provide natural side lighting throughout to research rooms on the upper levels and top lighting to the teaching areas below.

The grouping of the stacked accommodation on each side of a spine or route allows a central location for libraries, lecture rooms and servicing accommodation which, as it develops along the route, is likely to remain relatively unchanged. But varying quantities of accommodation and different arrangements to meet different teaching and research patterns can be provided as the system is extended, and various grid sizes could be considered.

If structuring routes are laid down and parcels of building development are identified, growth can be provided by extensions of the routes or by the provision

11. The Zoology building seen across the Merton playing fields. 12 indicates the uses within the general building form and 13 the structural tables from which the form is built up. Spaces between the tables form service ducts. 14 shows the model used in lighting tests and 15 is a general view of the two buildings in the central spine.

15

of spare space within the separate areas. In relation to routes there are probably some limits on depth of development coming directly from desirable lengths of sub-routes, servicing runs etc. There is a point at which each area of building land is fully developed and where new sub-groups begin to form themselves. Change can take place by addition and reallocation of space within the totality or within the developed building form itself.

The need for this is particularly important to the sciences. The development of complex and interacting research has led some universities to abandon departmental divisions. In Oxford, in the total layout plan for the science area, broad zones of interest have been grouped under such headings as the physical sciences, the biological sciences, technology etc., but the departmental structure remains as the administrative unit. Thus zoology and psychology are placed within the broader setting of biology. The pattern that emerges in the Department of Zoology itself indicates a development in which there 'are independent research groups under a professor or reader, with graduate students and post-doctoral workers forming a local focus for each of the many new branches of biology. These groups have always interacted in a productive way with related groups in other departments'.[5] Thus the Laboratory of Animal Behaviour in Zoology has close links with Experimental Psychology and the titles of other sub-groups – Molecular Biophysics, for instance – suggest their connections with associated fields in other departments.

The Zoology/Psychology building is not simply separated into two departmental halves: the sub-groups already overlap where the relationship is necessary and the pattern of the sub-groups is free to change.

16

The question that arises in relation to a building of this kind is whether this development and change within the sub-groups can be accommodated. Clearly some elements are likely to remain static, for instance animal rooms with extensive air conditioning and tanked floors. Other special areas or pieces of equipment can be distributed throughout the building so that they are available to any research group. In this Oxford building the general system was devised before the sub-grouping was completely established. The sub-grouping changed during the design and working drawing stages and will certainly be re-arranged again to meet the changing developments of biological research. The structural 'tables' and servicing systems appear to accommodate this change without difficulty. The required flexibility also extends on to the roof areas where a simple system has been devised to produce a variety of spaces which may be enclosed, netted or glazed.

These notes relate to a system rather than an individual building. Within the total system there are many interlocking and interacting factors. They include a knowledge of the effectiveness with which various building forms use the land available and their suitability for internal and external links; the consideration of structuring routes and the grouping patterns that can be developed around them; the study of the range of structural grids that can accommodate changing patterns of use and the sub-routes and servicing routes that are possible within these. To understand the interaction of these factors is to develop theory. And theory is as important to the development of architecture as it is to the sciences which the system and its buildings are designed to accommodate.

16. View from the Manor Road libraries. **17.** External areas and stair outside the Zoology common room areas. **18.** Staircases and connecting bridge between departments. **19.** The library in the central spine. **20.** View along the spine from one of the connecting bridges.

17

18

19

20

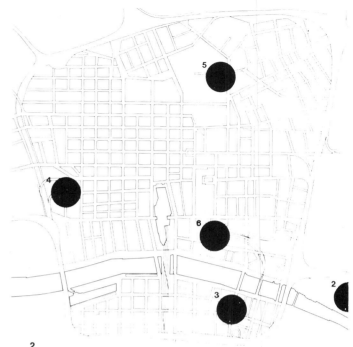

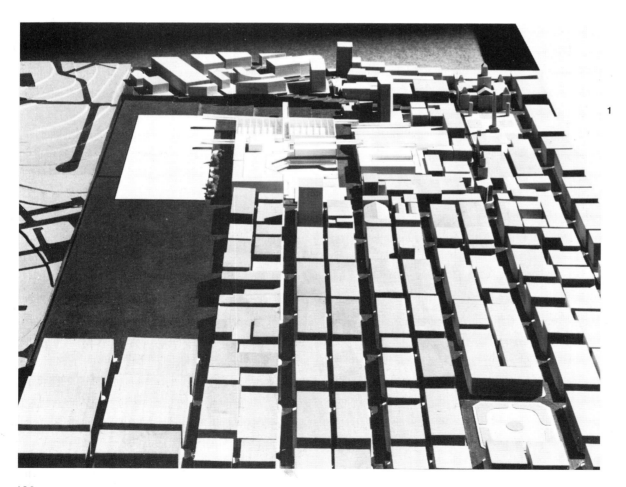

1   2

Concert hall and development, Glasgow
The 1968 Report

This work originated from an invitation by the Glasgow Corporation to advise on a possible site for what was then described as a new cultural centre for the city. At that time the scheme included a concert and conference hall, an exhibition hall, a civic theatre and a repertory theatre.

Proposals of this magnitude were clearly of great importance to the future of the city. The question raised was whether a major group of new buildings could be related to the older pattern of the city. The central issue seemed to be one of choosing a location in which the new buildings could reinvigorate a part of the city and in turn be supported by what already exists and works well.

What is in fact being studied is the effect of adding a new nodal point within a city. Clearly the problem

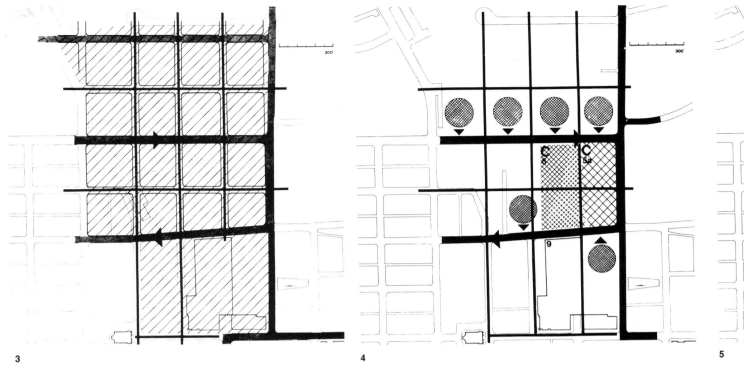

3

4

5

6

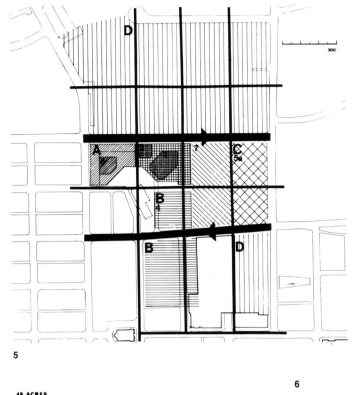

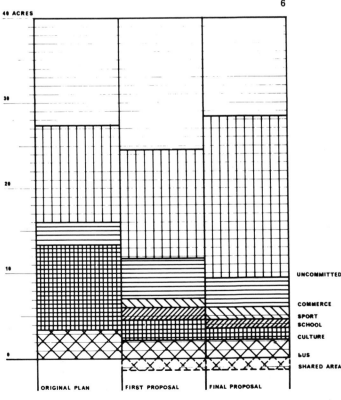

cannot be separated from access, transport etc. But beyond this we can also recognise that some city uses are interrelated. The placing of a major group of buildings of this kind in Glasgow was essentially a matter of considering whether it was to be an isolated monument or whether it could be a means of stimulating activities in its immediate surroundings. With this general point in mind a number of sites were examined, including one that had been selected for the initial proposal. The question of de-centralising activities in the arts was also considered. What became clear was that this group of buildings required a central position. The concert hall was to be a home for the Scottish National Orchestra and for many other civic interests. Good transport facilities by rail, underground, bus and car were essential.

1. The Glasgow grid extended to create the new site for the cultural centre and to create a new square at the junction of an extended Buchanan Street and Sauchiehall Street. **2.** Various sites considered before the final selection. **3 & 4.** The site selected had many advantages. It formed a nodal point at the junction of two busy streets. The building group could be seen along these streets and could form a new symbol in the city. Traffic and pedestrian streets could be segregated (3). Rail and underground connections existed to the south; a new bus station could be created to the north (4) and car parking could be associated with the new traffic routes. **5.** The elements of the new centre arranged around the new square and associated with commercial development to the south. **6.** A land use study illustrated the advantages of land conservation that became possible with this final proposal.

After several possible sites had been investigated a site at the junction point of two busy streets – Buchanan Street and Sauchiehall Street – was proposed. The Council's road plan had already suggested traffic proposals for the area and the suggestion had been made that these upper parts of Buchanan Street and Sauchiehall Street should become pedestrian areas. The site could be conveniently related to a new bus station to the north and Queen Street railway terminal and underground station to the south. Indeed, there could be a connecting route between these two transport centres and the new building itself would stand on elevated ground and would be seen along both Buchanan Street and Sauchiehall Street.

Adjoining sites also offered a possibility of redevelopment. The pedestrian route suggested some shopping and the adjacent transport facilities the possibility of some hotel accommodation.

It was suggested that the railway cutting adjoining the site might be covered in and that the floor space might be used for an internal sports hall which could be shared by the city and the University of Strathclyde. The larger floor area provided might also make some provision for an exhibition centre.

7

8

7. The model shows the existing grid extended, the new square, the curved roof of Queen Street station and the railway cutting above this covered to form a new Sports Centre. Pedestrian bridges lead from this to the railway station and the bus station (top). St George's Square appears on the bottom right-hand corner. **8.** General view. **9.** The components of the plan, preliminary scheme (1968): 1 Concert hall. 2 Theatre. 3 Commercial development. 4 Possible hotel site. 5 Temporary bus station (this was eventually placed within the dotted area (top) with an underground connection to the main buildings). 6 Buildings for the Royal Scottish Academy. 7 & 8 Sports Centre and exhibition buildings. **10.** Diagram of the scheme. Although the component parts have changed the principal ideas of siting, connecting pedestrian ways and combined civic and commercial uses and easy access from bus and rail still remain in the latest developments.

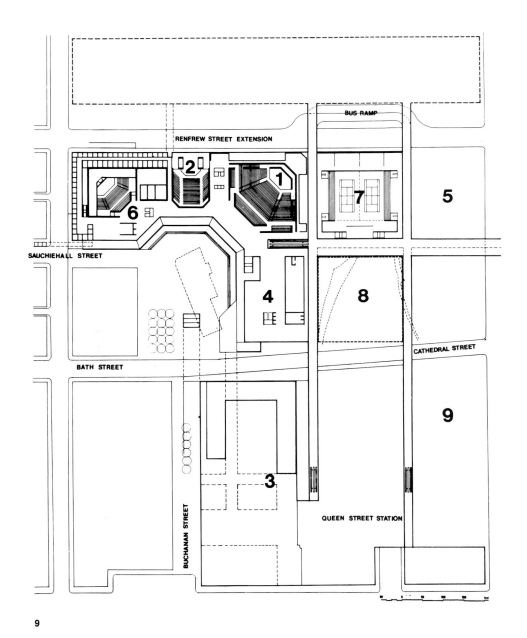

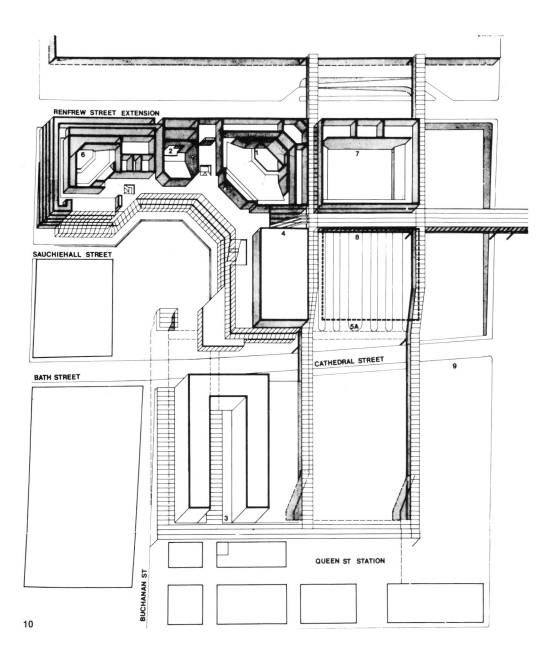

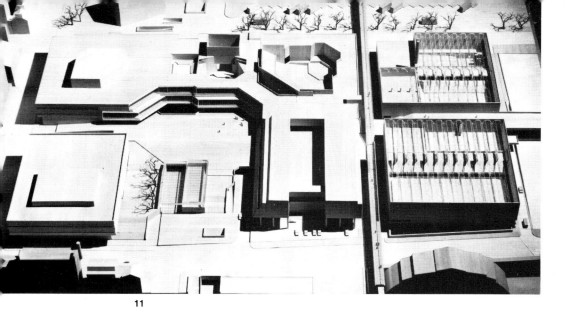

11

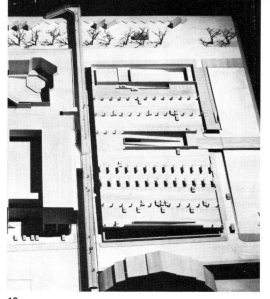

12

13

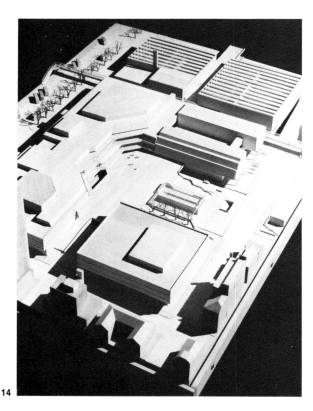

14

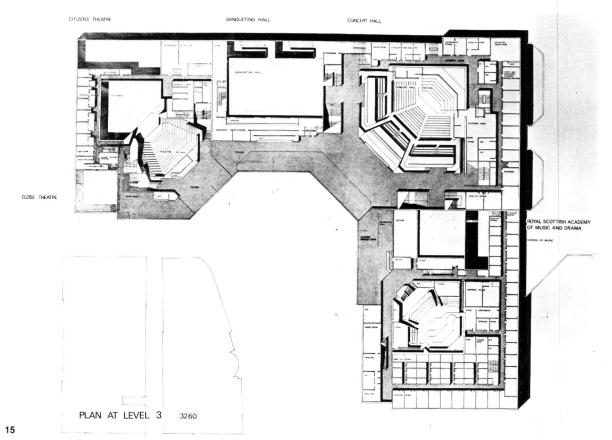

CITIZENS' THEATRE   BANQUETING HALL   CONCERT HALL

CLOSE THEATRE

ROYAL SCOTTISH ACADEMY
OF MUSIC AND DRAMA

SCHOOL OF MUSIC

PLAN AT LEVEL 3   3260

15

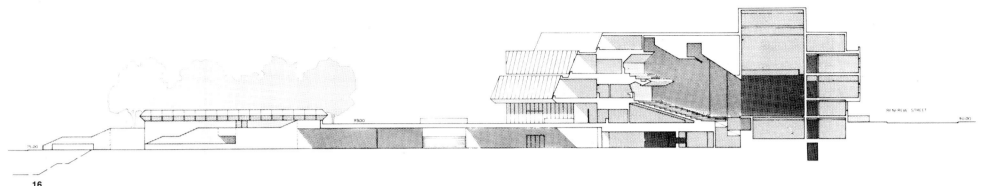

16

The 1971–9 development

In the central group, a number of related activities were brought together, including accommodation for the Royal Scottish Academy. This group formed the knuckle at the junction of Buchanan and Sauchiehall Streets; the concentration of the building form when compared with the earlier proposal showed a significant saving in the land area required. Clearly a related group of this kind could serve many functions including conferences and the associated development could produce a series of varied uses around a new public square within the city. In the years that followed this early report, the city took steps to carry out the proposals suggested and to create the new site. A derelict area was cleared; the bus station was transferred to a new site, Sauchiehall and Buchanan Streets were turned into pedestrian routes and a redesigned underground transport system has a major entrance related to the proposed site. Some adjacent sites have also been developed.

The design of the central group of buildings passed through a series of stages of development in which the requirements of the concert hall and theatre were studied in some detail and complete design drawings were presented. Owing to financial restrictions, however, work was indefinitely postponed at the working drawing stage.

11, 12 & 13. The 1971 proposals in which the earlier ideas were developed in more detail. 11 shows the total scheme with its adjacent sports and exhibition halls, 12 the car parking areas over the railway cutting and 13 the substructure spanning the cutting itself. In this scheme there is a hotel site adjoining the concert hall. **14.** A general view of the model. **15.** The project as developed in a later scheme which placed the Royal Scottish Academy building on the hotel site and introduced the Citizen's Theatre. **16, 17 & 18.** The square itself contains a covered shopping centre, shown in the long section and the sketch.

17

18

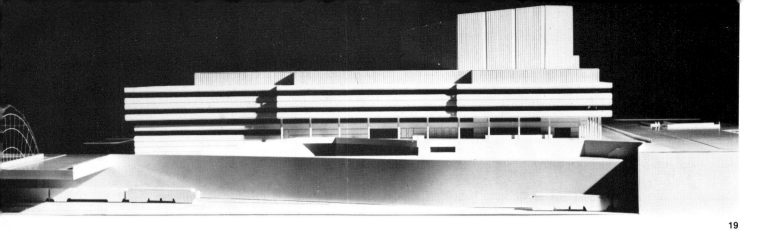

19

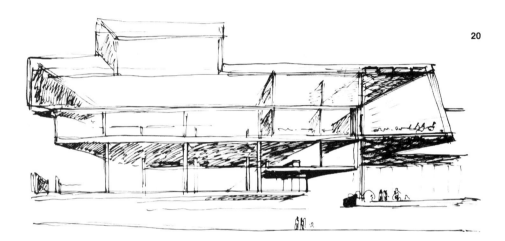

20

This pause resulted nevertheless in a further development. During this period it was decided that the Citizens' Theatre was likely to remain in its existing premises. The Royal Scottish Academy, which was funded independently, was considering an alternative site. But an available and attractive site remained for the main civic group and in 1979 the possibility arose of a combined development which would bring together this group of buildings and some suitable commercial uses on adjoining sites. It was envisaged that the whole group of buildings might be linked together by a covered shopping arcade which would also serve the civic buildings and connect the transport centres at the northern and southern ends of the site. The scheme in fact was remarkably similar in principle to some of the earliest proposals for development.

19. General massing in the 1978 scheme. 20. Preliminary sketch section developed in 21 to show the main entrance and terrace level, below this the connecting way from the bus station to the forecourt, and above the banquet suite and restaurant overlooking the city. The reinforced concrete structure and glazing system is shown below.

21

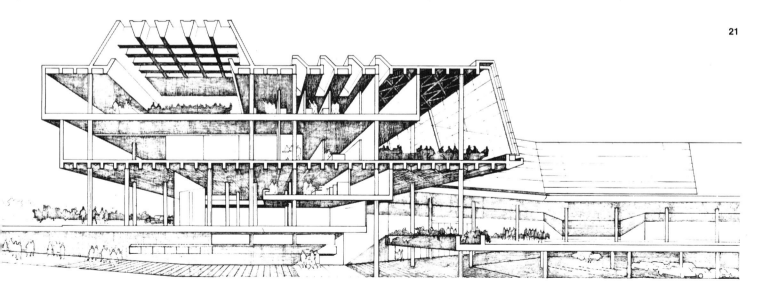

The 1979 proposals

The scheme was given a new impetus in 1979 when a combined scheme of civic and commercial development was studied. By this time the Citizens' Theatre was already established in its own building and the Royal Scottish Academy had made the decision to move to a separate site.

Important steps had, however, already been taken to establish the main site for redevelopment. The bus station had already been rebuilt to the north of the site and the new road alignments established. Parts of Buchanan Street and Sauchiehall Street had become pedestrian ways and the new underground station to the south had been built.

The civic content in the scheme was now the concert hall, which had to be developed in a way that would allow other types of use; the exhibition, reception and banquetting areas and a restaurant and coffee bar overlooking the view of the city to the south. This accommodation, accessible from Renfrew Street and the subway below, was planned in the north east corner of the site where good backstage access was also available.

Once this position for the civic area was established three sites remained for commercial development as stores, one in the east corner, the other two to the south. These stores are then connected together and to the civic group itself by a continuous glazed shopping arcade which provides a covered way from the underground or Queen Street station in the south to the new bus station at the north end of the site.

As the site slopes to the south the various levels can be conveniently connected and the new buildings occupy an important position in relation to the city and to the new square which they create. The south facing coffee shop, terrace and restaurant serve both the concert hall users and the general public. The foyers are spacious and provide extensive views across the city. The civic element remains a clear and self-contained entity within the total development.

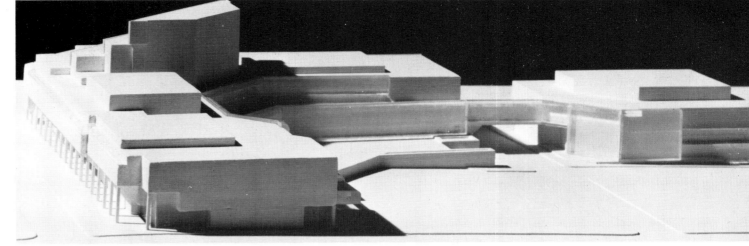

22

23

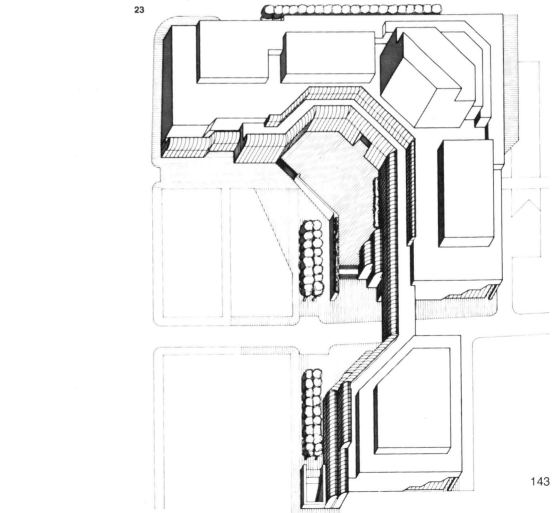

22. A general view of the development from the west. The north and south parts of the site are connected by the shopping mall which crosses the intermediate street. 23. Diagram of the total development, the new square, the civic group, the three stores and the connecting shopping mall.

143

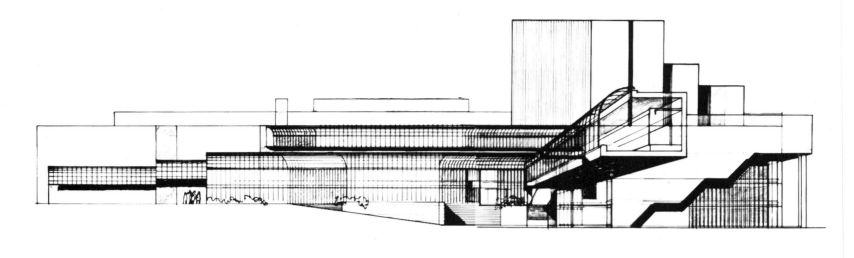

24

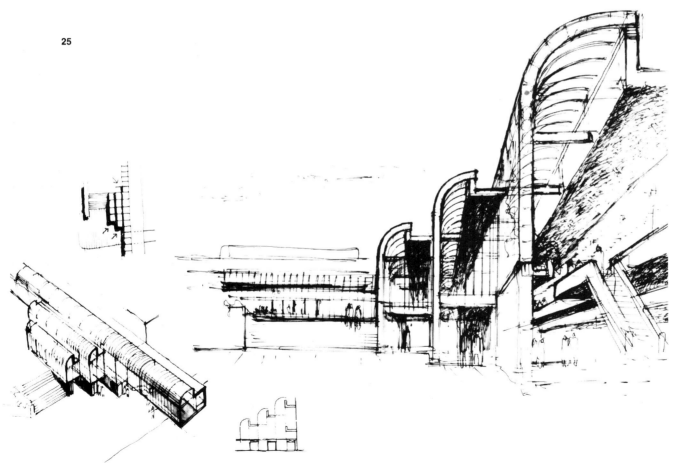

25

24 & 25. Preliminary sketches of the glazed mall, the road bridge and one of the entrances. **26.** South elevation from the intermediate road level. The drawing shows the bridge over the road and the entrances to the mall. **27.** The mall looking north, shops on each side. This level of shopping entered from the intermediate road level connects directly with the underpass to the bus station (to the left) and the car park (right). Stairs from this level lead to the terrace level and the entrance to the main entrance foyers of the concert hall. **28 & 29.** Views of the model.

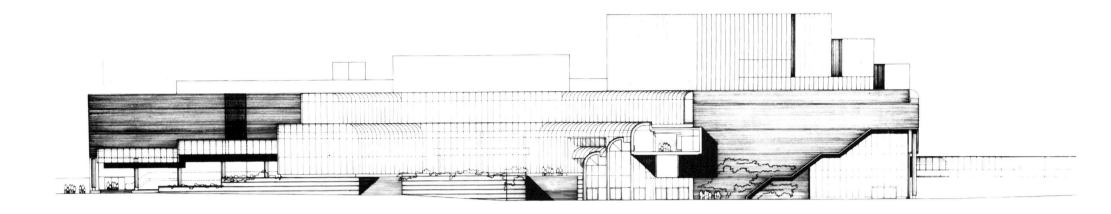

26

27

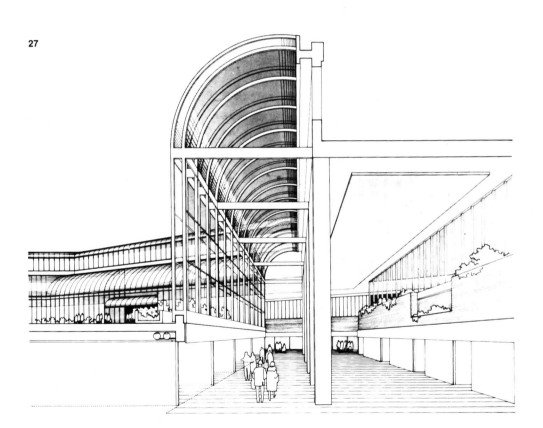

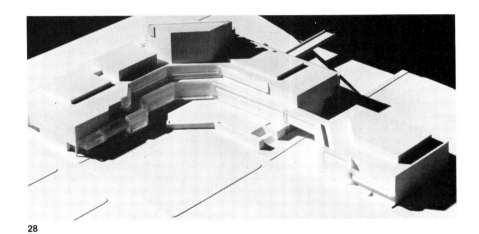

28

29

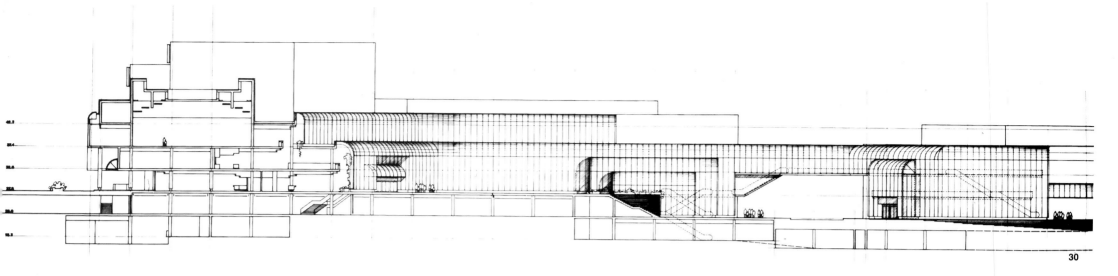

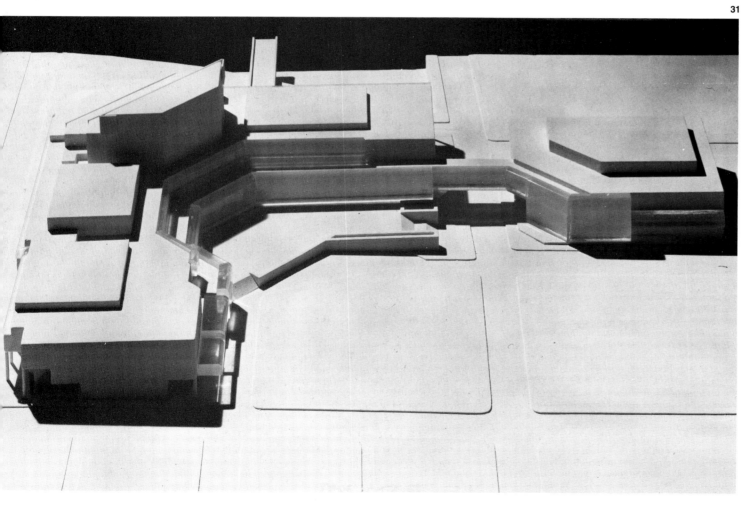

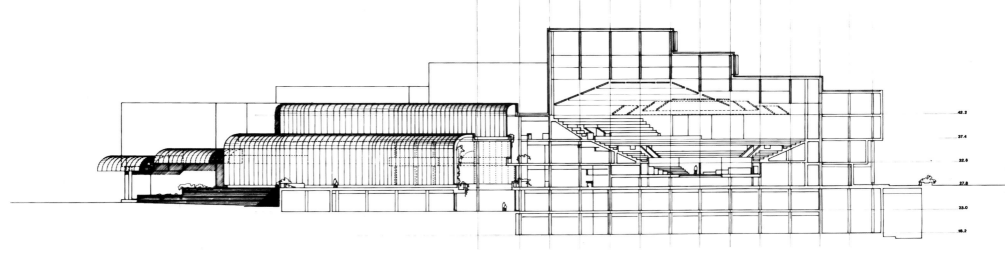

32

33

30. Section north–south through the banquetting suite and showing the elevation of the shopping link. The road level at the north becomes the terrace level on the south front of the building. The restaurant at first floor level overlooks this. The tunnel from the bus station under the road connects directly to the mall. **31.** General view of the model from the west. **32.** Section through the concert hall. **33.** General view from the south.

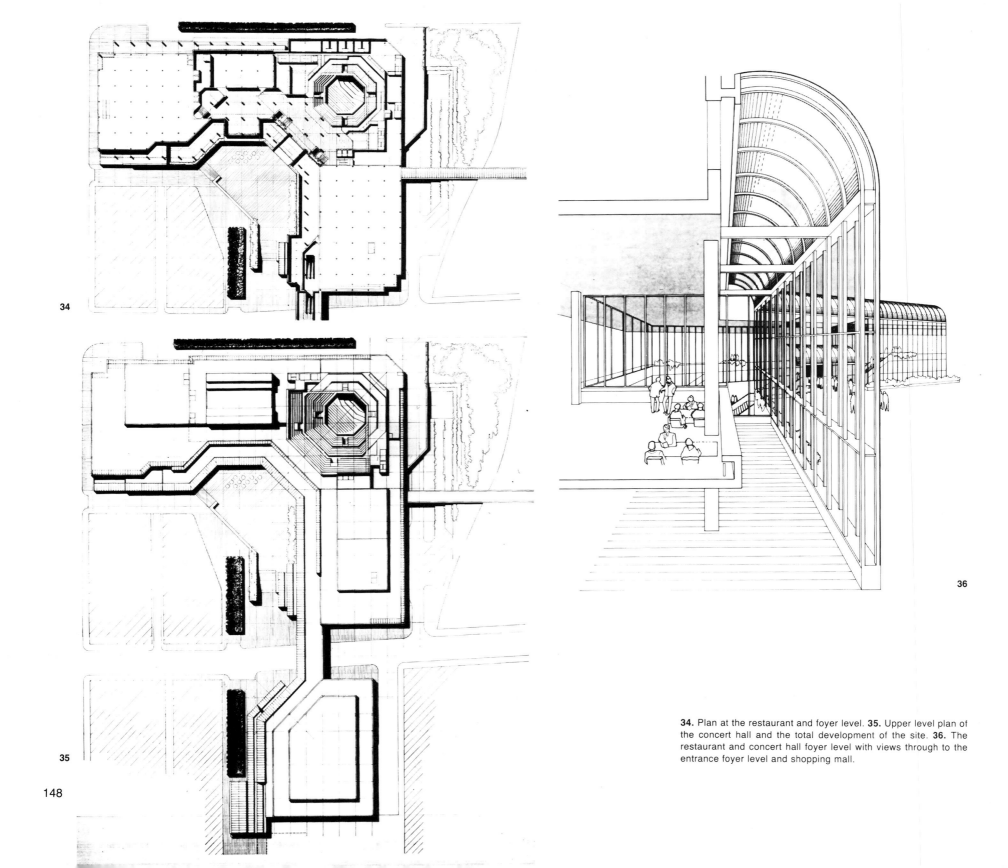

34. Plan at the restaurant and foyer level. **35.** Upper level plan of the concert hall and the total development of the site. **36.** The restaurant and concert hall foyer level with views through to the entrance foyer level and shopping mall.

34

35

148

36

The 1982 developments

The main contribution which resulted from the 1979 proposals was the establishment of a much firmer link between the civic and the commercial elements. In the earlier schemes the separate civic and commercial areas were held together by an overall architectural idea: in the 1979 scheme they were integrated within one single building group and firmly connected by the public shopping mall.

More recent proposals have developed this integration still further. The civic component is now placed at the head of Buchanan Street. In this new position the building is more self-contained but nevertheless still directly connected to the public activities of the commercial area. The new position allows greater freedom in the planning of foyers and the design of the auditorium for a variety of uses. The civic component is entered from Renfrew Street but has secondary entrances from Sauchiehall Street, the terrace and the shopping concourse.

The commercial element is linked by the glazed internal shopping mall and this still connects together the centres of transport: the bus station and public car park to the north and the underground and railway station immediately adjoining the southern boundary of the site.

The major ideas of the 1968 scheme have all remained constant. The junction point within the city grid is given emphasis by the new public space and its enclosing buildings and by the new vistas and focal points which these create. The pedestrian areas are increased and the total development is properly related to transport facilities. And finally civic, cultural and recreational activities are interconnected with the varying day to day needs of the public in a single comprehensive group of buildings.

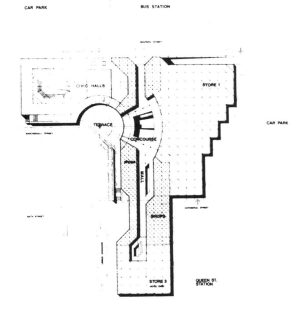

37

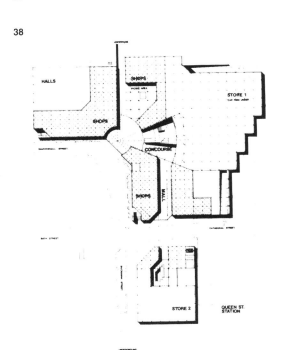

38

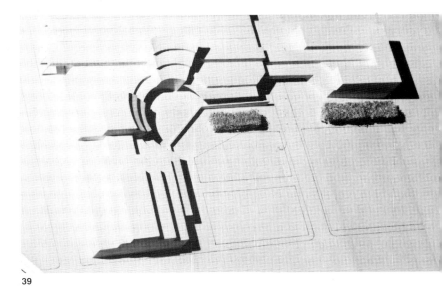

39

40

37 & 38. Plans of the general layout.
39 & 40. Views of the block model.

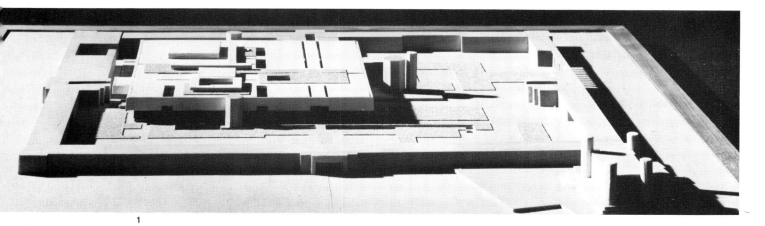

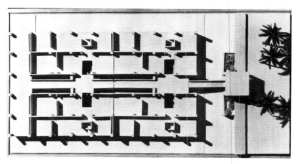

Government centre, Taif (1970–)

1

2

3

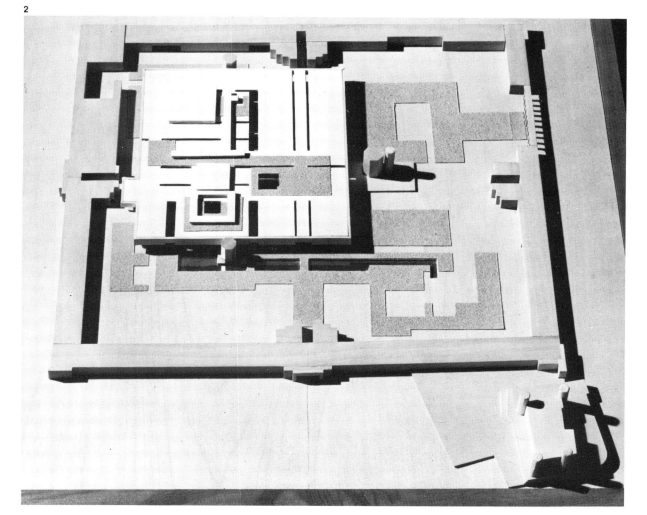

1 & 2. This first proposal established the idea of an overall shade-creating roof supported on a regular grid of columns. The columns were the equivalent of two storeys in height so that the structure allows a spreading colonnaded effect in public spaces, considerable height in the larger rooms and two storeys in offices. **3.** Preliminary model for the study of a central corridor serving several Ministries. **4** illustrates the position of the building in relation to the enclosing walls of the fort and the town itself. The gateways to the fort mark the principal entrances. **6.** The main public entrance is on the right and opens on to a public square. The Ministers' entrances are marked by the gateways in the walls at the top and bottom of the plan. The king's entrance is on the left. **5** shows the general disposition of accommodation within the plan. The public spaces within the building open up wide views of colonnaded spaces and are penetrated by open courts and small gardens. All rooms have views out on to planted areas. Their windows are shaded. The external space between the new building and the old walls of the fort is planted in a formal manner to create shaded areas and to screen car parks.

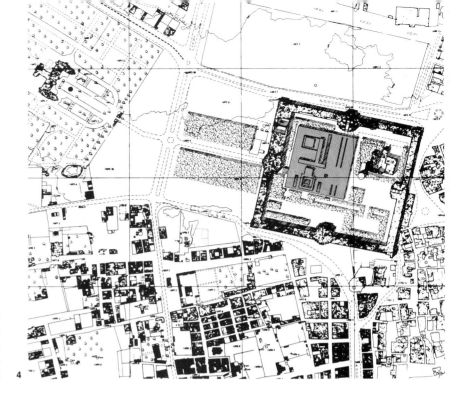

This building provided the opportunity to consider the appropriate character and form of a major Government centre; in this case within the background of a different culture and climate.

The purpose of this building was to provide accommodation for the executive section of the Saudi Arabian Government during the summer months, when it moves to the more favourable climate of Taif in the mountain area of the Western Region. The building houses Ministers and selected executive staff from the principal departments of Government and provides suitable accommodation for Government meetings.

The area selected for this building is an appropriate one. It is near the centre of the city adjoining open land close to the Royal Palace on one side and the souk on the other. The site itself formed a large square of land enclosed by walls with central entrances on the cardinal faces. Each one of these entrances has its appropriate use: that on the side facing the Royal Palace is clearly the principal ceremonial entrance. Opposite this on the other side of the square, the main public entrance relates to the town centre and the souk. The road to the north provides a convenient entrance for Ministers and visitors and the gate in the south wall provides the Bedouin entrance. The plan of the building within the court itself has always been related to these primary considerations.

The first scheme proposed for this building illustrates a spreading form based on a columnar structure and an overall roof. The main effect on entering the building is a continuous shaded space with many columns which extends right across the entire width of the

4

5

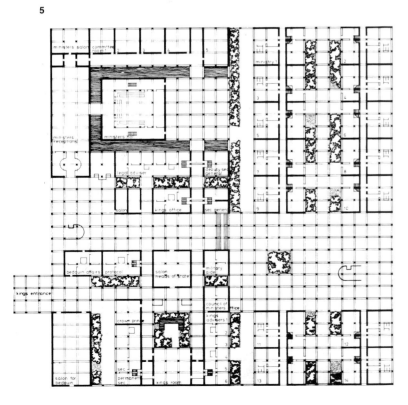

6

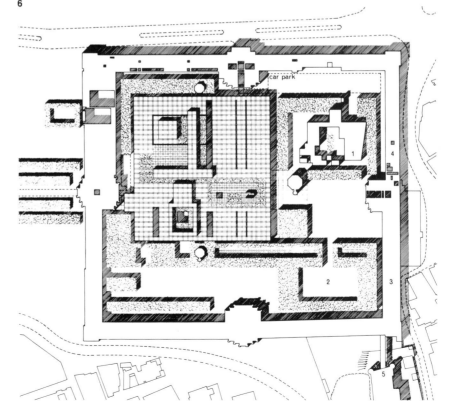

building. From this space the principal entrances to the working areas of the plan are clearly visible. The constructional form allows penetration of the roof where desirable and the public areas and most of the private rooms themselves open out on to internal but sunlit gardens.

Alternative alignments and layouts for the Ministry areas were developed within the overall structural system. The one illustrated shows the public access along a single corridor leading to groups of Ministries. A change of floor level provides each Minister's office with a double height, and each office is entered through a Secretary's room and waiting area. The supporting offices form a continuous strip at first floor level so that they may be attached to individual Ministries or used as general space. The structural system is designed in relation to simplicity and repetitive use. Air conditioning, lighting and roof insulating systems are adapted to this general constructional form.

8

7

152

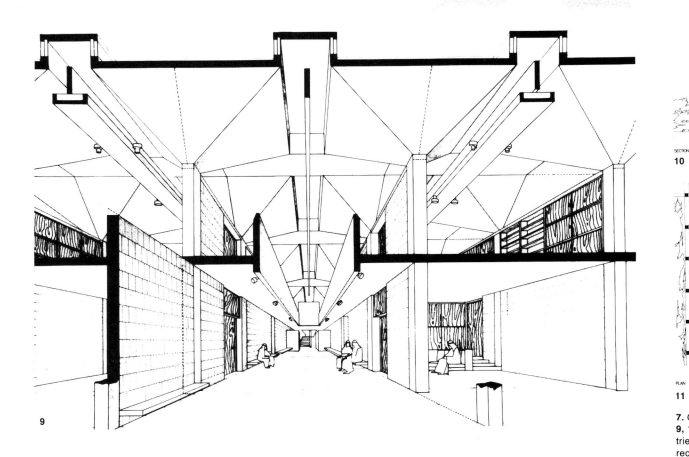

9

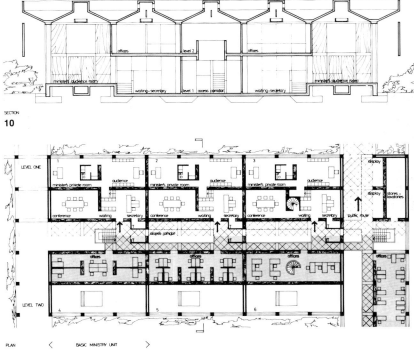

SECTION

10

PLAN ‹ BASIC MINISTRY UNIT ›

11

7. General view of the main public entry. **8.** The structural system. **9, 10 & 11.** The Ministry areas are planned with individual Ministries on either side of a Ministers' corridor. Each Ministry has a reception area and meeting room with offices over. The Ministers' suite is accessible through the reception area and has a double height. **12 & 13.** Alternative alignments that were tested before the plan on the previous page was selected. **14.** The roof structure is designed for insulation, to take planting, to act as pavement, to admit indirect daylight and to reflect artificial light.

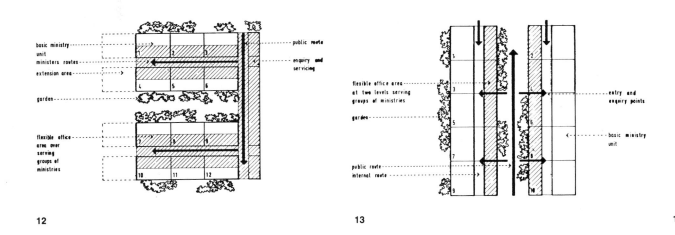

12

13

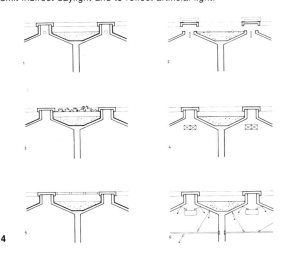

14

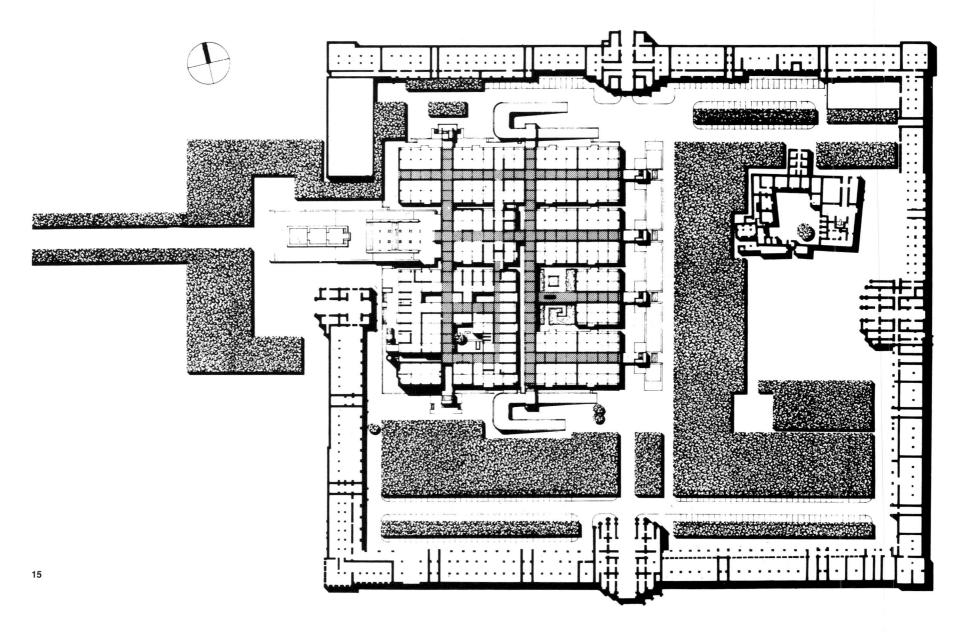

15

15. The fully developed plan. The building retains a spreading form but is now two storeys high. All the main rooms are at first floor level. A grid of cross routes or corridors at this level links the main rooms together. The four main public entrances of Ministries are at first floor level on the east front facing the entrance from the town itself. The Ministers arrive by car at the north and south entrances. The king's entrance is on the west and leads to his own area of the plan and the central rooms for the Council of Ministers. The Ministers' suites are identical. The rooms below have direct staircase connection to each Ministry but can vary in quantity to meet differing needs. **16.** General view from the public approach side. **17.** The king's entrance. The Council of Ministers' rooms are directly behind. The king's building is on the right with its private suite, inner garden, audience room, etc.

16

17

The final scheme, built between 1974 and 1977, was developed when it became necessary to increase the accommodation for Ministries. In these new circumstances it seemed desirable to produce a scheme on two levels. One advantage of this arrangement was that the increased accommodation could be planned without increase in the total area of building, thus leaving adequate surrounding space within the walls for future development. All the principal rooms were placed at first floor level and were linked by galleries which provide a predominantly horizontal movement throughout the building. The supporting offices are at ground floor level with internal staircase connections to the principal rooms over. This arrangement again provides great flexibility in the supporting accommodation to meet the varying requirements of different Ministries.

The arrangement places all principal entrances at first floor level. Each has its portico and is given its special significance within the overall building form. The ceremonial entrance is approached by a broad ramp leading to a shaded reception area. The Ministers' entrances on the north and south sides are approached directly by car ramps to first floor level. The public entrances to Ministries are marked by four porticos approached by broad staircases. These entrance points are connected within the building by the galleries and routes which link but also segregate the

various uses within the building. This produces a unified, shade-creating, interrelated mat of buildings and gardens. Slots in the roof provide sunlight for these garden areas in which some existing trees have been preserved. All rooms look out on to gardens but are protected from direct sunlight by overhanging roofs and hanging trellises. The larger principal rooms have a protected form of side lighting which can be built up into a stepped form to give additional height; this side lighting is again filtered internally by the fretted timber screens and ceilings.

Externally the building form responds easily and naturally to the interior uses. The overall mass and silhouette changes as it adapts to encompass the main audience rooms or the mosque. The granite ramps and screen walls emphasise the base; above this the walls are veneered in stone, screened by teak trellises shading the windows.

A second-stage building proposal within the enclosing walls of the Government Centre included a project for a separate and free-standing mosque. The proposed site for this was that previously occupied by an existing building in the forecourt which had become dilapidated beyond repair.

The mosque therefore occupied a key position in the foreground of the Government building when seen from the public approach. In this position it was available to all sections of the community. It could be partially isolated from the main approach itself by planting and by its own enclosing colonnade.

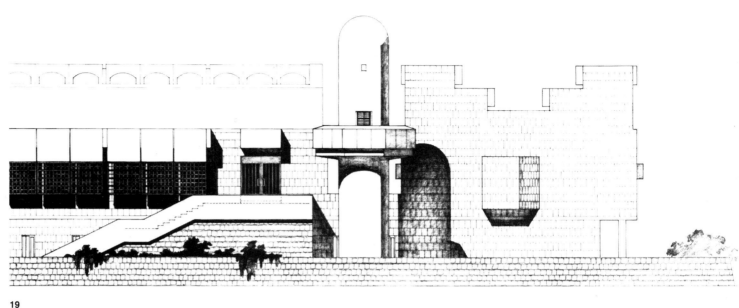

19

20

18. Close up of the king's entrance with porticoes to provide a shaded reception area. **19.** The Bedouin entrance to the main audience room and the end elevation of the mosque. **20.** General view from the west.

157

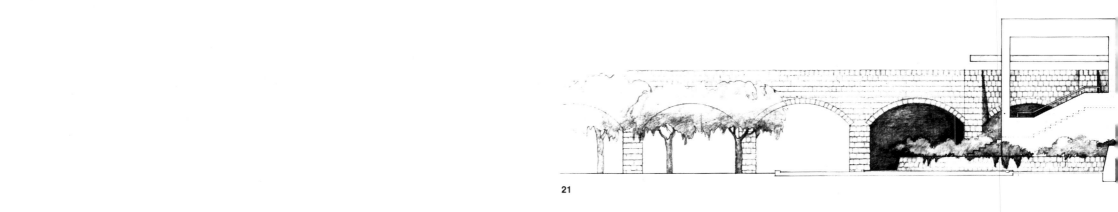

21

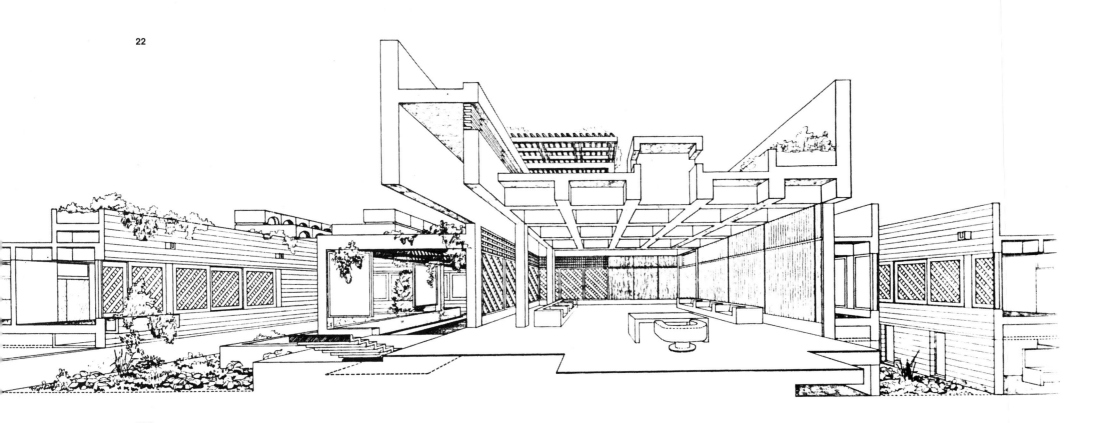

22

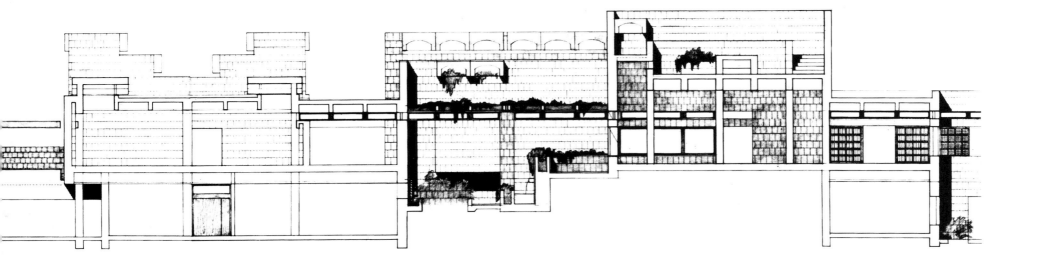

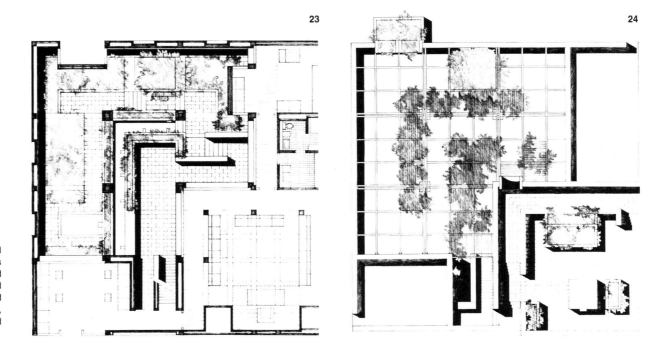

23

24

21. A section showing one of the entrances, an inner garden and the principal audience room with its roof terrace. The old wall is seen in the background on the left. The section shows the stepped form of roof used in the principal rooms. This allows shaded clerestory lighting which is again screened internally by wood lattices. **22** shows the audience room and its associated garden, **23** is a plan of the room and garden and **24** the roof terrace and pergola over the garden area.

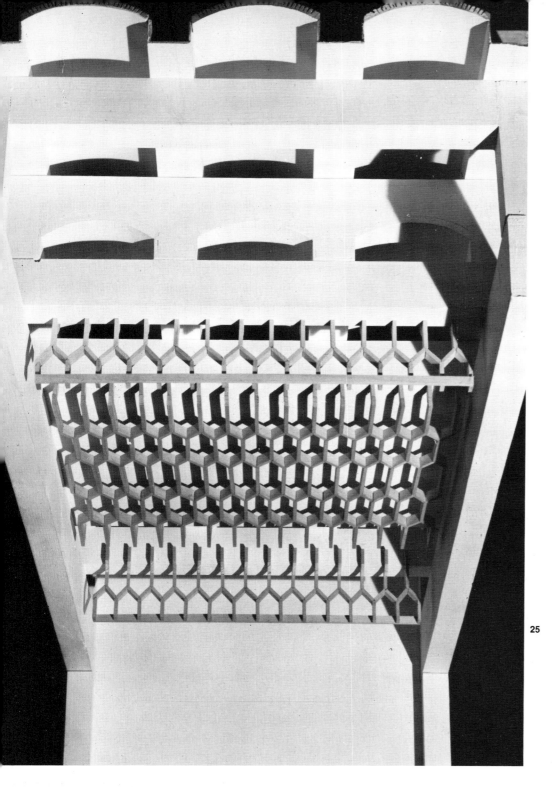

25

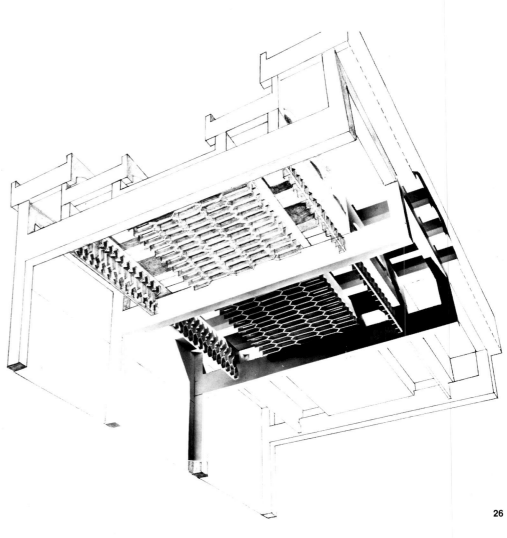

26

25, 26 & 28. Daylighting is introduced into main rooms through shaded clerestory windows. Most of the private suites look out on to shaded gardens. One of the problems nevertheless is to reduce glare. In all the main rooms where clerestory lighting is used, fretted ceilings made of teak form light baffles. In private rooms all windows have external grilles made of teak. Internally various types of timber infilling are used in the coffered ceilings (27 & 29).

27

28

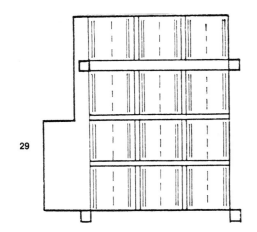

29

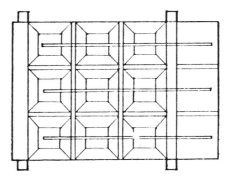

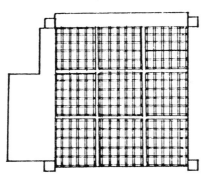

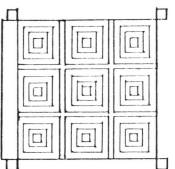

7 · Form and anonymity

Infilling

The original Kettle's Yard was a house where the owner, Mr H. S. Ede, demonstrated a manner in which works of art, paintings, sculpture, pottery, glass and a variety of natural objects might be brought together in a home whilst at the same time the total collection could be shared with others. For many years Mr Ede kept an open house for undergraduates and any friends who might be interested; in his own words, his collection was a kind of 'nursery to the visual arts' and a preparation for the more formal art gallery.

By 1966 Kettle's Yard had established itself. The University of Cambridge accepted the gift of Mr Ede's collection and in 1967 a fund was launched to provide a suitable extension. This extension took the form of a gallery built on the adjoining land – a builder's yard; and the original usable area of 1,600 square feet was expanded to approximately 6,000 square feet in which additional space was provided for the collection and a separate but interconnected gallery space for visiting exhibitions. This exhibition gallery had an additional extension in 1981.

The architectural problem was that of providing a suitable link between the existing house and the new gallery and designing the gallery in such a way that it was related in scale to the older rooms and to the special qualities of the work exhibited. The solution consists of a link to the house by means of a bridge connection at first floor level. The arrangement forms a

1

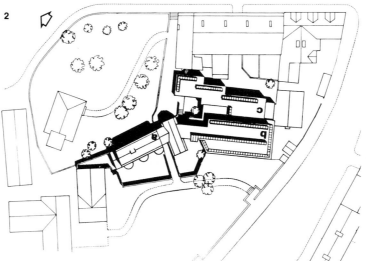

2

1. General view. The house which formed the home for the original collection is on the left, the new galleries are on the right. Internally the sequence of spaces forms a varied setting for the collection. Externally the new building is as anonymous as possible so that it takes its place in the general setting. The second-hand brick and stained weatherboarding have been chosen to harmonise with existing materials. 2. The plan shows the house, the new gallery and, entered separately, the gallery for visiting exhibitions. This exhibition gallery has now been extended (see later) to provide more space by filling in the remainder of the site. 3 & 4. Two views of the lower levels of the gallery. They are lit by top lights in the roof. The floors are brick paviors and the walls have a rough plaster finish.

162

3

4

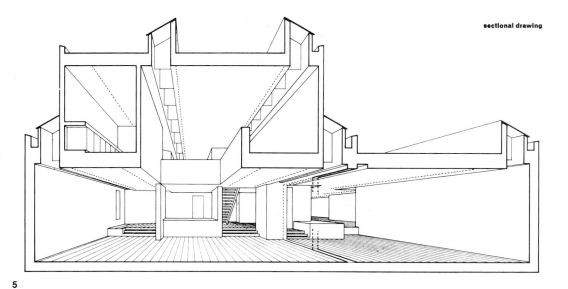

sectional drawing

5

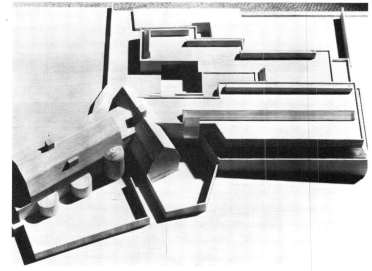

7

6

natural circulation from the house (which contains the main entrance) across the bridge over the entrance passageway and then into the new gallery which forms a series of descending levels. The larger areas of the new gallery open out from each other, and although the space as a whole can be sensed it is built up from a series of discrete and asymmetrically arranged volumes. The section of the building illustrates these varying volumes and the method of top lighting which is used throughout the building. The internal finishes are simple: the walls are finished in rough plaster, the floor with brick paviors.

Externally the gallery takes its place within the

5. The section showing the upper and lower galleries and the rooflight system. **6.** The gallery level. **7.** Model of the group. **8 & 9.** Views of the lower levels of the main gallery.

8

general setting. It is a piece of infilling behind a wall not dissimilar to the wall of the builder's yard which it replaced. The gallery is seen as an extension to the house: the house itself is subservient to St Peter's Church which is at a higher point on the hill. The whole group surmounts the grass bank which rises from Northampton Street.

The recent extension to the exhibition gallery completes the development of the site. This extended gallery, which has its own separate entrance, provides the considerable increase of wall space necessary for visiting exhibitions and, by its use of levels, an increase of height to accommodate larger works of art.

9

165

10

12

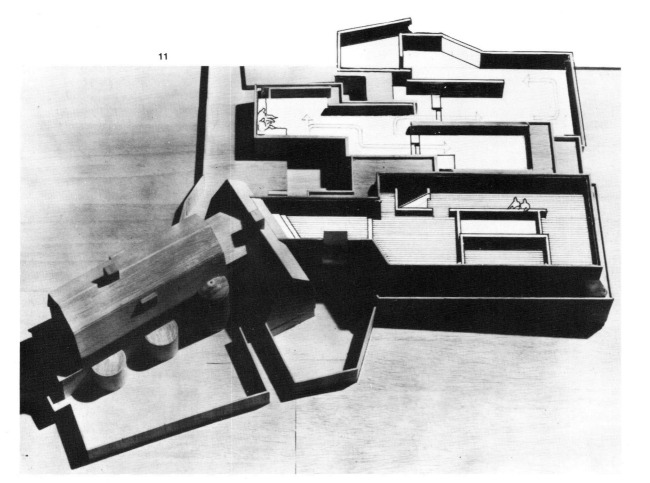

11

10. Plan of the recent extension to the exhibition gallery. Again the top-lit rooms have descending levels. The walls form a series of planes and open up long views across the total area. This device increases the variety of positions for display and extends the sense of space. 11. The house and the upper level of the main gallery are in the foreground. The courtyard entrance and the extended gallery are shown in relation to this. 12. View from inside the entrance looking out on to the courtyard. 13 & 14. The change of level within the extension. 15. View looking along the length of the extension from the entrance. 16. The reverse of 15 – view from the end of the gallery looking towards the entrance.

13

14

15

16

The McGowan Library, Pembroke College, Oxford (1972–)

The library at Pembroke was built on a piece of land between the college buildings and the Master's Lodge. Before 1972 this land contained washhouses and a garage. When these were removed an irregular area of land became available which was accessible through an archway from one of the college courts; opposite this a secondary entrance from the Master's garden was made possible. At the rear, the site along its Brewer Street frontage was bounded by the old city wall. An arch and gates in the wall on the road side provides a frontal approach to the new library site across a forecourt.

The site was certainly restricted. The need for adequate reading space, enclosed rare books room and study room, a librarian's control and workroom and a closed stackroom required at least three levels. The developed plan placed the entrance, librarian's accommodation, rare books and study rooms at the level of the entrance forecourt; one reading space and closed stack was provided below this (at the level of the Master's garden) and another in one large room at first floor level; this was cantilevered out on the two free faces to gain floorspace. The three levels of accommodation are interconnected by a staircase (and book lift) and a central top-lit well which provides additional daylighting to the whole of the interior and increases the general sense of space. The old city wall was left largely untouched, a top-lit area behind it providing

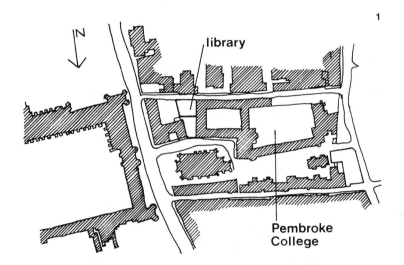

1

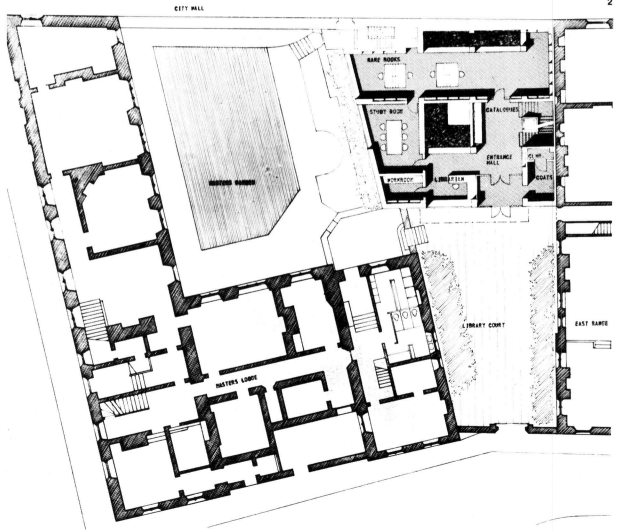

2

1. The Pembroke College site and two pieces of infilling: the library top left and the St Ebbes residential accommodation. 2. The plan shows the Master's Lodge and the new building approach through a new court. This ground floor level of the library contains the librarian's space, catalogues and two enclosed areas, the rare book room and adjoining study room. An open well in the centre of the plan gives top lighting to the whole of the interior and unites the three levels. 3. The lower reading room and closed stack. 4. The top level. 5 & 6. The general position and the new library seen over the old city wall.

natural light for the rare books room.

The building is an example of infilling. It is never seen as a whole. It is glimpsed through the gates of the college frontage or over the city wall along Brewer Street. Approaches from the college court or the Master's garden provide side glances and a sense of changing levels. The building has to relate to the changing angles of the existing buildings and to the outlook across the Master's garden. The external finish is ashlar, which matches the existing stone in colour. Internally the central lightwell relates the surrounding space on all levels into a single whole.

5

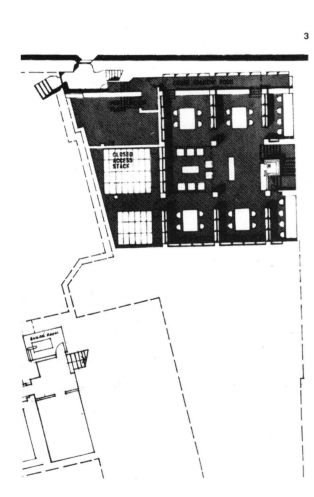

3

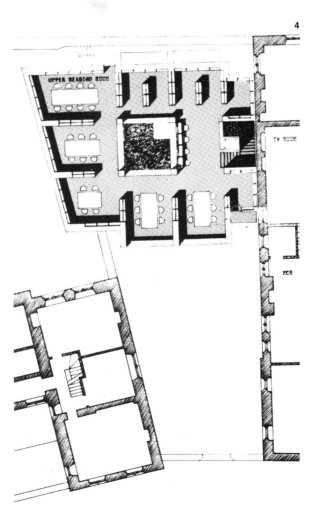

4

6

169

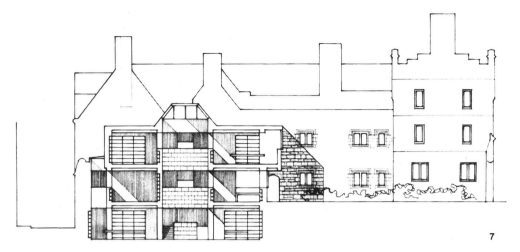

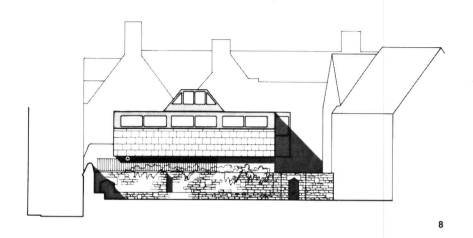

7

8

7. Cross section showing the three levels and the entrance court.
8. Elevation from the Master's garden. 9. Elevation from the
entrance court. 10. The building, the old city wall and the Master's
Lodge. 11. View of the library from the entrance gates. 12. The
library front from one of the college courts. 13. The entry point from
the Master's garden. 14. The building from the Master's garden.
The library is faced in stone, the metal windows are anodised dark
brown.

11

12

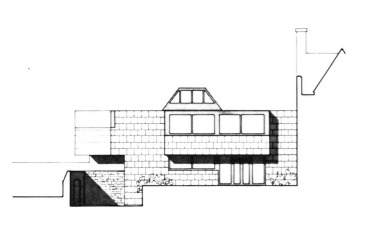

9

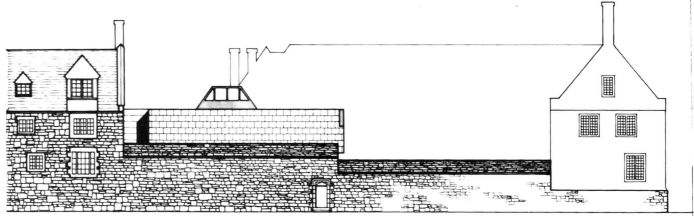

10

13

14

Houses and conversions

Preliminary model

4

The site is predominantly flat with some rising ground just beyond its northern boundary. This land is the source of a spring which feeds a small stream running across the site; the stream was widened out to form a water area behind the house.

The required accommodation in the main house included a large living/dining area and a private study; a bedroom suite and private sitting room for the owners; guest and children's rooms and generous kitchen and service areas. It was also desirable to provide adequate wall space for a large collection of paintings and drawings. A separate but adjacent building was to be provided for staff.

The main rooms are arranged around three sides of a galleried hall. The spatial effect of this hall is extended to the south west by a terrace which continues the marble floor outwards into a series of descending levels which lead to the garden. On the opposite axis the view from the entrance leads right through the building across the hall and dining area and on to an outdoor platform overhanging the water. The dining room, living room, conservatory and study form the main suite of rooms, with the private bedroom/sitting room area over. The guest rooms, with children's rooms over, are on the entrance side; the kitchen, with staff rooms over, connect these two main wings so that the accommodation forms a compact plan around the double height of the galleried hall. The accommodation in the staff annexe is arranged in a single-storey building built around a court and echoing the plan form of the main house itself.

The buildings form a varied group now seen across a carefully planted landscape. The load bearing walls are faced with buff brick, the window frames are teak and the pitched roof shapes are finished in zinc.

1, 2 & 3. The drawings illustrate the arrangement of rooms around the double height central hall, the view across this from the entrance to the lake and the terraces on the south west leading from the central hall to the garden. The staff flat and garage accommodation around its own courtyard is shown on the right. **4.** The entrance front. **5 & 6.** Two views of the south west terraces.

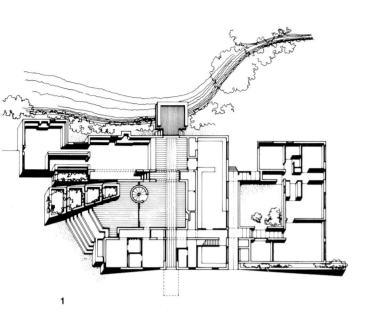

1

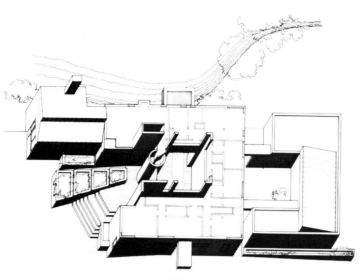

2

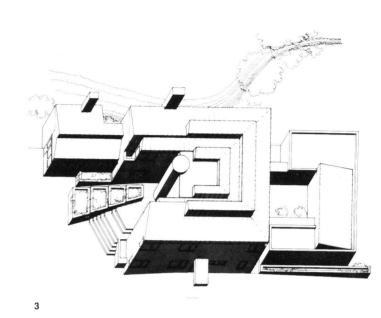

3

5

6

1

2

3

4

Small houses abroad (1961–)

Two of these houses are designed on steeply sloping sites; both make use of upper terrace levels.

The first house in Switzerland was designed in 1961 and is arranged along the contours of the site at three levels. A staircase cuts across the plan, providing the main connection between these levels and the link between the living/dining/kitchen area and the upper suite of rooms which includes bedrooms, studio etc. Externally the house appears as a cluster of single-storey buildings arranged at different levels around a terrace. The total form is held down in scale so that it has some relationship to other houses in the vicinity.

The second house designed and built in Portugal three years later is planned across the contours of the site to provide two separate terraces related to the principal rooms in the plan. Basically the plan consists of a central entrance level which accommodates the living room and kitchen and provides an external terrace as an extension to the living room itself. A stair up from this entrance level leads to the main bedroom and its terrace. A stair down from the living room leads to the guest rooms at the lowest level. All rooms have extensive views towards the Sierra. The house was designed so that it could be built simply and economically with a minimum number of drawings. It has a reinforced concrete frame and floors, and the walls are brick block rendered. The roof is tiled.

Another house on land adjoining the previously described house is in a small valley. It is designed around a sheltered courtyard and related to sun and view.

1 & 2. The house was designed in relation to a steeply sloping site in Switzerland. The design includes two studios at different levels and the various elements of the plan are arranged to form a group of buildings around an outdoor terrace. 3 & 4. A small house in Portugal. 5, 6 & 7 illustrate the plans and the formal arrangement.

5   6   7

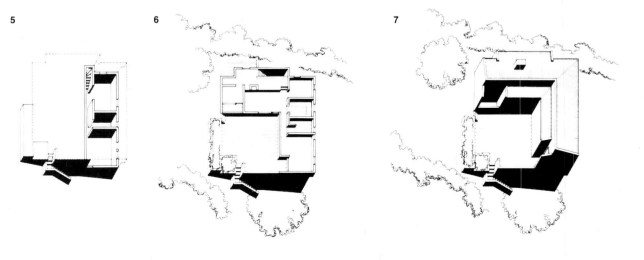

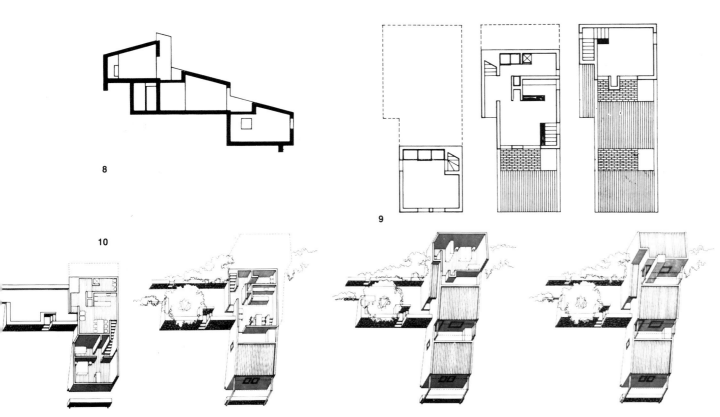

8

9

10

11

12

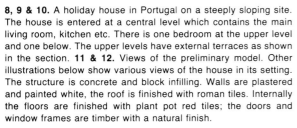

8, 9 & 10. A holiday house in Portugal on a steeply sloping site. The house is entered at a central level which contains the main living room, kitchen etc. There is one bedroom at the upper level and one below. The upper levels have external terraces as shown in the section. **11 & 12.** Views of the preliminary model. Other illustrations below show various views of the house in its setting. The structure is concrete and block infilling. Walls are plastered and painted white, the roof is finished with roman tiles. Internally the floors are finished with plant pot red tiles; the doors and window frames are timber with a natural finish.

The Mill: own house and studios, Shelford, Cambridge (1956–)

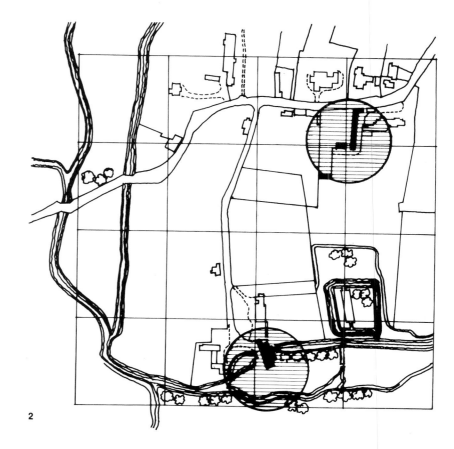

2

The mill consists of a composite group of buildings. The older part of the mill and miller's house is a two and three storeyed building built of timber and overlapping boarding. It stood beside the main mill stream which operated its mill wheel. In 1890 a larger four storeyed brick structure with cast iron windows was built on land on the opposite side of the stream; at this date a turbine was introduced to operate the new machinery. Finally the two separate buildings were connected by a heavily framed timber structure faced in corrugated iron; this accommodated the grain silos.

The mill was unused in 1956. The first part of the conversion started in the 1890 building. The four floors

1. General view of The Mill across the mill pond. 2. Plan of the neighbourhood showing The Mill (bottom) and The Barns (top right). 3. The elements which form the total group include the miller's house (top), the old mill (below this), the four storey brick

176

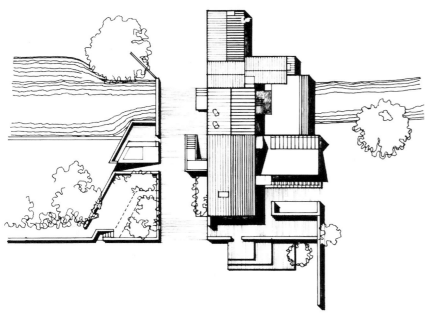

3

4

of this structure were supported on massive timber cross beams spanning the width and providing a clear floor space twenty-five feet wide by forty feet long on each floor.

The conversion starts from a new external staircase which leads to the entrance to the house at first floor level. The studios are at ground level and have a separate entrance. The house has four floors of accommodation: three are connected by single flights of open staircases placed one above another. One internal wall dividing the service from the living areas runs through all floors and contains the plumbing. Another brick structure forms a core which again runs

through all floors and contains the heating. One end bay of the second floor was cut away to make a double height: the living area at second floor level becomes a gallery overlooking this double height. The first and second floors are therefore part of the same volume and are open in plan. The bedroom floor is arranged to give a maximum sense of enclosure. Each room has two interconnecting areas and the total shape is never obvious.

This brick end structure which formed the original house and studio has shown itself to be flexible in use: it has been changed in plan on at least two occasions. The old mill and miller's house have been formed into

mill of 1890 (bottom) and connecting these, the silo house. The ground floor of the 1890 building forms the main studio. A second studio built within the walls of the old engine shed extends this space and is shown on the right of the plan. External terraces

complete the link to the garden area. **4.** A view from the rear of The Mill shows the river and the second studio. The roof shape is designed to introduce sunlight on to the studio wall.

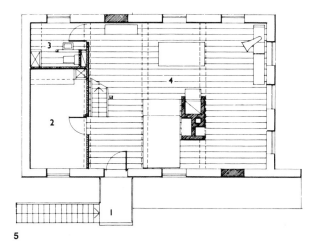
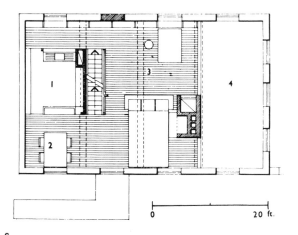
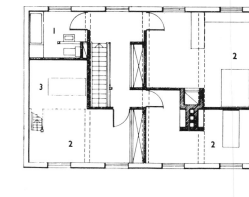

5   **6**   **7**

5. The entrance to the house at first floor level, main reception room, study and cloakroom. The studios are at ground level below this. **6.** Second floor level: the main living area: 1 Kitchen. 2 Dining and living space. 3 Writing. 4 Open space overlooking floor below. Walls painted brick, ceilings timber, carpets and upholstery natural colours. **7.** Third floor level: 1 Bathroom. 2 Bedrooms. 3 A gallery level over one of these. **8, 9 & 10.** The kitchen area. **11.** Bathroom. **12.** Entrance door and stair up to main living area. **13.** The first floor level. **14.** View up to first floor level from the entrance.

8   **9**   **10**

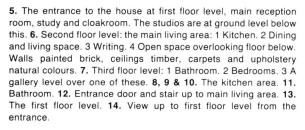

178

11

two separate dwellings, the mill itself forming an unusual elongated plan with varying internal volumes. The silo house connecting these two buildings has contained flats and, at its upper levels, rooms used by postgraduate students and colleagues from the studio. Again the planning has been changed on numerous occasions to meet changing needs.

What has been interesting and impressive about these conversions is the wide variety of accommodation that they have provided. This has allowed a considerable range of choice for the changing inhabitants, and it forms a sharp contrast to the conception of housing which has crystallised into the two or three bedroomed standard plan. The question that arises is whether a similar range and variety could be achieved by the imaginative planning of new housing.

12

13

14

179

15

16

15. The living room and gallery: long view. 16. The living area: cross view. 17 & 18. The double height and gallery from first floor level. The brick column contains heating ducts and flues. 19 & 20. Views of the second studio. The window provides a view along the river. The walls are painted brick, and the roof structure is timber with a boarded soffit. 21. The building in the centre of the main group was converted into flats, those in the roof space forming studios with sleeping galleries.

17

19

20

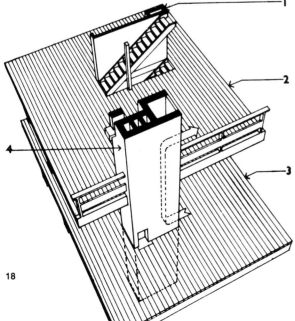

18

21

The Barn: own house, Shelford, Cambridge (1977–)

This barn, originally the village granary, was built around 1642. It runs at right angles to the village street, opposite the church. More recently it has been used as outbuildings adjoining the kitchen garden of the neighbouring house.

The total length of the granary and its barn extension is about 150 feet; its width is fifteen feet. The granary had storage at ground level. A heavily constructed first floor with open timber roof members over formed the lofty room in which the grain was kept. This long storage building had a later extension at the road end at right angles to the main block and with a greater height at ground floor level.

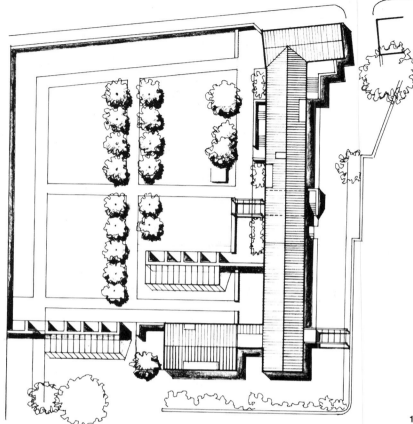

1

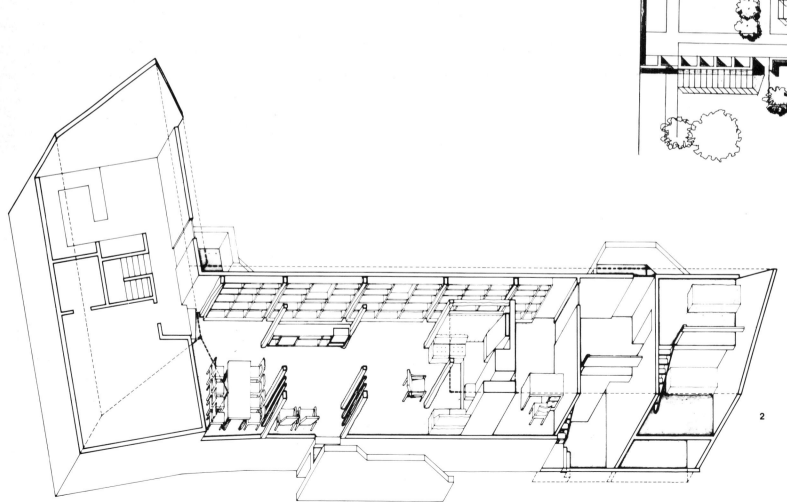

2

3

4

1. Plan of the buildings and adjoining garden. The granary, which is the conversion illustrated, occupies about 80 feet of the end of the buildings nearest the road. The remaining area and an adjoining outbuilding have been converted into a separate house. 2. The main living room of the converted barn: bedrooms left, entrance hall and guest flat right. 3. The main entrance; the kitchen entrance can be seen beyond. 4. The pergola marking the entrance to the adjoining house and a view along the entrance front.

The conversion is simple. The entrances are at first floor level. This main floor forms the living space which is subdivided into writing and living areas by a fireplace recess which projects across the room. The main room has a further suggestion of subdivision from the pairs of columns which run along and emphasise its length: on one side of the room these columns form part of the timber screens which stiffen the structure and define the dining end, on the other side they mark off the passage area along the bookcase wall.

The main entrance stair gives access to a double height entrance hall. Beyond the entrance hall there are self-contained guest rooms, bathroom and kitchenette. The bedroom area for the main house is in the extension along the road front. This *T*-shaped end also contains the kitchen with its separate external entrance. There are studios on the ground floor of these areas of the plan.

6

6 & 7. The living room. The old timbers were cleaned and left in their natural finish. As the living room runs from north to south, top side lighting is introduced into the sloping ceiling at two points. This allows some south east and south west sun to penetrate the living room.

The construction of the top light is simple. A strip of roof and ceiling is cut away in the lower part of the ceiling of one of the bays; the rafters are left exposed and the opening is glazed with one large pane of double glazing. Windows in the wall are small and mainly for outlook.

6 shows a view along the living room from the higher level of the kitchen floor. The line of supporting columns forms a passageway along the front of the bookcase wall. The light strip allows a flexible arrangement to suit books or paintings. 7. The bookcase wall, left, and the cabinet to hold television and record player between columns in front of this. The screens and diagonal braces on the right stiffen the timber structure. 8. Diagram of the TV and record player cabinet. 5 shows, above, contrasting materials, textures, etc. and, below, the studio.

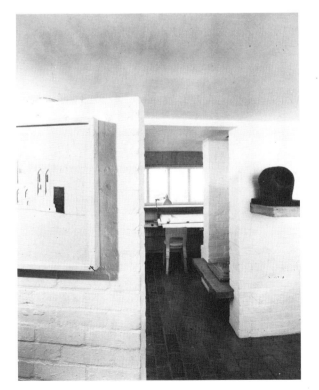

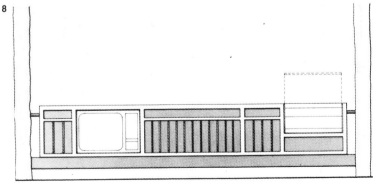

8

5

9

10

186

9 & 10. The area around the fireplace has a lowered ceiling. The brick fireplace recess has a metal hood over the exposed fire. The raised hearth is finished with brick paviors. On the right of the fireplace the wall is penetrated (10) to create a sense of the writing space beyond. **11.** The fireplace recess. The general colour effect is subdued. The walls and ceiling are white (brick and plaster). The timber is left in its natural condition and is light in tone. The floor coverings and seating fabrics are white, cream and warm grey; their effect depends on texture. This neutral background allows the paintings to have their own natural setting and to provide their own emphasis. The view above shows the studio passage: the cane chair is by Franco Albini.

11

12

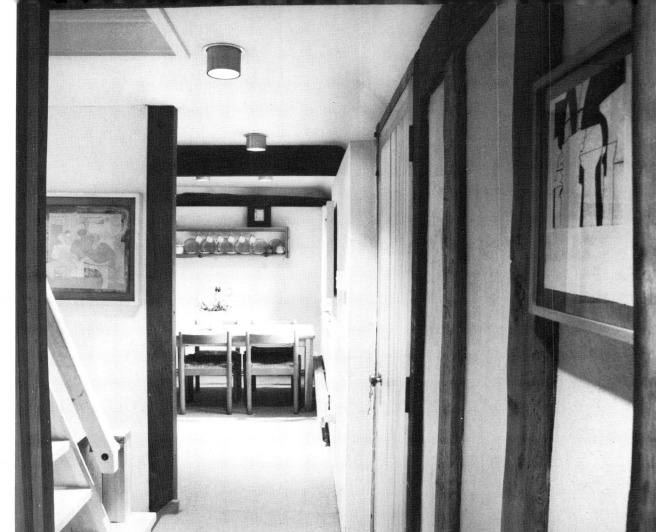

13

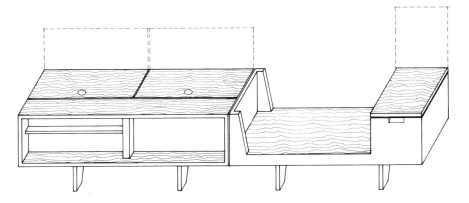

14

15

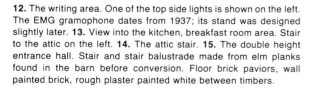

12. The writing area. One of the top side lights is shown on the left. The EMG gramophone dates from 1937; its stand was designed slightly later. **13.** View into the kitchen, breakfast room area. Stair to the attic on the left. **14.** The attic stair. **15.** The double height entrance hall. Stair and stair balustrade made from elm planks found in the barn before conversion. Floor brick paviors, wall painted brick, rough plaster painted white between timbers.

Housing, Saudi Arabia (scheme, 1975)

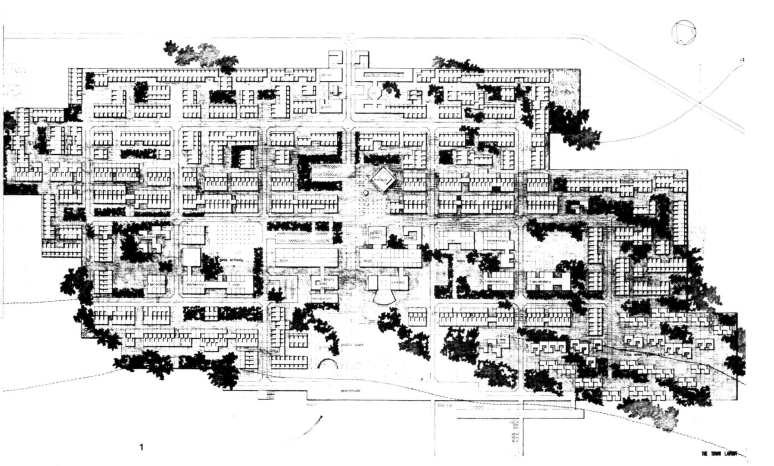

1

2

These proposals for housing were developed to meet the needs of one of the communities associated with the operation of a large industrial plant. The site is on the coast. The community will have its traditional mosque and souk, and some schools and public buildings are proposed. But the houses themselves are intended for the employees. Some of these may be residents from outside the Kingdom, perhaps European or American. Other houses are for specialist technicians or engineers. Most of the houses will require space for cars. The total community is not large; about 2,000 dwellings of various types were required.

The general plan has a simple circulatory road system which gives access to the houses and the car

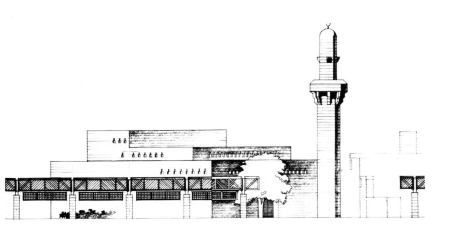

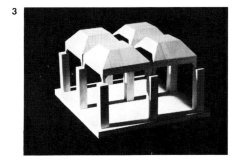

3

190

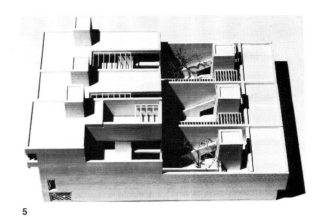

4

5

park which serve the central buildings. The cars do not penetrate this central area. The central square is pedestrian and contains the mosque and its minaret, the administrative offices and clinic and the souk. This area will be paved and planted with shade-creating trees. Connecting this central area to the shore there is a public park and recreational area, and running across the town in the opposite direction there is a pedestrian street which contains the apartment dwellings. This pedestrian walk is also shaded by the form of the dwellings themselves and focuses on the minaret of the mosque. The villas are placed close to the sea front. Most of the dwellings are planned so that they can be built either singly or in compact groups of varying forms to suit their position in the total layout.

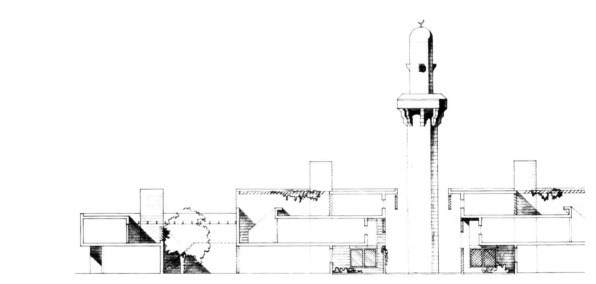

6

1. The general plan. An open pedestrian square with its mosque (**2**) is at the centre. This is associated with the souk and a park leading down to the waterfront. A circulatory road system keeps the centre free from through traffic. Pedestrian streets, areas and diagonal routes are maintained throughout the scheme. One main pedestrian street is lined by the high density housing. **6.** The minaret of the mosque can be seen throughout its length and becomes a focal point of the layout. **4 & 5** show the block form of this housing. The illustrations (**3**) come from a series of studies of shade-creating structures.

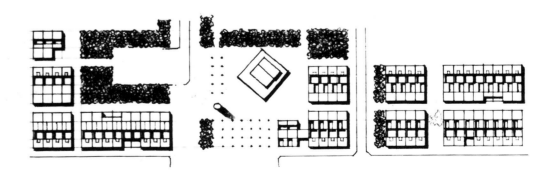

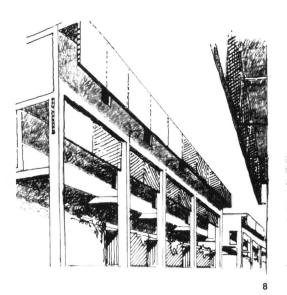

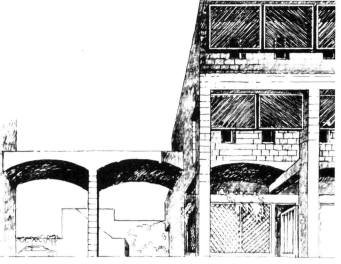

The high density proposal develops an overlapping form of apartment, accessible from small private courts along the main pedestrian street; the car access and garage accommodation is at the rear. In this type a long narrow plan is developed around an internal court used by the ground floor occupants of the apartment who have their bedrooms over the garages at the rear. The apartment over this is again entered from the pedestrian street but directly connected to the first and second floors on which main accommodation is provided. A passageway at first floor level along one side of the courtyard (but screened from it) connects this apartment to its garage at the rear.

The general form of these apartments again makes full use of private courts and screened sleeping ter-

8

9

7

races. Along the frontage on to the pedestrian street, the houses have a stepped and oversailing form with all windows protected by hanging wooden trellises.

Other types of dwelling designed to meet different family needs are again planned around courts and capable of being grouped so that they can be arranged around pedestrian ways with cul-de-sac approaches for cars. Some of these in their planning follow traditional forms of arrangement within the dwelling, other plans show several variants on the villa form in two-storey and single-storey types. Most of these types lend themselves to a compact grouping without loss of privacy. Two forms of single room or two room dwelling are suggested for unmarried residents.

The characteristic element in traditional housing is the court. More recently various architects have explored the possibilities of the narrow fronted house with courts, notably Serge Chermayeff in his pioneering work *Community and Privacy* and George Candilis in his use of the court in housing in hot climates. The plans that follow are simply modifications of the type forms adapted to specific family groupings and uses. They provide shaded court areas as a means of control of internal temperatures: air movement across rooms and the use of sleeping terraces. 7 shows the high density housing. Each plan width provides two separate dwelling entrances from the pedestrian street at the front, a separate entrance for each dwelling by car from the rear. 8 & 9 show the main street frontage. 10 shows the overlapping form of the plan. Heights are three or four storeys depending on the size of the upper dwelling.

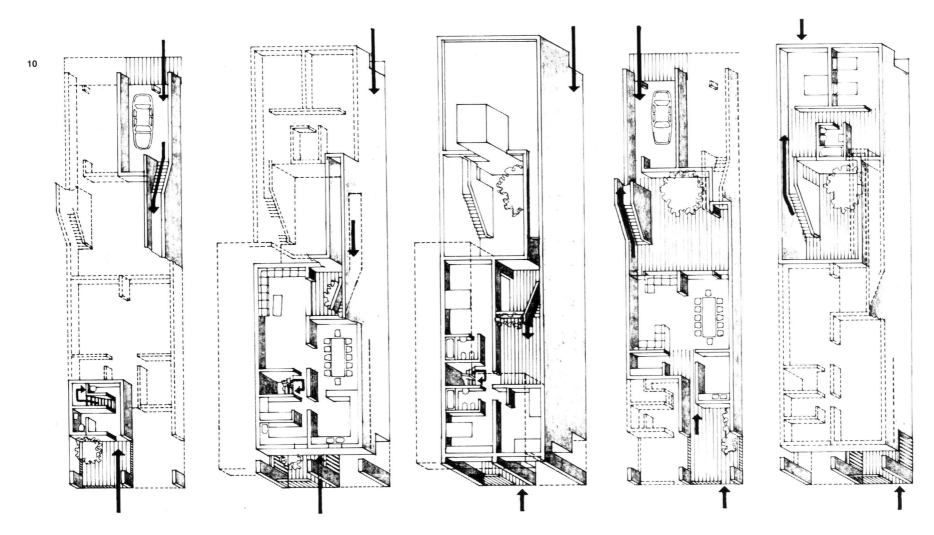

10

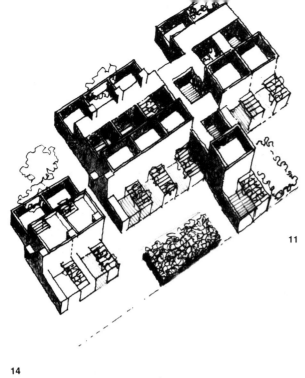

11

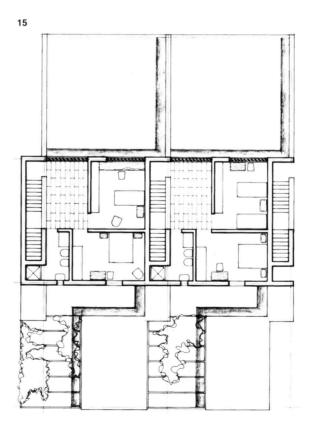

16

14

15

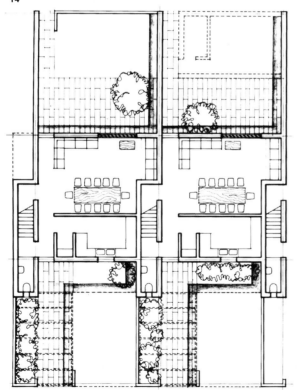

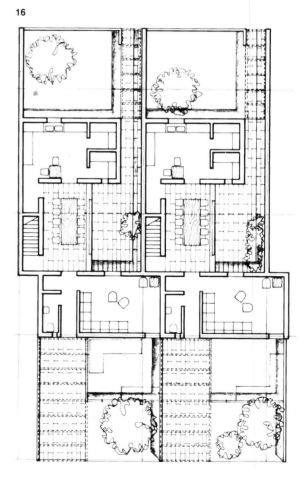

194

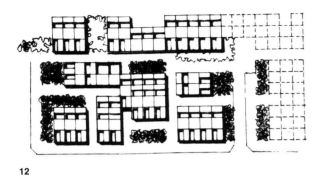

12

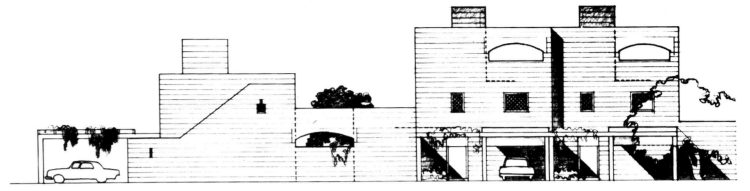

13

17

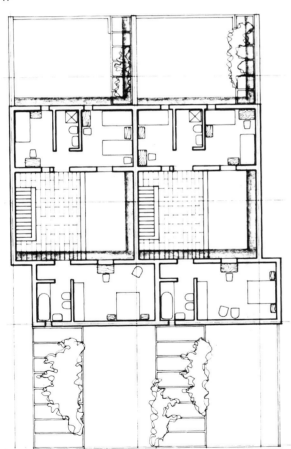

11. Narrow fronted dwelling. **14 & 15.** Minimum two bedroom type. Open car port in front. **16 & 17.** Three bedroom type: with shared sleeping terrace: men's area in front, children's court at rear. Typical grouping of two and three bedroom types shown in **12** opposite. A deep plan, five bedroom, large family type was also developed. Two courts retain cross ventilation. Servants' room at ground floor rear. Sleeping terrace or additional bedroom at roof level. Grouping on elevations shown in **13** above.

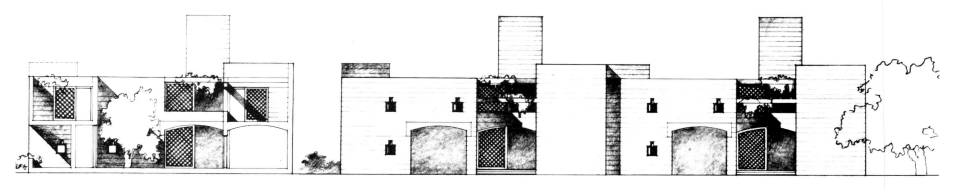

20

23

24

25

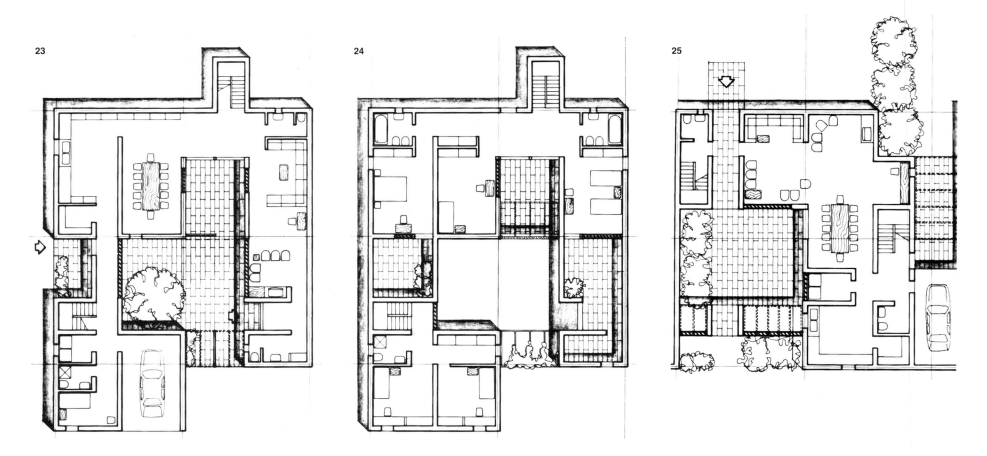

The villas. These are of various sizes and can be free standing or grouped. They have concrete block walls and teak trellises. All have internal courts. **23 & 24.** The larger two storey villas have spacious living areas with three main bedrooms with individual terraces over. The lower level of the house is linked to a separate garage building with accommodation for staff over. **25 & 26.** Two storey villas with a court, sleeping terraces at first floor level and the possibility of echelon arrangement. **27 & 28.** Single-storey types: grouping as shown in **21 & 22.**

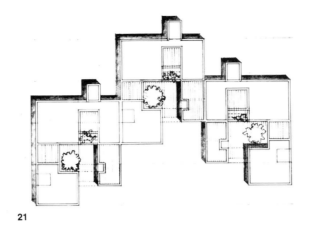

21

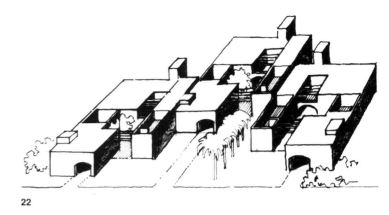

22

26

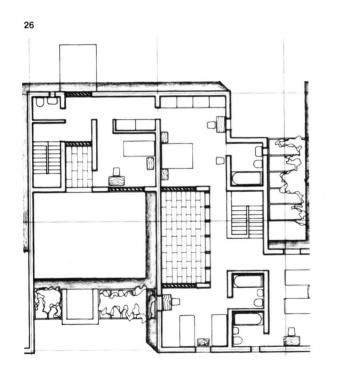

27

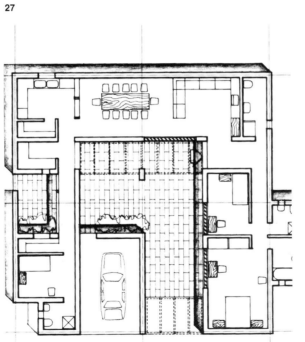

28

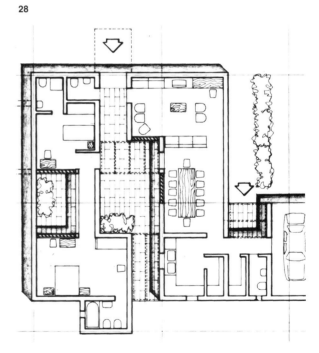

29

Groups of bachelor dwellings are placed near the main entrance to the town. **29** shows a studio type with internal open access and external balconies. **30 & 31** develop a two storey type with external car ports. **32.** The general effect of the constructional system used throughout all the types: the illustration shows the living area opening on to a courtyard in one of the high density types. **33.** The elements of the constructional system: white concrete block walls; pre-cast units for floors and roofs over standard bays; teak window elements and external screens.

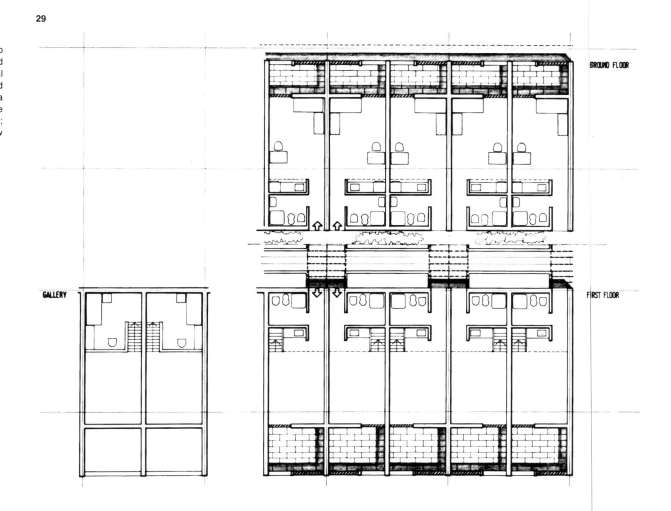

GROUND FLOOR

GALLERY

FIRST FLOOR

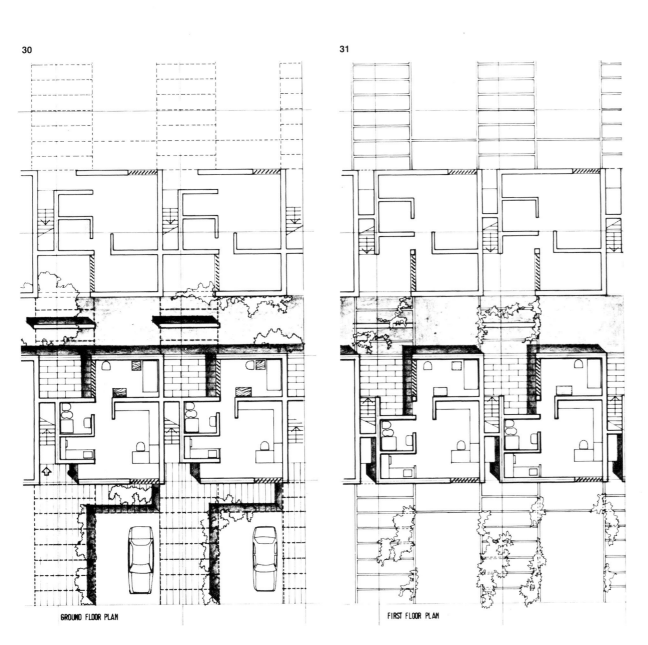

30

31

GROUND FLOOR PLAN

FIRST FLOOR PLAN

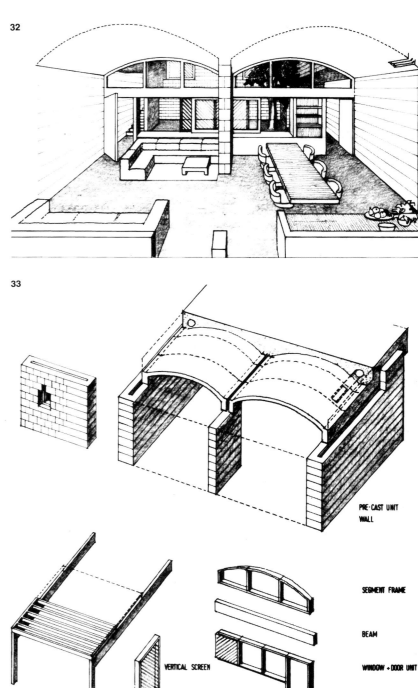

32

33

PRE-CAST UNIT
WALL

SEGMENT FRAME

BEAM

WINDOW + DOOR UNIT

HORIZONTAL SCREEN

VERTICAL SCREEN

199

1

2

3

4

1. The author: Head of the School of Architecture, Hull, 1934;
2 & 3, at the Cambridge School, Le Corbusier talks to students
1957; Henry Moore draws portrait of Le Corbusier without looking;
4, at the Royal Institute of British Architects, presentation of the
Royal Gold Medal to Alvar Aalto 1957; 5, at Ronchamp with his wife,
Sadie Speight.

5

3 APPENDIX

1

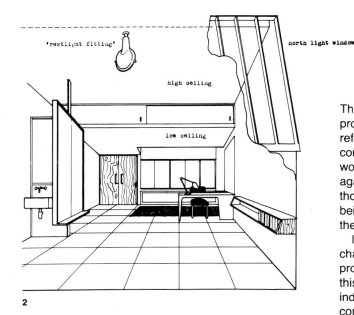

'restlight fitting'

north light window

high ceiling

low ceiling

2

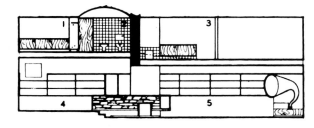

3

4

The work illustrated and described in these notes was produced partly in private practice. Other buildings referred to include those with which I was directly connected during my service in a public office. The work after this period, from 1956 on, was produced again in private practice but it is in part connected with those national programmes of building which were being carried out both in public and private offices in the sixties.

It is certainly not the intention here to document the changes in the way that buildings were sponsored, programmed at a national level and executed during this period, except to note that one scholar at least has indicated that the changes taking place were considerable.[1] They represent changes in the pattern of relationships that happened almost unnoticed in the same way that, at an earlier date, the patron became simply the client. So too, within the building industry, the position of the building tradesmen changed, when Thomas Cubitt (1788–1855) founded what might be described as the first firm of general contractors.[2]

What is relevant here is that the early work designed between 1934 and 1939 is modest, dispersed and built for private clients who were interested in a special problem on a special site. The work that I refer to later in public offices is large-scaled and publicly sponsored. I have said before that in both contexts I have never been conscious of any difference in the way that I have worked as an architect. I continued to design and to work with a small group of colleagues. The work in a public office involved some administration, but not a great deal and there was appropriate staff to help with this. The work in private practice is equally demanding in relation to administrative skills. And in my time at least as Deputy Architect and later Architect to the LCC, we public architects were glad to share with our private architect colleagues the immense responsibility of building new homes or meeting the building needs of a vastly expanded programme of educational building.

The changes that I describe reflect, to some extent, not only my own employment but changes in the scale of opportunity for young architects before and after the war. The individual projects in the group of buildings built before the war are so small that I have chosen to represent the work as a composite group of illustrations. They speak for a period and illustrate a number of houses which respond to very different requirements

The illustrations on this page show various drawings and photographs relating to small houses and extensions built between 1937 and 1939. **1, 7 & 9.** The general form of the Morton house and studio built at Brampton, Cumberland. The house is built of brick. Stone retaining walls and canopy supports link the building to the landscape. **2 & 5.** The interior of the studio. **3 & 4.** Extensions to a

5

6

7

8

9

and were built in very different landscapes. There is an extension to a house in Cumberland built in the dry stone walling of the area; another in a more sophisticated landscape near Carlisle where the brick structure is linked to the setting by protecting canopies and local stone walling. A third is in a village near Hull where the material is predominantly brick. Work of this kind, though small, provided the opportunity to compose buildings around differing needs and to think about materials and the effects of different sites.

The school at Northwich had other implications. It was built at a time when there was considerable interest in classrooms with good natural light, variable ventilation, internal flexibility and plan growth. It was at that time unusual to build a school which brought together standardised products, like metal windows, and a simple structural system that used mainly dry construction, in this case timber. Because of this departure from the standard forms of construction that were then acceptable, it was regarded as a temporary structure. The actual building consisted of four classrooms with their cloakrooms, lavatories etc. The possible method of enlargement is classical in its form: it consists of a series of mirror images which finally end

stone house at Dockray and **6** a suite of rooms and terrace added to a house at Brampton; both in Cumberland. **8.** A house built in Ferriby, Yorkshire.

10

11

12

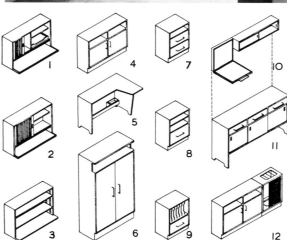

12a

in a completely balanced plan built up around cross axes.

The other work illustrated is an early range of unit furniture designed at a time when there was not, to my knowledge, anything of this kind available. The range proved, as we demonstrated in an exhibition at Messrs Rowntree's showrooms in Scarborough, that it could be related to many different needs and settings and that it could readily be combined with the early Aalto, Plan and Isokon furniture then becoming available.

Compared with the quality of the many smaller houses that have since been built, or with the great quantity of school building that has been constructed in this country since the sixties, or with the carefully designed and elaborated unit furniture that has now become available, this early work can certainly be regarded as trivial. I am glad that this can be said. It emphasises the contrast between then and now. These things were certainly important to me then, and perhaps it is worth pointing out that in spite of much talk of new techniques and concrete structure at that time, the materials used in these early buildings are basically traditional: brick or local stone and timber.

I joined a public office, the architect's office of the LMS Railway, precisely because I realised that a change was taking place in the whole range of building work and the scale of its production. It seemed obvious that developments of this kind should be preceded by some investigation of the problems involved. Sir Harold Hartley, an Oxford scientist, had joined the LMS as a Vice-President and had established research work in a number of technical fields. We were able to build up a research and development section in the architect's office with the object ultimately of investigating new technical methods for use after the war. Meanwhile we were fully engaged on war-time problems.

10. Scheme for a series of shops with standardised display windows and interior furniture. **11, 12 & 12a.** Unit furniture. A series of timber bookshelves, cupboards with roller shutter fronts, sideboard, wardrobe fittings etc., all based on a standard module, painting by Arthur Jackson. **13, 14, 15, 16 & 17.** Nursery School at

Northwich, Cheshire, 1937–8. Four classrooms were required. These could be converted into a larger floor area by removing a folding partition. Lavatories, cloakrooms and kitchen were planned in line with the classrooms. A lower roof over these servicing areas allows cross ventilation to the classrooms. The plan was capable

The immediate post-war period produced the large programmes of housing and schools that had been envisaged and for some years they were the only types of building to be constructed. The shortages of materials continued for some years and Research and Development sections made their contributions to the investigation of programmes and methods in both public offices and Ministries.

When I joined the LCC in 1948 there was a problem of a different kind. The LCC, in considering its plan for the development of London,[3] had laid some stress on the development of the South Bank. Ideas included the possibility of building a new concert hall for London (the old Queen's Hall had been destroyed during the war) or possibly a new National Theatre between the Hungerford Railway Bridge and Waterloo Bridge; in fact in 1948 Dr Charles Holden was preparing a plan for this development. At the same time consideration had been given to a suitable London site for the Festival of Britain Exhibition which had Government support and was being planned under the direction of the Lord President of the Council, Mr Herbert Morrison.

The two ideas of finding a site for the Festival and leaving a permanent contribution to the development of the South Bank in the form of a new river wall and a concert hall happened to complement each other and Robert Matthew, architect to the Council, had the courage to say that the concert hall could be built on the South Bank site by May 1951, and he carried throughout the overall responsibility.

I joined Matthew as Deputy Architect in October 1948 and was asked by him to regard the work on the concert hall as a special task. My immediate colleagues included Edwin Williams, the senior architect responsible for overall production, and Peter Moro, who came from private practice as associated architect

of extension by a series of mirror images; one of these is illustrated in 13, the service area becoming a spine between two rows of classrooms. The constructional frame is timber. Sliding wooden window frames carry standard metal windows.

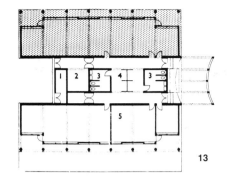

13

14

15

16

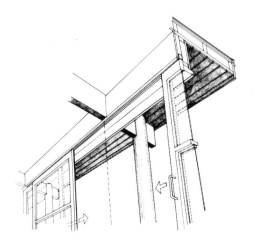

17

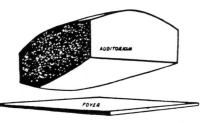

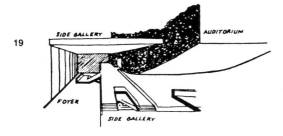

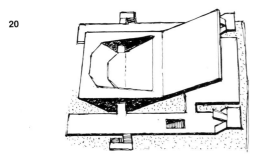

on the design side. Our supporting team included some established members of the LCC staff and an enthusiastic group of young architects specially appointed for the project.

There were several conditioning factors connected with this early stage of the project. The main concert hall itself was to seat not less than 3,000, and at that time a small hall for 500 was also proposed. Dr Holden's plan had suggested the site area and the frontage line for the building in relation to the site for the proposed National Theatre. This plan also suggested that the Hungerford Railway Bridge would be replaced by a new road bridge. Since this was unlikely to happen for many years, clearly the design of a concert hall on this site would have to take into account the noise from the adjoining railway. And of course the timing was critical. The whole project would have to be designed, built and in operation within a period of thirty months. I have described aspects of this operation and the acoustic and sound insulation problems elsewhere.[4]

Here it is sufficient to say that at that time although some general principles regarding the effect of acoustic considerations on the shape of the hall could be

stated, the effects of its internal shape on the clarity, echo, or reverberation could not then (as they could now) be predicted in advance by model testing.[5] What could be predicted (and indeed was proved by an experimental building on the site itself before the work was started) was that the auditorium would require massive enclosing walls to resist sound penetration from external noise.

From the point of view of the design conception it could be shown that the major auditorium form would in itself occupy a large area of the available site. This would have a special shape, a raked floor etc. and it would require the heavy construction that has been described. The limited site area was always one of the main problems. Given the fact that the auditorium must occupy a major position, where do you place the necessary foyer which, in turn, is connected to other uses, for instance an exhibition area and a restaurant that preferably should overlook the river?

Clearly the foyer must be linked to points of entry. At the time of the design conception, the most convenient points of entry were from the sides of the site: one at ground level from a new square between the proposed concert hall and the future National Theatre, the other

18, 19 & 20. The initial gain of space obtained by placing the auditorium over the main foyer area. The large foyer can be used for various functions: at the Belvedere Road end of the building its sunken floor area can be used for exhibitions, receptions etc. It contains the main bar and is connected to the restaurant on the riverside front. In relation to the concert hall the foyer acts principally as a means of bringing together the flow of movement

from the two side entrances, one below and one at the level of the foyer itself. From this central foyer area side galleries, with staircases on the river frontage, give access to all levels of the auditorium and provide promenades and refreshment areas at all levels. As the movement through the foyer progresses the visitor is presented with a succession of views across the total volume. **21.** View from the lower entrance level: the cloakroom is on the right,

23

on the opposite side and at a higher level to serve the Hungerford footbridge and, in the future, the roadway proposed in the Holden Plan.

One central and major solution became clear. The two levels of the entrances at the sides could connect with a large foyer space which, with its associated restaurants and so on, would occupy the whole of the site area. The auditorium itself could be centrally placed over the foyer space. It was this suspended auditorium within the main volume of the surrounding foyers and galleries that became known as the 'egg in the box'. And however incompletely it was realised, it is this central idea that provides the building with its major attributes: the great sense of space that is opened out within the building, the flowing circulation from the symmetrically placed staircases and galleries which give access to all parts of the auditorium, the changing spatial volumes and views that are presented from these different access levels, and, within and enclosed by all this, the mass of the auditorium itself.

That was the architectural conception as it was first envisaged and which we attempted to retain in spite of all kinds of problems arising from the building regulations, structure, air conditioning and not least the

24

the ascending stairs to the main foyer on the left. **22.** View looking down on to the foyer from the connecting bridge between the two sides galleries. **23.** The foyer from the access stair. **24.** The main foyer area with the raking floor of the auditorium over. **25.** View into the riverside restaurant from one of the staircases at the end of the side galleries.

25

207

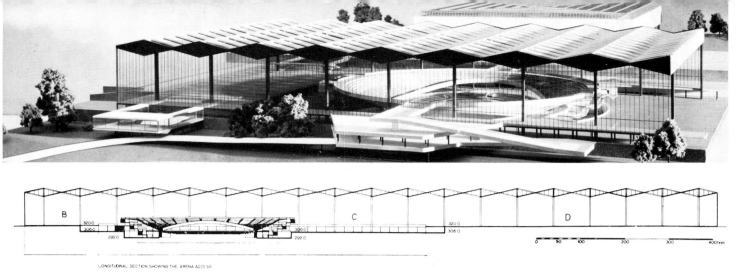

B C D

LONGITUDINAL SECTION SHOWING THE ARENA ACCESS

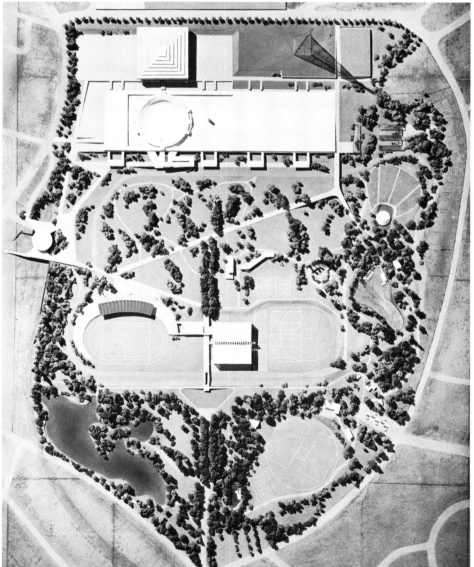

27

speed with which the building had to be constructed whilst the design ideas for all parts of the building were still being developed.[6]

The first concert was held in May 1951. We had decided before starting that it would not be possible to build the small hall and it was clear during the progress of the work that we would be unable to build the backstage administration and changing room areas. This necessitated a temporary end on the Belvedere Road frontage. The line of the river frontage (fixed by the Holden Plan) had restricted the restaurant area and it was clear that when we did complete the backstage accommodation this river frontage also required extension. These limitations were known and a plan for the completion of the building preserving the approaches and movement patterns through the foyer was developed and published later during my period as architect to the Council.[7] This plan also suggested the removal of the small hall on to the site that had been

This first scheme for the proposed LCC development of the Crystal Palace site included a permanent exhibition centre on an international scale. The proposed main buildings include a small hall to the north and, along the ridge of the site where the old Crystal Palace used to stand, the main exhibition hall spanning 400 ft by 1,000 ft long. Within this total volume there is an arena and amphitheatre for sporting events. Outside the hall are terraces that could accommodate outdoor exhibits, temporary pavilions etc. Restaurants and bars are incorporated and the building takes its

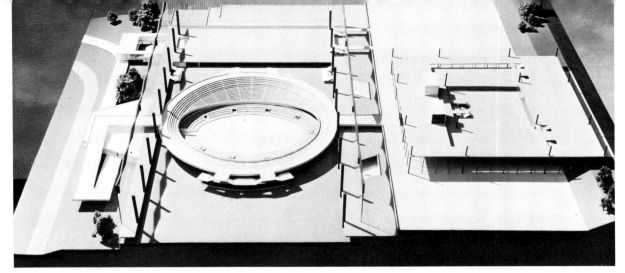

28

allocated to the National Theatre.

Finally, again during my time as architect to the Council, I worked with Norman Englebach, Bryn Jones and John Attenborough on proposals for the development of the Crystal Palace site. The idea of using the site for an Exhibition and Sports Centre had been suggested to the LCC by Sir Gerald Barry in a Report produced in 1952–3. The design for this total project was worked out and published in 1956.[8] The main Exhibition building consisted of one large structure running the whole length of the terraces at the upper levels of the site. Within this total enclosure, various types of use are made possible by changes of floor level and the sculptural form of the amphitheatre and its access ways. The idea of the Exhibition Hall was never developed. The Sports Centre became a reality and was very ably developed into detailed design and construction by members of the General Division LCC.

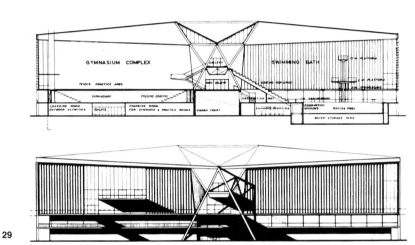

29

30

place in a total site development which could produce a comprehensive recreation area. The car racing track was to be lengthened, there were facilities for boating and riding, and an outdoor theatre was included in the scheme. **27.** The total layout including the Sports Centre which has now been built. **26 & 28.** The ideas behind the general form of the main exhibition building. **29 & 30.** The scheme drawings and first model for the Sports Centre with its viewing gallery running along the central spine.

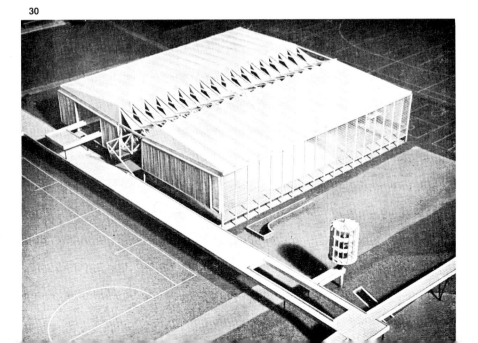

9

Notes on a developing architecture

This essay, originally published in the *Architectural Review* (July 1978), pp. 11–17, developed from the William Townsend Memorial Lecture given at University College, London. The object of that lecture was to give some account of the ideas about architecture that evolved in Britain in the 1930s, and the reassessment and elaboration of those ideas that has since taken place. What I am writing is not art history. I do not believe that can be written until the work I am describing can be seen within what Professor Gombrich has called the context of its time. This essay is nothing more than an outline of a set of developing ideas that have seemed to me to be important and that I believe to be relevant today.

I have said elsewhere that I am old enough to have seen in practice some of the last stages of the Arts and Crafts movement at a time when training had not yet ceased to be a matter of apprenticeship. So long as there were masters, and so long as there was a limited range of buildings to be built, the apprenticeship system worked. The great merit of the movement, which was so forcefully demonstrated in the work of the English Free School, was that all-embracing approach to design in which everything mattered and everything was worthy of the designer's consideration. It is not for nothing that Muthesius[1] rated it so highly and that its influence abroad was so profound.

Of course it is possible to start from that line of thought, and to establish the clear connection with the foundation of the Deutsche Werkbund in 1907. It is possible to trace the long debate in Germany between the individualist and collectivist positions or the intuitive and rationalist arguments, which occupied so many sessions at the Werkbund meetings before the First World War. From that it is only a step to the resolution of the debate in an educational process with the declared intention of training a new kind of designer (the artist technician) and then finally to the establishment of the International Style. I do not believe that things happened like that nor do I believe in this teleological presentation of history. The interesting thing about history, when it is actually being made, is that it is full of complex and confusing influences and pressures. On the broad international front of architectural development, of course, there were parallels: each country was undoubtedly making some reassessment of human needs. There was certainly some common ground in the view that these needs could best be met by the use of a new technology. There was clearly in each country a changing attitude to the process of design. But when the developments in architecture and art in each country in Europe are set down side by side, the important things to be noted are not just the common elements which build up the generalised conception of the International Style, but

the differences. What can so often be overlooked are differences of timing, and above all differences in the background of assumptions within which the architects of each country were working.

The point is well illustrated by Catherine Bauer's comparison between the ideas of the development of the English superblock from Unwin onwards, and the German attitude to the layout of the superblock of *Zeilenbau*.[2] Or compare for example the Russian interest in the building of the industrial city with the entrenched idea in England of the city as something to be escaped from or re-built as soon as possible.[3]

There are important differences of background that are essential to any complete understanding of the architectural changes that were taking place, just as there are important differences of timing and communication. The Russian work, for example, where the events of 1917 found a revolutionary art already established from 1914 (as Tatlin was to observe) and where during the 1920s a wide range of architectural problems had been discussed, could not have been widely accessible outside Russia. The Berlin exhibition of 1922, Melnikov's pavilion in the Paris Exhibition of 1925 and publications in *L'Architecture Vivante* in 1926 and 1928 certainly provided some illustrations, but I do not think that any general survey of what was happening existed in this country until the publication of Lubetkin's article in the *Architectural Review* in May 1932.

Similarly, a decade of work from 1920 to 1930 in Holland or in Germany was not known to many in this country before 1930, in spite of the importance of the housing contribution, the Bauhaus and its industrial products, and the Weissenhof Siedlung of 1927. A few individuals would have seen Le Corbusier's Pavillon de L'Esprit Nouveau in the 1925 exhibition,[4] but the great significance of that seminal work packed with ideas about planning, housing and design was certainly not widely understood. When we consider generally the architecture and art in England in the twenties, we must conclude that these European movements which were achieving so much were virtually unknown. But I think it is also true that the effects of the 1914–18 war, which had resulted in such profound social and artistic changes in Russia and in Germany, were the start of equally profound changes of attitude in England, though the form of those changes had its roots in a totally different set of influences and background. There was without question a break with the past; and what consolidated that break was the Great War itself.

For those who lived in England through the twenties there can be no doubt about the effects of change. This made itself clear in the break with Edwardianism, the general feeling of emancipation, the greater freedom of speech, of manner and of dress; in changes of attitude and relationships – and there was after all the women's vote. At this distance from the events, and when so many things are taken for granted, it is perhaps worth recalling a few of the remarkable advances that were made, particularly in communications and technology. Regular air flights for passengers and mail to Paris and Brussels started in 1919. Nigel Gresley's Pacific Class 4472 made its high-speed runs to Edinburgh in 1920. The first public broadcasting and the foundation of the BBC (2LO, then called· the 'wireless') happened in 1922. This was the era of the film and in every town the super cinema. Ford, Morris and Austin popular cars date from 1925, and of course it was the era of jazz, of the big band, of new styles of dance.

Before the war there had been a Vorticist movement built up around Wyndham Lewis, with Roberts, Epstein, Gaudier-Brezka, Wadsworth, Nevinson and Pound all contributing. If it left any public impression after the war it was simply that all advanced art could be called 'futurist', and that it was in some way associated with zig-zagging decoration. In the twenties it left its mark on new angular fashions in furniture, on the cinema organ and the design of the magazine jacket. Much of that is the world of change and the fashion that accompanied it. But in terms of architecture there was a more sombre background in the condition of the urban areas and a range of work

which gave architects something new to think about. And it gave to architecture itself an entirely different dimension.

Professor Napper has described a general scene that could be typical of so many towns in the Midlands and the north, and has pointed out how difficult it must be for anyone born, let us say, since 1940 to recapture

The depressing effect of towns and cities especially in the large conurbations. Masses of desolate unkempt sub-standard soot-blackened and decrepit buildings of depressing monotony . . . low-rise high-density bricks and mortar. The silhouette of the town showed only the church spires and factory chimneys piercing the sky above rows of domestic chimneys and slate roofs.[5]

'Leeds' suns', wrote Mr Betjeman at the time, 'are always setting', and those paintings by Lowry are a kindly and understanding comment on a tragic human situation. It is important to keep this picture in mind in any attempt to understand the ideas of the thirties. In contrast to this, a project like Maxwell Fry's housing built on the site of a gas works (under the Slum Clearance Act), with its adjoining nursery school, clearly spoke for a different world. And it is not surprising that the vision of Le Corbusier's Ville Radieuse, when it became available, should have had such a profound appeal.

And there certainly was throughout the twenties a positive effort to develop house building both in terms of programme and technology. The decade 1920–30 laid remarkable stress on new house building. The 1919 Housing and Town Planning Act introduced state subsidies to Local Government and builders in an effort to produce more homes at costs that those in need could afford. At the same time the Ministry of Health (then responsible for housing) published its manual of standards for state-aided housing. For the first time the Government itself was involved in a firm housing commitment.

From 1919 to 1939 political parties changed; the emphasis on state-aided or private building changed;

1

2

1. View of an industrial town. 2. Arnos Grove underground station, by Charles Holden, 1932–3.

211

3. Russian pavilion, Paris Exhibition of Decoration, Art and Industrial Design, 1925. Alexander Melnikov. **4 & 5.** Pavillon de l'Esprit Nouveau, Paris Exhibition of Decoration, Art and Industrial Design, 1925. Le Corbusier.

the cost of building changed; the method of subsidy or rent control changed; but the emphasis on the housing need provided a lasting commitment throughout the twenties and thirties with considerable influences on the range of architectural effort. There are two aspects of this, one the extent of the programme and the other the degree of innovation and invention in the work itself. The first has been set out in some detail by Cullingworth.[6] By 1931, 1·5 million new houses had been built and housing was linked to slum clearance and overcrowding. By this time all the principal local authorities (LCC, Liverpool, Birmingham, Manchester, Sheffield and Leeds) were involved, though never from 1922 equalling the output of private builders. That remarkable housing effort continued into the thirties. By 1939 over four million new houses had been built; by 1938 a peak figure of 340,878 houses produced an annual total not exceeded in any of the twenty years following the Second World War.[7]

This extensive housing effort left its mark on the form of the town itself. At the centre the normal type of urban development was the block of flats. There is sometimes a considerable time lag: Beresford records that back-to-back houses were still being built in Leeds in the thirties.[8] The alternative form of housing is in the suburbs. The twelve-to-the-acre layout became the generally adopted form. At its best, it owes much to Raymond Unwin, whose earlier mathematical and geometrical studies of the density contained the seeds of many ideas for development. It was also Unwin who was instrumental in introducing investigation into the technical aspects of the problem.[9] He can certainly be connected directly with the establishment of the Building Research Station as a branch of the DSIR in 1919. Building research had its origins in the housing programme and established a link that had such important implications for the early ideas of the Modern Movement.

And there were new methods. Some of them were as advanced as the methods used in the famous Weissenhof Siedlung. But without exception in England the appearance followed a traditional form.

There is an interesting contrast here. By 1927 the Germans were demonstrating quite clearly that architecture should look as though it had been built by new techniques. In England the process had not even begun. Moreover the twelve-to-the-acre layout, which Unwin had developed with such competence and done so much to foster, found itself translated and degraded (with a few notable exceptions) into a sprawling suburbia, quite unacceptable as the offspring of the garden city movement. What were the architects doing? Turn the pages of the *Architectural Review* for 1925 and you will find that there is little evidence of change. Only Adelaide House by Burnet shows some leaning towards a stripped and more severe form that has some reflection of the structure. As Gerald Heard was to comment later, 'It is almost as though a generation of unparalleled change had been using its powers to make that change as little evident as possible.'[10]

There are, of course, distinguished exceptions, for example Charles Holden who, in 1925, began to build the first of some thirty stations for London Transport, where the square or circular box of the booking hall with its concrete lid became 'the quiet focal point in a generally uninspired suburbia'.[11] Holden, of course, was a founder member of the Design and Industries Association (1916), itself derived from the Deutsche Werkbund and dedicated to simple design in all things of everyday use. Its slogan was 'fitness for purpose', and Holden extended this principle into the design of outdoor equipment, interior fittings, lettering, etc. With the help of Frank Pick good design became the recognisable hallmark of London Transport.

The Paris Exhibition of Decoration, Art and Industrial Design took place in 1925. When the *Architectural Review* illustrated the exhibition its main concern was the style of decoration (the Art Deco) that for several years found its way through into furnishing, the elevator doors at Selfridges, the cinema organs and the stream-lining, zig-zag and chrome of some London hotels. The isolation of England from the Modern Movement abroad is illustrated by the fact that two buildings of great seminal interest in the exhibition were not described. The Russian Pavilion by Melnikov, from which so much could have been learned about the Russian ideas, found its way into one of the illustrations. It was an important example of the principles that had run right through constructivist art. Its alternating roof planes were not simply a striking form. They indicated a major constructive invention in widespan roof construction used in Russian buildings elsewhere.

Le Corbusier's Pavillon de l'Esprit Nouveau is not even mentioned. The point about this is that the Pavillon was not just an exhibition building.[12] It was in itself Le Corbusier's idea of a dwelling (double-height living rooms, enclosed garden space, etc.). Alongside this was a room that contained dioramas of his projects for a city. In the dwelling each object, each piece of equipment and furniture, was a selection from the mass-produced articles that were available. They were the *objets-types*, the type forms which were the end-products of design centred around function. These Le Corbusier and Ozenfant extended into the substance of their paintings: the bottle, the glass, the pipe were the 'absolute objects beyond the reach of accident'.

Some twenty-three years earlier Parker and Unwin in their *Art of Building a Home*, first published in 1901, illustrated a lofty living room equal in height to the two storeys of supporting accommodation: kitchen and sanctum on the ground floor with bedrooms over. ('A good living room', they wrote, 'is the first essential: all other rooms should be considered in relation to it.') An open stair off the living room connects these levels. The house is completely furnished. Both the Pavillon and Unwin's design are derived from considerations of how people might live. The contrast in the total result illustrates the change that had taken place. While Unwin looks back to the medieval hall, Le Corbusier

looks to the future. Unwin's furniture comes from craft when craft can no longer supply all that is necessary. The objects in the Pavillon are already in mass production. Both believe in a new kind of setting: for Unwin it is the house on the ground in the garden city. For Le Corbusier, who also set groups of houses on the ground, it is in addition an opening up of ideas about what could be available and what is still worth working for within the building blocks of the city itself.

So by 1930 there was in Great Britain a major concern with housing and the extension of the social programme. There had been demonstrations of new constructional methods, an important research centre had been established and knowledge of what had been built in Europe was beginning to infiltrate. But there was little that could be described as modern architecture. By 1934, however, and from then until the outbreak of war, the Modern Movement in Britain was established by a comparatively small group of people of widely different backgrounds. It was not too difficult to make a list of the architects concerned with this development by referring to published work between the early 1930s and 1939. Most of them were born between 1895 (Wells Coates) and 1914 (Clarke-Hall and Lasdun). To this group should be added the engineers: Sir Owen Williams (born 1890), who pioneered reinforced concrete structure in this country with his Boots factory, Wembley Swimming Pool and the Peckham Health Centre; Ove Arup (born 1895), originally designer with Christiani and Nielson and engineer for Tecton's buildings; and finally Felix Samuely. Then there are the writers most closely concerned with the establishment of modern architecture in this country: P. Morton Shand, Herbert Read, poet and art critic, and J. M. Richards, assistant editor and later editor of the *Architectural Review*.[13]

Amongst the future architects who were to make this transformation of viewpoint in the thirties there were men of very different interests and skills. Some like Wells Coates and Chermayeff came from outside the

6

7

8

6. Studio for Augustus John, Fordingbridge, Hampshire, 1935. Christopher Nicholson. 7. 'The Hopfield', St Mary's Platt, Kent, 1933. Colin Lucas. 8. Factory for Boots, Beeston, Nottingham, 1932. Owen Williams.

213

9

10

11

9. Swimming pool, Wembley, 1922. Owen Williams. 10. Peckham Health Centre, London, 1935. Owen Williams. 11. Penguin Pool, Regent's Park Zoo, London, 1934. Lubetkin and Tecton.

subject as it was then taught. Perhaps only Lubetkin (from Russia via Paris) had by training and experience a developed theoretical point of view. Amyas Connell, Basil Ward and Raymond McGrath had come to England from the other side of the world. Others were finding their way through schools of varying calibre.

But with the possible exception of the Architectural Association, there could not have been a school in this country in 1930 that would, through its leadership or instruction, have led any student to take an interest in a changing view of architecture. The AA, thanks to its origins and its principal, Howard Robertson, was liberal and eclectic. Within the universities the subject had an uneasy acceptance, requiring usually a five-year course rather than the three-year degree course, and usually a special type of degree (BArch). Liverpool, the strongest university school in the country, relied heavily on American classicism, though it had a distinguished school of planning, led in succession by Adshead and Abercrombie and clearly associated with the housing movement. Richardson at University College had well-known enthusiasms and prejudices but could design with distinction. Professor Dickie at Manchester was by early training an Egyptologist. Theodore Fyfe at Cambridge had been surveyor to Arthur Evans at Knossos. And yet George Checkley came to Cambridge and built one of the houses illustrated in the 1934 edition of F. R. S. Yorke's *The Modern House*, and Nicholson, a student at Cambridge, immediately on leaving the school produced Augustus John's studio, and later some original plywood furniture. Another student, Colin Lucas, built a small house of real distinction for its day.

How then did this change come about? The point that has to be realised is that in terms of architecture the change was not just a change of fashion. Widening problems extending from town planning at one end of the scale to industrial design at the other were beginning to present themselves as architectural problems, and in relation to this the educational system had no

effective answer. There were for example design problems which could not be solved in terms of the older formal training or the craft techniques; nor had the schools established any theoretical basis which would have allowed design to develop from first principles. There were, however, some types of design that Wells Coates (with a Japanese upbringing, which gave him an unusual conception of the arts in relation to things of use, a doctorate in science and an interest in mechanisms), though without formal training, was uniquely well qualified to deal with. Similarly Serge Chermayeff could move naturally into architecture through sheer design ability. The point is that there was something new to work on which had to be thought out afresh. And there was a reassessment of what architecture was about.

This kind of reassessment was not happening in isolation. In many disciplines the accepted doctrine within a subject was being questioned. Look for example at art history. The accepted way of looking at the history of architecture in the schools in the twenties was to treat it as a series of peaks of achievement (Renaissance) followed by depressions or valleys (Baroque). This presentation was now superseded. The publication of Wölfflin's *Principles of Art History* in English in 1932[14] made it quite clear that the difference between these two manifestations of architecture is one of totally different intentions. Each period had its own values. Studies of this kind had two effects: the first provided a deeper understanding of historical periods; the second gave some justification for a new set of values for our own time.

There is also an exact parallel in literature. The revised course in the Faculty of English at Cambridge had laid particular stress on contemporary literature and a new approach to critical assessment. The *Calendar of Modern Letters*,[15] a literary review published by a younger generation of writers, was introducing to the public a newer type of poetry (for instance Eliot) and also reassessing the older values in the work of Donne, for example, or Gerard Manley Hopkins. The critical standards which the editors set themselves were high. They regarded criticism, to use Eliot's own phrase, 'not merely as a series of random conjectures or a catalogue of successive actions, but as a process of re-adjustment between poetry and the world in and for which it is produced'. For the word 'poetry' it was easy to substitute 'architecture'.

I take this evidence from my own bookshelves at the time; but if this interconnection of ideas seems remote, there is something more concrete. In November 1932 Wells Coates published an article in the *Architectural Review* under the title 'Response to Tradition'. In this he quotes at length from what he calls a brilliant and original work by I. A. Richards, namely *Principles of Literary Criticism*.[16] Richards was in fact teaching in the Faculty of English at Cambridge, having been introduced into that faculty from Moral Sciences, and he had played a major part in establishing the new standards of critical assessment. It is partly from this that Coates built up his own theoretical position. It is by 'bringing Art and Science together in architecture that architects must find a way' and 'it is between these two that they may lose themselves'. They must 'respond to the old forms of materials and perceive their true intent in their own age ... and remembering everything ... start again. That is the essential intention of Tradition.'[17]

For that same number of the *Architectural Review* Morton Shand wrote his distinguished article on the historical development of steel and concrete. Some important illustrations were shown, including some of Maillart's bridges and photographs of the most important building of the early years in England, the Boots factory at Nottingham which was in construction between 1930 and 1936. Other British buildings illustrated included Amyas Connell's 'High and Over', 'White Walls' at Torquay by William Wood, and Joseph Emberton's yacht club at Burnham. Wells Coates' design for an airport was illustrated, as was a scheme

for a house (fully furnished) by Serge Chermayeff and a house and block of flats by McGrath. Add to this the knowledge that Coates had already completed his Cresta shops and that the BBC studios by Chermayeff, McGrath and Coates had been illustrated in the *Architectural Review* in that same year and you have a representative impression of actual achievement at this time. But from 1933 to 1939 some of the initial ideas were developed in buildings which, when seen as a whole, have an impressive range. To dismiss this period as a new fashion of square-box architecture is not to have looked closely at the buildings themselves and the ideas that they embodied. Nor do I think that the work can be regarded as a series of importations from abroad. That did indeed happen, but the way in which the work developed in Britain also had its own roots. As the work is examined more thoroughly it becomes, I think, quite clear that it is not just an attempt to impose a fixed revolutionary style (although the propaganda was often evident) but, more fundamentally, a spontaneous growth of a new way of designing buildings around changing needs.

Consider the buildings but, more particularly, consider the ideas that they carried. Owen Williams' Boots factory, with its mushroom construction and completely glazed wall, or his Wembley Swimming Pool, with its counter-weighted roof span of 236 ft 6 in. planned on a 2 ft 9 in. grid (1934), were remarkably well worked out concrete buildings and major works by any standards: in this country the first of their kind. The Peckham Health Centre, again by Williams (1935), and later the Finsbury Health Centre by Lubetkin and Tecton, brought together a pioneering social effort and a new building form. The buildings for the London Zoo, by Lubetkin and Tecton (1934), are there to underline the fact that this new form of building art had its own range of formal elements: the Penguin Pool is a pure constructivist work, as I seem to remember J. M. Richards pointing out at the time of its construction. Add to this list Chermayeff's offices for Gilbey, his laboratories for

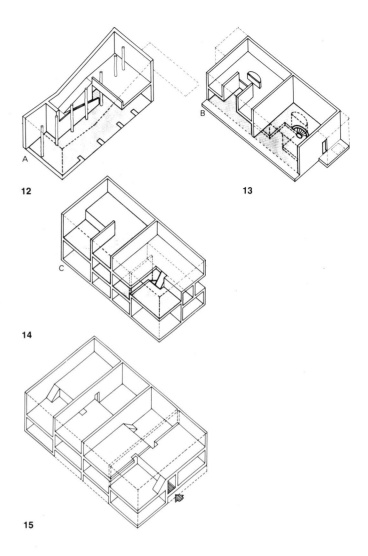

12 **13**

14

15

12, 13, 14 & 15. These four diagrams illustrate developing ideas. The difference between ideas and external impressions is central to the argument developed in this essay. 'Ideas generate forms and by extending them we create a tradition. The imitation of superficial form is fashion.' 12 is a house designed for Madame Errazuriz in Chile by Le Corbusier, 1930. 13 shows the interior arrangement of the flats in Lubetkin and Tecton's Highpoint Two with their double-height living rooms, 1938. 14 shows the three–two section used by Wells Coates in his Palace Gate flats, 1939. 15 shows a cross over type of dwelling which allows high density in low-rise building, flexibility of plan arrangement to meet different needs, and external play spaces adjoining living rooms.

16

17

16. Sound effects studio, Broadcasting House, London, 1932. Wells Coates. 17. The Studio, 18 Yeomans Row, London, 1937. Wells Coates.

ICI at Blackley, and the Mendelsohn and Chermayeff Bexhill Pavilion, and the range of buildings covered by the designers is fairly complete; indeed Yorke and Breuer put together a part of a town in 1939. I have intentionally left until the end the conception of housing, and all that goes with it, and educational building. They deserve special attention and are of some significance in relation to the post-war years.

I think that a convenient starting point for any discussion on housing can be made by reference to F. R. S. Yorke's book *The Modern House* (1934).[18] In the introduction Yorke noted three things: first, that the isolated villa was preferred as a dwelling and that it gave an important opportunity for experiment; second, that it was often chosen because there was no attractive alternative offered in new urban housing; and third, that any change was unlikely to take place without new legislation affecting land use.[19]

How the opportunities for experiment (Yorke's first point) were followed up may be tested by anyone who cares to refer to the periodicals, or trace from them the villas produced, from the early Connell and Ward houses (1928–33) to the Wells Coates and Patrick Gwynne house at Esher (1938). That list would include some distinguished buildings (for instance the Whipsnade bungalows by Lubetkin), not all by any means built in materials like concrete, but including timber, brick and stone. Yorke himself, though following Le Corbusier's *Précisions* in his references to the influence of new techniques on form, also illustrates in his text Le Corbusier's house in South America for Madame Errazuris. This house was to be built in the local materials of stone and timber and with a double-pitch pantile roof. What is remarkable about it is the use of the pitch along the length of the plan, the beautiful section that results from this, the double-height living room and balcony-type bedroom space. What we are talking about then are ideas about the ways in which different types of people may live in different types of houses – that they need not all live in

boxes either on the ground or in the air: there are options.

Yorke noted in December 1936 (in an article in the *Architectural Review*) that in the two years since the publication of *The Modern House* he had probably accumulated enough material from England alone to fill a book. He classified these new examples in relation to their constructional materials, brick, timber or concrete. Breuer later explained his small exhibition house for Gane's of Bristol with this statement:

There are of course new materials . . . [and] the modern designer tries to understand their laws without prejudice. He endeavours to find the language of their forms. But the basis of modern architecture is not the new materials; not even the new form but the new mentality. Modern Architecture would exist even without reinforced concrete. It would exist in stone, wood or brick.

That is from *Circle* (1937) in which Breuer also draws attention to the vernacular building.

If at this point we pick up Yorke's second and third observations about wider choice in urban building and planning we find, I think, that they are ultimately interrelated. Some steps in this process can at least be traced. First, there are two house types that are not just planned as isolated villas: Coates' 'Sunspan' house (1934–6) was accompanied by a layout of an estate; the Tecton house in the Gidea Park Exhibition had an *L*-shaped plan which, when joined to adjacent houses, produced gardens protected from overlooking. Sliding one plan against another could have introduced an original and adaptable layout for the urban dwelling.

But the principal advance is Lawn Road flats by Wells Coates, which was being completed in 1934. The block contained twenty-two balcony access flats planned and furnished with all Coates' ingenuity and attention to detail, four double flats, three studio flats and a penthouse. It provided for the first time a form of completely furnished single-room accommodation, much in demand but difficult to find, and also the idea of combining different types of unit. Highpoint One contains flats, but these are given some sense of isolation from each other and moved forward into a new conception by the ingenious plan form; it is a part of the radiant city in which dwellings look out on to trees and grass. So is Highpoint Two, but now with the inclusion of the double-height living room. This line of thought depending on the section was taken considerably further at Palace Gate (completed 1939), where Coates developed his three–two section in which three eight foot high levels of access corridor, with bedrooms, bathrooms, kitchens above and below, equal two twelve foot high living rooms. If one of the central points in the design of dwellings is to increase the range of options, Palace Gate is an important advance.

Apart from the initial gain in the living room itself, a system of interlocking allowed an inbuilt variety in which flats could have anything from one to six bedrooms without structural alteration.[20] The Palace Gate block is a single-sided block on a restricted site. But given this line of thought the idea can be taken further: suppose the arrangement is double-sided; suppose that some cross-over type of development is introduced; suppose that play spaces are included adjoining the living rooms. It might then be possible to show in the options available that families or individuals could have far more choice in the accommodation that they need, and that the higher densities can be obtained with far greater amenity and without tall buildings.[21] I show this by diagrams (p 215) and put the argument in this sequence to illustrate developing ideas. The difference between ideas and external impressions is central to the argument. Ideas generate the forms and by extending them we create a tradition. The imitation of superficial form is fashion. The same point could be made in another line of development, educational building, by showing ideas that changed the form of schools from the *News Chronicle* competition (1937) onwards. Clarke-Hall's winning design was translated into building at Richmond, Yorkshire. The

ideas were extended again in village colleges (Impington, by Gropius and Fry), one or two small schools, and finally developed by a more complete analysis of educational building in the 1950s. The examples that I have given are highly selective. New work was on the whole small-scaled and the mass of building in the country was generally unaffected by these new ideas.

The *Architectural Review* was to comment that exhibitions of good housing seem to have had little effect on those concerned with slum clearance. The six to eight storey block of flats remained the normal form of public authority building, and private housing continued to extend suburbia on a considerable scale. But what was developing was a broader front. The most obvious example of this was the natural extension of the new design consciousness into furnishing and industrial design. The ground for this was already prepared by the Design and Industries Association, whose principles had been so well demonstrated in the typography, furnishings and rolling stock of the LPTB. The furnishing of the dwelling had become the mainspring of a number of DIA exhibitions.

Herbert Read's book *Art and Industry* published in 1934 had set the new tone. The work of a number of architects at the start of their careers had been shop or exhibition design in which the architectural form, the display and the furnishing had formed a complete unity. Chermayeff had moved into architecture through furniture and his work and that of Wells Coates at the BBC demonstrated the connections. In the sound effects studio or the gramophone turn-table bench by Wells Coates, it is impossible to say where the architecture ends and the industrial design begins: it is all of a piece. The problem can suggest the need for a new piece of furniture; and as a result unit wall-fittings, desks, chairs, storage and radio cabinets are specially designed and some become the standard products of Pel, Gane, etc. There could be no better example of this total integration than the home that Coates made for himself at 18 Yeoman's Row, London. One further

aspect of the widening thought comes from a simple process of sharing ideas and sensing some common ground. The *Architectural Review* played an important part in this. Under H. de C. Hastings and J. M. Richards it maintained its special role of broadening ideas. Quite apart from the quality of its special numbers (that on steel and concrete has already been mentioned), articles by Richards himself, the brilliant historical series on the pioneers Loos, Wright, etc. by Shand, or the contributions on landscape and art continuously extended comment and understanding beyond a normal architectural range.

The grouping of individuals and ideas was also happening elsewhere. Unit One (1933), under the able direction of Paul Nash, brought together a distinguished group of painters, sculptors and two architects (Wells Coates and Lucas) in an effort to show 'the expression of a truly contemporary spirit'. But it did not require much insight to see that the work of some of these artists was quite different in intention. The exhibition of 1936, 'Abstract Art in Contemporary Settings', at Duncan Miller's showrooms, and those exhibitions of abstract art organised by Nicolette Gray moved away from this. The first brought a particular kind of art and architecture nearer together; the second showed the work of artists who were closer to a common viewpoint. What seemed to be lacking was some more adequate description to indicate the content of the work and some means of demonstrating this.

The idea behind the publication *Circle*[22] was to put together one particular manifestation of art and architecture, to put side by side work which appeared to have one common idea and one common aim: the constructive trend in the art of our day. The idea was to try to place the work of art as an essential part of constructive thought, as the counterpart of architecture and the sciences. What we were talking about was content, with the work of art or architecture as a symbol of a particular attitude of mind.[23] But from the point of view of architecture the most powerful widening of the

18

19

18. Detail of the underside of leaf of the Victoria Regia water lily.
19. Concrete construction at the Fiat Factory, Turin: compare with 18.

front was the foundation of a group of modern architects with the title MARS, with international contacts and a collective emphasis on the 'R' in the initial letters: that is, on Research. MARS was formed in 1933[24] as a branch of CIAM, the International Congress of Architects. The Congress established common methods of study which could be used by each national group in relation to a common problem: the 'minimum dwelling' and 'rational methods of siting' had already been investigated. The membership of MARS was small, but enthusiastic. In 1937 it held its first exhibition and at the end of the decade was working on a plan for London.

Between 1934 and 1939 what had been achieved? Above all I think the idea had been established that designing a building was no longer a question of imposing an applied form. In every problem, the yacht club, the airport, the laboratory, or in schools and housing, the appropriate form could be discovered in the problem itself. What had resulted was a different method of thinking about architecture, and it was this design attitude that gave to the movement its extended range and its great potential for future development. The work itself was recognisably individual, small-scaled and limited, and the offices that produced it were themselves small. But what could also be seen was the possibility of applying these design ideas to the established social programme in housing and educational buildings. And it seemed clear that through the application of research the limited thought about problems and the inadequate techniques could be corrected. In the late 1940s a new generation moved in to consolidate the earlier ideas and to link them firmly to the new social programmes of building. Indeed there was little else. The immediate demand was for housing and buildings for education, and a generation of young architects, trained just before the war, joined the Hertfordshire County Council or the LCC and, later, various Ministries. Each group had its development section; each group used new techniques of production as well as new standards of design, and in the case of school building at least there was an important influence on building in Italy and Germany, and on the American SCSD achievement. I do not want to suggest that these efforts came entirely from the public offices. They did not. Many of the schools within the LCC programme were built by private architects, and in the case of one school the economies of traditional brick and timber were demonstrated with remarkable effectiveness. The same is true of housing. While the standards set by the public offices at their best did give some idea of what housing in the green city of the early Modern Movement could be like, there were contributions like Lasdun's cluster block or, at the other end of the scale, his flats overlooking St James's Park, which developed and enriched housing ideas.

But the overall range of buildings had widened too. This was the period of the new towns and later the new universities. Quite unlike their restricted work of the pre-war period, when every building was a struggle, the architects of the fifties found themselves able to work with remarkable freedom on important projects. There is no doubt about it, the fifties established modern architecture as a method, perhaps the method of building.[25] It was the very scale on which modern architecture was being built, the rapid rate of its expansion, the number of individuals and the size of the organisations involved that carried with it and highlighted some inherent dangers. These had in fact already been demonstrated by the dreary quality of some mass housing in Europe before the war. They were perhaps present in the early implications of the CIAM conferences when it sometimes appeared that everything could be solved by rational analysis and improved technical production. They began to show themselves in this country during the fifties in the growing belief that through analysis alone towns and their needs could be mapped once and for all; in standards for housing so fixed that they could not be changed; in the increasing size of each development;

in the enormous emphasis given to speed (though not necessarily economy) of production and in the effects of repetitive forms. The outstanding example of this in housing is the transformation of the ten storey point block (which was used in the early fifties in combination with four storey and two storey dwellings in order to bring people nearer to the ground) into a universal housing solution consistently increasing in height (and taking people further away from it), even when this could not be justified in terms of density.

It was the growing sense of dangers of this kind that throughout the post-war period spurred individuals and groups to try to give modern architecture a new sense of direction. An early warning note had been sounded by Aldo Van Eyck, I seem to remember, at Bridgwater where CIAM held its first post-war conference. He spoke about the non-rational aims of modern architecture. He meant, I think, the need for more speculation, for imaginative questioning of what was becoming accepted. The MARS group extinguished itself in 1957. In 1962 Team 10 came together because of the inadequacies of the architectural thought that they had inherited. The members laid stress on the need to develop thought processes and the language of building and to try to work this out on a scale which would be really effective in terms of modes of life and the structure of the community, that is to say in terms of a down-to-earth realism and a sense of involvement.

These ideas themselves have in turn been moved forward in a number of different directions and this essay is no place for a catalogue. In comparing the work of the thirties with that of a more recent past, it is not I think the way in which designers work or the open ended design method that has changed. Nor is it merely that there is more technical competence. What has changed is, first, the much wider range of issues that are now integrated and the much richer vein of thought in the design process and, second, the different levels of emphasis that designers give to their work within the total range. As an example of the first, it

now seems inconceivable that the form of housing could have been derived, as it was, almost exclusively from density: flats in the town, twelve-to-the-acre in suburbia. I have tried to indicate how, by thought about options within the plan, that concept was eroded. Once that process is started, a whole new set of considerations emerge: what family groupings can be accommodated, what ranges of space within the dwelling can be provided, how much private open space and how much public space, what balance of privacy or neighbourliness, what degree of urbanity and what kind of environment, etc. Add to this the extension of choice by imaginative conversion of existing property, and building (any building) becomes part of the re-creation and renewal of the urban fabric.

But it is more than that. My second point is that there is now far more thought about the different levels at which architecture should operate. All buildings are not solved in exactly the same terms. There are different degrees of emphasis. One may be public and may give significance in an area; others may more appropriately be anonymous and may add to the general cohesion of environment for the community. There are a number of lines of thought that individual designers have followed with sincerity and conviction: there have been designs developed with great sculptural quality, others with an emphasis on sheer technical perfection which have produced buildings of real distinction. And above all there is a very great deal of work throughout the country, small in scale and often anonymous, that is creating a new small-scale environment.

All these things seem to me to be branches of a line of thought reached by criticism, reassessment and creative action. I understand the conviction and the single mindedness with which each is separately pursued. A firm conviction is necessary for any good building; it is part of the mix of thought that moves ideas forward. What seems to me to be certainly true is that none of these buildings could have been built in these various forms in the thirties, but also that none of

them would have been what they are without that new starting point and those early ideas. When history can be written (and that certainly cannot happen as it is being made) we may be able to see these developments as different currents within the broad stream of a developing 'modern' architecture. But since we are now some forty years or so away from its beginning, perhaps we had better drop that dated term and talk about developments in the creative architectural thought of our time.

If it is true that the freedom to work out a problem in its own terms is valid, and that we can add to this from a growing and inherited vocabulary of ideas, forms and techniques which are part of the designer's stock in trade, then we are talking about the development of a tradition. What has then to be distinguished is the difference between this creative line of thought and changes that are no more than changes of fashion. And perhaps more important than this is the difference between work in this creative tradition and its opposite, the far greater mass of building which makes no advance and which turns every dwelling into a box (of whatever fashion) or produces the standard block of flats or offices. It is the flood of building development of this latter kind that has shaped the form of most cities of the Western world and it is this phenomenon that we must learn to understand. Perhaps some day the urban geographers and historians may study the changing pattern of a city in the sixties in the same depth that the pattern of the medieval town has been studied. When they have done this we might be able to see more clearly the forces that are at work, who commissioned the buildings, who built them, what were the effects of legislation, what were the social goals and so on. We may then see that the city is the product of the mixed society that builds it. The vision of the thirties that all this could be changed by architecture alone is an illusion. But architects can help to forward a better human condition of living and environment by working with vision on what is within their grasp.

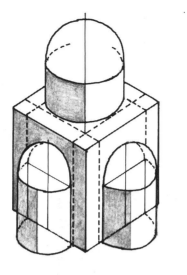

1

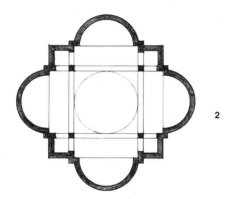

2

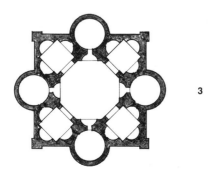

3

10 · **A sketch by Leonardo**

These notes are not intended to be art history. They are simply an architect's interpretation of what he sees in a series of historical documents – in fact in one particular facet of the work of one exceptional man, Leonardo da Vinci. The work examined comes from a considerable number of drawings which are devoted to the study of the centralised church and illustrated and classified by Richter.[1] They appear to date from 1488–9. Richter makes the point that since these drawings are not projects for any particular building they are in fact 'theoretical'; a kind of 'ideal designing' around a particular problem. Wittkower[2] speaks of Leonardo's 'preoccupation' with this particular problem and refers to the drawings as 'systematic studies' which are 'above all documents of Renaissance religion'.

The deep symbolism behind the centralised church has been convincingly argued by Wittkower. Here it is completely accepted as the most powerful influence on the architectural conception. But given this fundamental starting point the interest lies in the way in which the centralised church is developed as a piece of architecture. Leonardo's own comment 'that a building should always be detached on all sides so that its true form can be seen' establishes the first principle. The building must be seen and appreciated as a whole. Its total form is critical. The drawings themselves confirm this. These drawings are not just sets of plans, such as those presented by Francesco di Giorgio or much later in Serlio's fifth book on Architecture (1547). They are sketches which in the main show the diagrammatic plan and at the same time present its total volumetric form. In essence the drawings demonstrate with absolute clarity a series of manipulations of pure geometric solids: the cube, the cylinder and the half or quarter sphere. For an architect the formal process is quite clear. Each one of these drawings is a complete

visualisation of a totally comprehended building. The drawing which may have suggested the built form of S. Maria della Consolazione at Todi (1504) illustrates the process in its simplest form. The main body of the church is a pure cube within which four piers and their pendentives support the central dome, a half sphere mounted on its cylindrical drum. On each side of the cube is a half cylinder roofed by its quarter sphere, and one of these contains the entrance. The whole composition is indicated by the simple diagram shown in the top left corner of one of the drawings and is developed in the central plan. The only question that remains to be considered is how the corner squares of the cube should be developed: whether they should be finished internally with a splay to create a modified octagon or developed as pure squares each supporting its cupola. The octagon theme remains in the mind and, in another drawing, each face of the pure octagon is given its own separate apse, and this clearly leads to an elaborate superimposed plan with its eight radial forms around the central dome.

A similar process starting from the square and developing into the octagon is again illustrated by other drawings. In one case the square or enclosing cube is turned on to the diagonal. The apses on each of the four faces of this cube, one of which contains the entrance, are generated from pure cylinders and domes within the plan, and the four corners of the cube are built up in volume from cubes and apses. The total plan pattern generates a central octagon covered by an eight sided dome.

These drawings are not concerned only with volumetric forms. In another drawing a further question is introduced. What happens to a total form based on these principles if, for example, one church is placed above another (or at least above a crypt)? The question of two levels, of external and internal staircase access and a surrounding access gallery is introduced into the total concept.

There could be no clearer indication of the questioning attitude of mind than the studies which illustrate the forms of a church designed 'for preaching and the celebration of the mass'.[3] Although these drawings are simplified to the point of being diagrammatic they illustrate the creative process of Leonardo's thought in the clearest possible way. A church designed especially for preaching or for the celebration of the mass has two special requirements: first that the speaker should be clearly heard, second that the ceremony should be seen.

One of the drawings illustrates an attempt to meet these conditions within the type of plan studied in some of the previous examples, for instance the cube with apses. Curved rows and seats are introduced into the apses: these are arranged with a stepped section shown in a sketch, a device which would make both vision and sound path direct and without interruption. At one point Leonardo wrote 'Theatre to hear Mass'.

But it is the 'design for a place for preaching' that suggests a fundamental change and illustrates the remarkable force and completeness of Leonardo's thought. The preacher is to speak from a central rostrum in an elevated position reached by a spiral staircase. It is from this point that the whole geometry of the plan and section is evolved. It may have started from Leonardo's stated notions of acoustics, for instance his concept of 'the whole circle made in the air by the sound of a man's voice'.[4] If this can be translated into the idea that sound travels with a spherical wave front it would explain at once the hollow sphere that forms the interior of this building. If the seats are arranged in six galleries around this hollow sphere there will be a direct sound path to every seat. Moreover every seat will have direct vision and the speaker

and his audience will be in total contact.

It is at this point that the formal imagination really takes flight. The galleries will require access for each separate level and from the point of view of convenience the access points at each level should be evenly distributed around the circular plan. The precedent for this might well have been some recollection of the Roman amphitheatre but in this case reversed. In the Roman building the galleries give access to the internal stepped seating; in these diagrams the external stepping leads directly to points of access in the galleries themselves.

The external view suggests a building in the form of a gigantic cone, articulated by the radiating access ways and steps. The sketch also suggests that the building might be crowned at its centre by a dome. The deeply emotional symbol of the centralised church remains, but the total form is transmuted not merely by new questioning and new knowledge but perhaps also by some memory of a traditional past.

These are some of the constituent elements that appear to be held together in this architectural form suggested by these simple diagrams. They are in themselves clear enough to allow the total idea to be reconstructed in its elementary form. One question remains. The diagram which is associated with the two drawings appears to indicate a plan and leaves an element of doubt about the total form. If this diagram is taken literally it could suggest an audience arranged around two-thirds of the circle only and in that case facing the speaker himself.

Leonardo's church was never built to add its new conception to the developing architectural ideas. And soon the architecture of static, geometric and centralised volumes, which is so brilliantly demonstrated in this series of drawings, is being replaced by an architecture of quite different intention.

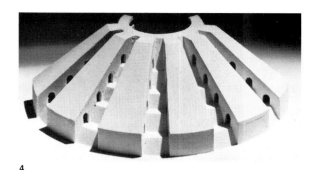

4

5

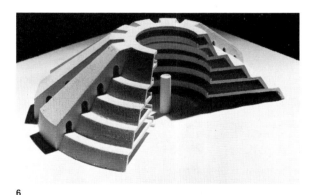

6

The diagrams are based on Leonardo's sketches. **1** shows a volumetric form which may have been followed in S. Maria Della Consolazione at Todi. **2** illustrates the plan of this cubic building with apses and a central dome, and **3** an octagonal elaboration. **4, 5 & 6** show a model which is an attempt to give a form to Leonardo's diagrams for a 'place for preaching' with its central speaker's column, spherical section, surrounding internal galleries and external stepped access leading to these.

11 · Extracts from papers

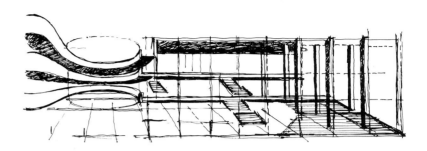

I. An architect's drawings (1982)

In a note (3) to the Introduction, I made a reference to the way in which architects draw their buildings. There is an important distinction between this and the professional renderings which have been so frequently used for public presentation. By architects' drawings I mean the type of drawing used by the designer to clarify his own mind and to illustrate the particular values that are considered to be important in the design intention: and the method of drawing is likely to change as the design intention changes.

As a starting point in my argument I have in mind the direct and obvious link between the organised formal systems, the volumetric relationship of Beaux Arts design and the elaborate techniques of rendering and shadow projection by means of which they were presented. These formed the perfect media for the description of the architectural intention. On the other hand I have a drawing of a Gothic Revival building, by the architect, in which the stress on the total concept has already changed. The drawing presents an impression of changing surfaces and changing light: it is an exact parallel to the architecture itself.

Alvar Aalto's own drawings and his painting illustrate an extreme example in which the relationship is difficult to describe but there is no doubt that for him at least his drawings and his paintings represented the equivalents of his architectural work. But perhaps the clearest demonstration of changing techniques occurred in the thirties when it became necessary to visualise complex subdivisions within the cubic volume of the building itself which were difficult to visualise adequately from plan or perspective.

In these circumstances the axonometric projection allows the plan and total volume, with all its subdivisions of space, to be considered in one single drawing. It formed a direct means of visualising relationships which could eventually only be considered by the slower process of model building.

Many drawings used in this book are directly related to the way in which the design of the building has been considered. Throughout the work in the Studio we have used various three-dimensional methods of projection as part of the design process. The Oxford libraries are best understood, in architectural terms, when they are thought of as a series of interlocking volumes around a rising access way. That kind of architectural conception can be represented in simple diagrams which integrate plan section and volume and we have used this method of projection in the general illustrations of library designs, auditoria etc.

The method of drawing is adapted in relation to the way in which the design is developed and explored. One drawing of the Royal Scottish Academy building for instance (p. 95) is simply a working attempt to relate, on a single drawing, different formal relationships within a series of planes inside and outside the building. It has something to do with movement from the street and through the building. It arose directly from an earlier sketch in which the main ideas about the internal volumes of the foyer and theatre areas are related to access points, flow of staircases between levels etc. The drawing in these cases is a means of exploring the design intentions. These in turn condition and change the method of drawing as it is being made.

II. From 'An Architect's Approach to Architecture'[1] (1967)

To study the contribution of the 1920s and the 1930s at the level of 'forms' is to isolate these end results from the ideas that caused them to exist, and which gave them, for their generation, their significant content.[2] For there is no doubt that they were valued precisely for the ideas they carried, and they remained significant only so long as the ideas behind them were valid. The important contribution of the 1920s and the 1930s was not the creation of a set of forms to be adopted and manipulated: it was the demonstration of a new attitude and a new method of work.

That method represents a revolutionary change and, however incomplete, hesitant or tentative it may have been, the change is there. James Marston Fitch underlined this shift of thought when he said that 'when one looks at the decade as a whole [the 1930s] one must recognize that there has seldom been another time when the problems of architecture and urbanism have been approached from so many different points of view. It is astonishing how complete – how synoptic – the investigation was.'[3]

What James Marston Fitch is describing are the results of new attitudes which break away very sharply from those of an earlier generation. The change from art and craft intuition towards rational analysis, measurement, technical innovations and speculative thought about these things is one manifestation of this. The change is there at an early date in the work of Loos, with its opposition to the intuitive craft approach, and in which buildings are 'built to a purpose' and thought out, rather than drawn. It is this matter-of-factness in which the act of design cannot be separated out as a form-making process that remains central. It is re-echoed in the various catch phrases around which theory (and particularly German theory) was discussed, and it finds its way ultimately into the declarations of CIAM.

But history is never clear cut. Against this attempt to re-introduce rationalism as a basis for architecture, there is, all along the line, the opposition of a powerful wing of 'individualist' creators. The situation is confused. Rational thought about needs and processes by one school was in some way considered by another to be dangerous and inhibiting. Practical reason and intuition were seen as opposites. And it is also true that just as the products of practical reason were being demonstrated on an impressive scale in the housing projects of Holland and Germany (as both James Marston Fitch and Catherine Wurster have noted),[4] the developing theory became dogma. The principles that I outlined at the beginning of this article required a continuous reassessment of every aspect of a problem. Knowledge would be established by analysis, advanced by experiment and confirmed or corrected by test. A ruthless reassessment of each achievement was an essential part of this process. But, in that important and major housing achievement of the 1930s, the process stopped. The speculative thought that could have extended the range of built forms into totally new environments dried up. We were left in Germany and elsewhere with a set housing solution solidified into parallel rows of slab blocks.

The fact that this happened was of enormous consequence. The rational approach was at once suspect. The end result of practical reason appeared to be sterility; and it was assumed that this could be countered only by intuitive processes – by feeling. Thus the old nineteenth-century oppositions were continued. The subsequent argument that developed (and still flourishes), is a prolonged confirmation of this opposition. For some of us, this is a futile argument in which we have no wish to take part. What was wrong with parallel slab layout was not the rational thought that it contained, but the failure to extend this by further speculative, formal invention. As A. N. Whitehead once pointed out,[5] it is speculation that makes rational thought live, and it is rational thought that gives speculative invention its basis and its roots. To analyse, to measure and to rationalise the problem is an essential part of the process of scientific thought. And, in the scientific process, intuition (or what Alfred North Whitehead prefers to call conjecture or speculative reason) is itself entirely arbitrary unless it is guided by thought or system. Practical reason is the means by which methods are developed for dealing with different kinds of facts. Speculative reason is an extension of this into theoretical activity. Progress depends on a lively interest in speculative reason. Through the interaction of these two forms of thought, factual assessment can take its place within an overall scheme of things; speculative reason is robbed of its anarchic character without destroying its function of reaching out beyond set bounds.[6] Whitehead goes on to add that the massive advance of modern technology is due to the fact that these two forms of thought (rational and speculative) 'have at last made contact'. That, translated into architectural terms, is equivalent to saying that the rational understanding of a problem and the extension of this into speculative (intuitive) thought is one single process: that is, that thought and intuition are not opposed but complementary. We may recognise at once an older (pre-nineteenth century) concept of architecture in which the design process cannot be isolated from the thought processes by which the problem is analysed and solved. The attempt to re-establish this in the 1920s and 1930s, whatever its failures, was fundamentally associated with a reassessment of method.

III. From 'An Architect's Approach to Architecture'[7] (1967)

The interesting point about Dutch and German housing in the 1930s is that it was at least a preliminary study of the relationship of the built form to the land that it occupies. It was, therefore, potentially a starting point for speculative thought, and the fact that it ossified at this stage is all the more surprising since Le Corbusier had already given several demonstrations of method far in advance of these narrow limits. Behind Le Corbusier's project for a city for three million is the same belief that everything is measurable.[8] But the comparison between the parallel rows of the German Siedlungen and the environmental areas formed by Le Corbusier's housing with setbacks (in all its modulations) is a telling illustration of his theoretical advance and the quality of his speculative thought. The project brings together a whole range of ideas about related uses (the generating principles of built forms, what is possible within them, the kinds of space outside them and the traffic that they generate). The overall speculation relates all the problems. We may not like the assumptions; in that case, we have the opportunity to challenge these in factual terms or to extend the process of speculation.

To see this project for a city, as so many have done, as some vague image of a city of towers (without even troubling to ask what they are for), is entirely to misunderstand the full implication of the ideas themselves. And yet it is around such vague images that we have built up so many impressions, for instance, of housing in towers at remarkably high densities. If we turn from the 'images' to an examination of the content of the proposals, we find that in a city for three million nobody is housed in towers. The housing density of the city is 120 people per acre. The nearest approach to residential high rise is to be found in the ten storey maisonettes which house 20 to 30 per cent of the population. The remaining 70 to 80 per cent of the inhabitants are to live in garden cities, probably on the lines of Pessac. The range of housing choice is considerable and much is on the ground. This remains true of the later studies, for instance, the scheme for St Dié, which certainly does include large collective blocks but where 60 per cent of the population is still to

be accommodated in family houses.

These plans are not just 'images'. They are packed with ideas about housing, about environment, about traffic. They demonstrate that these things can be set down in measurable terms and can be given a clear physical form. They also make clear that it is only through this physical form that ideas about individual component parts can be brought into relationship and ultimately assessed. And it is this method that distinguished the work of the 1920s and the 1930s so sharply from romanticism, and that is at the root of Le Corbusier's opposition to the visual imagery of Camillo Sitte (the attempt to build a picture), or the imagery of mechanisms that the futurists were so ready to accept.

If, instead of the attempt to examine the architecture of the 1930s in terms of forms, we had asked what the aims were and how problems were tackled, we would, I think, have been left with a series of propositions and some methods of work which would still be relevant now. We would have seen the essential relationship between buildings and cities, and how the interdependent parts of a city can be studied consistently in balanced relationship. In short, we would have recognised a framework: a framework of an open ended kind within which our own conjectures could be based, elaborated and criticised in turn. And we would have added to our knowledge. But we have preferred, in the main, to continue the old argument and to separate rational assessment from form-making. Behind this, without question, lies a nineteenth-century fear: the fear that 'intuition' might in some way be weakened by knowledge.[9] Indeed, this view seems to be so prevalent in the field of architecture that the rational attempt to learn more about the built form and to extend this by speculative thought (in short to develop theory) is, with one or two distinguished exceptions, practically non-existent. We are left instead with 'images'; as we increasingly rely on these, we are left with an architecture that moves towards a marginal activity incapable of taking its proper and central place in setting out alternative choices and methods of attack on our environment.

IV. From 'The Grid as Generator'[10] (1969–72)

Lionel March is responsible for several research studies associated with this paper.

In the case of American cities the grid or framework can be regarded as an ordering principle. It sets out the rules of the environmental game. It allows the player the freedom to play with individual skill. The argument can now be extended by saying that the grid, which is so apparent in American examples, is no less controlling and no less important in cities nearer home that would normally be called organic: London, Liverpool or Manchester. They too have a network of streets and however much the grid is distorted, it is there. At a certain scale and under certain pressures the grid combined with floor space limits and daylight controls is just as likely to force tall building solutions. And it is just as likely to congeal. It lends itself just as readily to regenerative action. The theoretical understanding of the interaction between the grid and the built form is therefore fundamental in considering either existing towns or the developing metropolitan regions.

The process of understanding this theoretical basis rests in measurement and relationships, and it goes back certainly to the work of Ebenezer Howard. Lionel March has recently pointed out a number of interesting things about Howard's book, *Tomorrow: A Peaceful Path to Real Reform*, first published in 1898. It is a book about how people might live in towns and how these might be distributed. But the important thing is that there is no image of what a town might look like. We know the type of housing, the size of plot, the sizes of avenues. We know that shopping, schools and places of work are all within walking distance of the residential areas. On the basis of these measurements we know the size of a town and the size of Howard's cluster of towns which he calls a 'City Federation'. We know the choice that is offered and we know the measurements that relate to these. If we disagree with the choice we can change the measurements. Lionel March's studies in 1967 took Howard's open centred city pattern linked by railways and showed that it could be reversed into a linear pattern linked by roads and that such patterns could be tested against the land occupied by our present stock of building and our future needs.[11]

Now that is theory. It contains a body of ideas which

are set down in measurable terms. It is open to rational argument. And as we challenge it successfully we develop its power. The results are frequently surprising and sometimes astonishingly simple. Ebenezer Howard's direct successor in this field was Raymond Unwin. The strength of his argument always rests in a simple demonstration of a mathematical fact. In his essay 'Nothing Gained by Overcrowding',[12] he presents two diagrams of development of ten acres of land. One is a typical development of parallel rows of dwellings: the other places dwellings round the perimeter. The second places fewer houses on the land, but when all the variables are taken into account (including the savings on road costs) total development costs can be cut. From the point of view of theory, the important aspect of this study is the recognition of related factors: the land available, the built form placed on this, and the roads necessary to serve these. He demonstrated this in a simple diagram.

Unwin began a lecture on tall building by a reference to a controversy that had profoundly moved the theological world of its day, namely, how many angels could stand on a needle point. His method of confounding the urban theologians by whom he was surrounded was to measure out the space required in the streets and sidewalks by the people and cars generated by five-, ten- and twenty-storey buildings on an identical site. The interrelationship of measurable factors is again clearly demonstrated. But one of Unwin's most forceful contributions to theory is his recognition of the fact that 'the area of a circle is increased not in the direct proportion to the distance to be travelled from the centre to the circumference, but in proportion to the square of that distance'. Unwin used this geometrical principle to make a neat point about commuting time: as the population increases round the perimeter of a town, the commuting time is not increased in direct proportion to this.

The importance of this geometrical principle is profound. Unwin did not pursue its implications. He was too concerned to make his limited point about low density. But suppose this proposition is subjected to close examination. The principle is demonstrated again in Fresnel's diagram (Fig. 1) in which each successive annular ring diminishes in width but has exactly the same area as its predecessor. The outer band in the square form of this diagram has exactly the same areas as the central square. And this lies at the

root of our understanding of an important principle in relation to the way in which buildings are placed on the land.

Suppose now that the central square and the outer annulus of the Fresnel diagram are considered as two possible ways of placing the same amount of floor space on the same site area. At once it is clear that the two buildings so arranged would pose totally different questions of access, of how the free space is distributed around them and what natural lighting and view the rooms within them might have. By this process a number of parameters have been defined which need to be considered in any theoretical attempt to understand land use by buildings.

This central square (which can be called the pavilion) and the outer annulus (which can be called the court) are two ways of placing building on the land. Let us now extend this. On any large site a development covering fifty per cent of the site could be plotted as forty-nine pavilions, as shown in Fig. 2, and exactly the same site cover can be plotted in court form. A contrast in the ground space available and the use that can be made of it is at once apparent. But this contrast can be extended further: the forty-nine pavilions can be plotted in a form which is closer to that which they would assume as buildings (that is, low slab with a tower form over this). This can now be compared with its antiform, the same floor space planned as courts (Fig. 3). The comparison must be exact: the same site area, the same volume of building, the same internal depth of room. And when this is done we find that the antiform places the same amount of floor space into buildings which are exactly one third the total height of those in pavilion form.[13] Fig. 4 shows the widely different effects of placing exactly the same amount of floor space on the same site area. Clearly there are choices.

This brings the argument directly back to the question of the grid and its influence on the building form. Let us think of New York. The grid is developing a certain form: the tall building. The land may appear to be thoroughly used. Consider an area of the city. Seen on plan there is an absolutely even pattern of rectangular sites. Now assume that every one of those sites is completely occupied by a building: and that all these buildings have the same tower form and are twenty-one storeys in height. That would undoubtedly look like a pretty full occupation of the land. But if the size of the road net were to be enlarged by omitting some of the

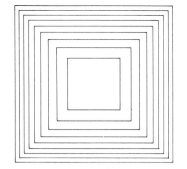

1

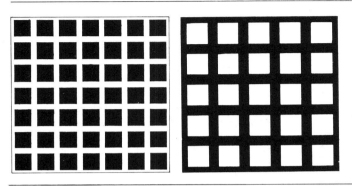

2

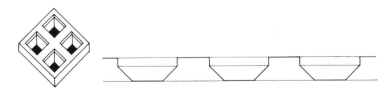

3

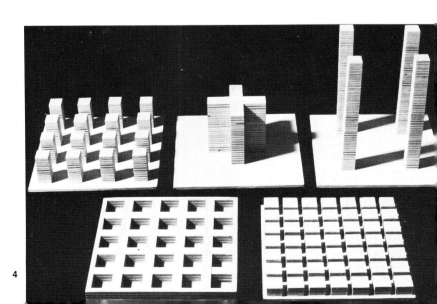

4

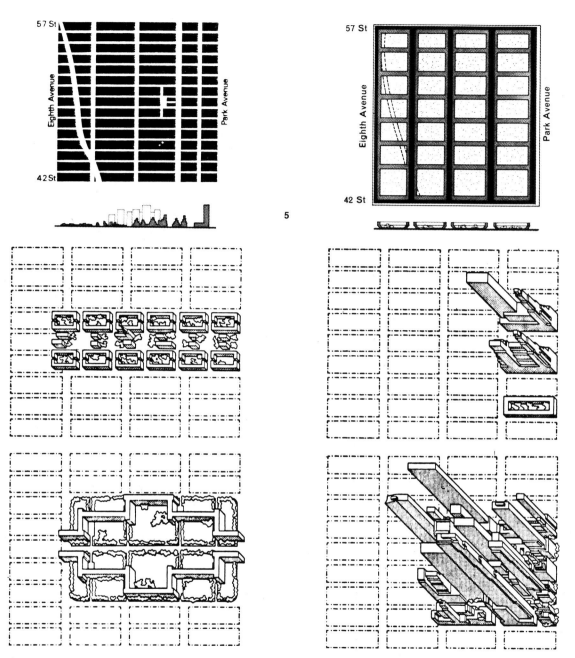

In the four diagrams above, the Manhattan grid is shown with dotted lines. In the top left, the type of development used in Savannah has been superimposed. The example shows the effective way in which this layout opens broad bands of green space and public buildings running across the developed area. Top right shows three stages of development in Manhattan; the four to six-storey perimeter form with a central garden typical of the 1850s and more intensive building during the present century. Bottom left shows Le Corbusier's residential development in his city for three million people and, right, the present plot development.

cross streets, a new building form is possible. Exactly the same amount of floor space that was contained in the towers can be arranged in another form. If this floor space is placed in buildings around the edges of our enlarged grid then the same quantity of floor space that was contained in the twenty-one-storey towers now needs only seven-storey buildings. And large open spaces are left at the centre.

Let us be more specific. If the area bounded by Park Avenue and Eighth Avenue, and between 42nd and 57th Street, is used as a base and the whole area were developed in the form of Seagram buildings thirty-six storeys high, this would certainly open up some ground space along the streets. If, however, the Seagram buildings were replaced by court forms (Fig. 5) then this type of development, while using the same built volume, would produce buildings only eight storeys high. But the courts thus provided would be roughly equivalent in area to Washington Square; and there could be twenty-eight Washington Squares in this total area. Within squares of this size there could be large trees, perhaps some housing, and other buildings such as schools.

Of course no one may want this alternative. But it is important to know that the possibility exists, and that, when high buildings and their skyline are being described, the talk is precisely about this and not about the best way of putting built space on to ground space. The alternative form of courts, taken in this test, is not a universal panacea. It suggests an alternative which would at once raise far-reaching questions. For instance, the open space provided in the present block-by-block (or pavilion) form is simply a series of traffic corridors. In the court form, it could become traffic-free courts. In this situation the question which needs answering is: at what point could we regard a larger area as a traffic-free room surrounded by external traffic routes?

In all this the attempt has been simply to give a demonstration of procedure. The full repercussions of the questions are not obvious. They are highly complicated. But the factual aspect of the study establishes a better position from which to understand the nature of the complication and the limits of historical assumptions. What is left is something that can be built upon and decisions are brought back to the problem of the built form, which is critical in a number of ways, not least as a means of securing a new unity of conception.

V. From the Introduction to the Catalogue of the Circle Exhibition[14] (1982)

I have been asked to say something about the ideas that brought *Circle* into being. In the first place I think that it is important to say what was *not* intended. *Circle* was not a manifesto in the sense that contributors were asked to support a particular point of view or some written document with which they all agreed. They came from a number of different countries; they had their own very definite ideas about what they were doing (Mondrian for instance would certainly have called himself a neo-plasticist); there were considerable differences of background and without doubt of religious or political points of view.

There was, therefore, no attempt on the part of the editors to circulate any statement. Nicholson, Gabo and I agreed quite simply that amongst the many forms of painting and sculpture that were being produced at that time, there were certain works which were not purely decorative, nor were they examples of realism or surrealism. The descriptive terms applied to this kind of work, for instance 'abstract' or 'non-representational', seemed to us to be inadequate and to remove the idea of content. We believed that such works were positive and affirmative: they were symbols built up around the attempt to construct the work of art, in whatever material, into some sense of wholeness and coherence of form. This type of art represented, as we said in our editorial, work which 'appeared to have a common idea and a common spirit: the constructive trend in the art of our day'. We considered that it was important to demonstrate this attitude of mind by showing examples of this kind of painting and sculpture side by side, and we extended the idea by illustrating a range of architectural solutions to varying problems, again selected from the work of individuals in various countries.

The written material was supplementary. Some articles had already appeared and were reprinted, others were specially written, each author being free to write a short note about the subject that they found interesting. Articles like Karl Honzig's 'Note on Biotechnics' which emphasised a parallel between technical structure and natural forms, or Siegfried Giedions' 'Construction and Aesthetics' which discussed the work of the brilliant Swiss engineer Maillart, were deliberately included to broaden the range of possible discussion.

Above all else *Circle* was, I think, an attempt, in a period of considerable confusion, to achieve a clarification and to demonstrate by illustration examples of a particular attitude of mind that seemed to be valid and at work in the art and architecture that we saw around us. It spoke for its time – or rather for a particular set of ideas that seemed to us to be relevant then. And it is for this reason that when *Circle* was reprinted thirty-four years after its original publication in 1937 we, the editors, felt that it should remain a facsimile without any attempt on our part to re-edit or to add a second introduction.

That is not to say that the individual artists ceased to develop and elaborate their work. Gabo himself during his lifetime broadened his range from objects in perspex and transparent constructions to stone carvings in which the problems of defining space and volume were always central and were no less constructive art in his own terms. Nicholson, throughout his considerable output since 1937, has consistently elaborated the complexity of his work but has always from time to time reflected again in a new form the serene work that we illustrated in the middle thirties. For many of those artists and architects who were able to continue their work, and not all of them did, there is no doubt that the work illustrated in *Circle* was at least some kind of a base for further development.

I can illustrate the point more clearly and perhaps speak with a little more authority in terms of architecture. The work illustrated includes buildings from Finland, Holland, France, Switzerland, the USA and England. It does not take much insight to see, even at this early date, some special characteristics in the work from Holland or Finland, or some quite distinct differences of interest and emphasis. With the benefit of hindsight we can recognise the beginnings of a series of lines of thought that have since been continuously elaborated and widened. In retrospect we now know how Aalto's work rooted itself more and more deeply in those influences of landscape and materials that came directly from his own background and his own country. At another extreme we can see in Richard Neutra's work within industrialised technology the beginnings of an interest that has today transformed high technology into a poetic expression. Each succeeding generation has widened the range and added a new and a deeper contribution.

And perhaps the whole process is already indicated at least in Marcel Breuer's article on 'Architecture and Material'. He described the new materials and new processes by which buildings and furniture could be produced. He illustrated the effects of this in his own early development of tubular metal tables and chairs. He shows the development of technique and of form in his aluminium chaise-longue. He illustrates the change of form that results when an old material (wood) is given a new application in bent-plywood. And finally, he illustrates a small exhibition pavilion built almost entirely from traditional materials. It is, as he says, not the new materials that matter but the new mentality which will use the materials that are most appropriate for the task and will produce the new content and the new form.

I am glad that some of the paintings and sculpture that we illustrated have now become the classics of their time. It is of some satisfaction also to know that Aalto's Paimio Sanatorium and several other buildings still seem to have a validity and that his housing is cared for by its occupants as he would have wished, and is now garlanded with climbing plants. Some of Breuer's furniture is so lasting in its use and appeal that (like the remarkable bent-wood furniture of Thonet before him) it is still being reproduced today. So, too, is the furniture of Alvar Aalto.

On the other hand I am equally glad that some of the work that we illustrated in 1937 at such an early stage has been widely developed and elaborated into new and appropriate forms by each new generation and with a richness that we could not possibly have envisaged. What has remained for me and others of my generation is a confirmation of the belief that art, whether it is painting, sculpture or architecture, can be one of the great constructive and unifying forces in our lives. That is what we intended *Circle* to express.

Notes

Foreword

1 *Building Design* (2 Feb. 1973), pp. 10–11.
2 Leslie Martin and Sadie Speight, *The Flat Book* (London 1939). This foreshadowed, in some ways, the Design Centre idea, by presenting designed objects of diverse source but common integrity. Some of these objects have become classics, even commercial successes.
3 *1930s Exhibition*, Hayward Gallery Arts Council Catalogue (1979).
4 *Ibid.*
5 *RIBA Journal* (Aug. 1973), pp. 382–3.

Introduction

1 Frank Lloyd Wright, *An Organic Architecture* (London 1970).
2 *Alvar Aalto 1898–1976*, Museum of Finnish Architecture (Helsinki 1978), p. 25.
3 It is of some interest to note that the method of drawing used by designers is itself to some extent related to design principles. The presentation drawings by English Free School designers were themselves 'picturesque'. The presentation associated with a Beaux Arts training, as Lou Kahn was the first to acknowledge, concentrated through its elaborate rendering and shadow projection on the complete understanding of form and volume. When subdivision of the volume became more complex in the thirties the isometric and axonometric projections were increasingly used to describe the volumetric relationships within the architecture itself.
4 The English Free School architects could never have achieved the formal impressiveness of New Delhi. But it is at least arguable that the informal style of Webb, Voysey or Mackintosh was at least as lasting an influence on British Domestic architecture as the formal houses of Lutyens.
5 Allan Greenberg, 'Lutyens' Architecture Re-studied', *Perspecta*, 12 (1969), pp. 129–52.
6 Examples of this criticism may be seen in one single volume of *Perspecta* referred to in note 5 which contains, in addition to Greenberg's article, Alan Colquhoun on 'Typology and Design Method' and Kenneth Frampton on the 'Maison de Verre'. An earlier number (no. 8) contained Rowe and Stutzky's brilliant analysis of Le Corbusier's villa at Garches.

7 *Le Corbusier 1910–29* (Zurich 1930), p. 193.
8 For this see Colin Rowe, 'The Mathematics of the Ideal Villa', *Architectural Review* (March 1947), pp. 101–4, and Greenberg, 'Lutyens' Architecture Re-studied'.
9 Robert Lutyens, *Six Great Architects* (London 1959), p. 146.
10 Peter Inskip, *Edwin Lutyens*, Architectural Monographs 6 (London 1981), p. 29.
11 Quoted by John Archer, Introduction to *Catalogue of the Work of Edgar Wood and J. H. Sellars*, Manchester City Art Gallery (Oct.–Nov. 1975).
12 For more on this subject see Ada Louise Huxtable, 'The Troubled State of Modern Architecture', *Architectural Design* 1/2 (1981), pp. 9–17.
13 *Franco Albini, Architettura e Design 1930–1970*, ed. Franca Helg (Milan 1979).
14 Cesare De Seta, 'Franco Albini architetto, fra razionalismo e tecnologia', in *ibid.*
15 Giancarlo de Carlo and Pierluigi Nicolin, 'Conversation on Urbino', *Lotus International*, 18 (1978), pp. 6–41.
16 *Alvar Aalto 1898–1976*, p. 25.
17 E. H. Gombrich, *The Sense of Order* (Oxford 1979), p. 64.
18 *Ibid.*, p. 230.

Part I. Buildings and form 1956–1982

1 J. N. L. Durand, *Recueil et Parallèle des Edifices* (Paris, 1801) and *Leçons d'Architecture* (Paris 1819).
2 Philip Steadman, *The Evolution of Designs* (Cambridge 1979), pp. 28–31.
3 See n.3 to Chapter 3. See also Dean Hawkes, 'Precedent and Theory in the Design of Auditoria', in *Transactions of the Martin Centre for Architectural and Urban Studies*, vol. 4 (Cambridge 1980).
4 William C. Miller, 'Alvar Aalto: From Viipuri to Mount Angel', *Architectural Association Quarterly*, 10: 3 (1978), pp. 30–41. Other more general examples might be cited from the work of architects who have over a number of years worked on the development of special types such as housing or the theatre, for example Peter Moro, 'Fifteen Years of Theatre Design', *RIBA Journal* (Feb. 1979).
5 Robert Geddes, 'Theory in Practice', *Architectural Forum* (Sept. 1972), pp. 34–41.
6 'Housing Development, St Pancras, London NW', *Architectural Design* (July 1959), pp. 279–81, and Leslie

Martin and Lionel March, 'Land Use and Built Forms', *Cambridge Research* (April 1966).
7 See Part 2. Also Leslie Martin, 'Science Buildings: Notes on the Study of a Building Type', *Architectural Design* (Dec. 1964), pp. 595–602.
8 'The Collegiate Plan', *Architectural Review* (July 1959), pp. 42–8.

2. The library: generic plans

1 *Alvar Aalto 1898–1976*, p. 25.
2 William C. Miller, 'From Viipuri to Mount Angel'.

3. Auditoria: variations on a theme

1 Hope Bagenal and Alex Wood, *Planning for Good Acoustics* (London 1931) and various papers, especially Bagenal's address to the acoustics group of the Physical Society, 1948.
2 See *ibid.*, pp. 145–9.
3 See also Michael Barron, 'The Role of Acoustic Models in Auditoria', *Transactions of the Martin Centre for Architectural and Urban Guides*, vol. 4 (Cambridge 1980).
4 Michael Barron has very kindly contributed the following notes on his tests relating to acoustic models and the auditorium of the Music School in Cambridge.
   'The 1 : 50 scale model of the Music School auditorium proved extremely valuable for an acoustic modelling experiment. The study of the acoustics of auditoria remains an imprecise art and one of the problems is the extreme complexity of acoustic behaviour in an enclosed space. To clarify this acoustic behaviour, acoustic models of auditoria have been developed since the 1930s; the model scales used have generally been 1 : 8 or 1 : 10. At this scale considerable precision of modelling can be achieved: as well as objective tests which produce numerical results one can also conduct subjective tests by playing music or speech 'through' the model and listening to the results over headphones. Acoustic models enable many measurements to be made prior to construction which cannot be predicted from drawings or by computer. For instance, one characteristic which is generally strived for in music auditoria is good diffusion, a uniform spatial flow of sound energy; the degree of surface treatment, diffusing elements as they are called,

required for good diffusion can only be determined by precedent or with a model. The value of models at scales of 1 : 10 is now widely appreciated.

'There are however several problems with models at these scales. The first of these is expense: the whole testing exercise is likely to cost in the order of 1% of the total building cost. The space required for the model is also large, requiring more than standard room height. A third problem is that to build a model in great detail implies that there is a substantial commitment to the design before the model can be constructed. This tends to limit the number of variations which can be tried in the model, and for fast building programmes such large models often perform only a confirmatory role, though they are also available for development of remedial measures should these be required once the auditorium is in use.

'A smaller model does not suffer from these drawbacks and offers the possibility of acoustic model testing becoming more intimately involved in the design process. The gain in flexibility is however at the loss of some measurement precision as well as at the loss of the subjective testing facility. The scale of 1 : 50 is very frequently used for architectural models, and investigations were started by the Acoustic Modelling Group at the Department of Architecture, Cambridge, into the feasibility of acoustic model testing at this scale. By chance this work coincided with the completion of the Music School auditorium and the model was very kindly made available to be converted for use for acoustic purposes. Apart from access holes for acoustic sources and microphones, the only additional requirement for acoustic tests was that all interior surfaces had to be thoroughly varnished.

'The particular value of this model was that it enabled the acoustics of the model to be compared with those of the real auditorium to determine the accuracy of 1 : 50 scale models. A series of identical acoustic measurements was made in the model and in the full-size auditorium, good use being made of the variable elements around the stage to provide additional comparison conditions. The measurements included reverberation time and impulse measurements for which loudspeakers are used in the full-size condition and a weak spark source in the 1 : 50 model. The results of these tests have been reported in detail in an acoustic journal (*Applied Acoustics*, 12 (1979), pp. 361–75). The agreement proved to be good, with errors small relative to the smallest differences perceptible with our ears.

'Two examples of physical "errors" in the original

model serve to illustrate the sensitivity of the techniques. The original model omitted eight ventilation supply dropper ducts and their subsequent inclusion significantly reduced the errors between the model and full-size. Poor agreement was also found at one of the measuring positions, which proved to be due to the precise location of a surface containing an entrance door being different in the model, which affected a particularly prominent reflection.

'These tests with the Music School auditorium appear to validate the technique of acoustic modelling at 1 : 50 scale. They have given confidence in the model tests successfully conducted since on several other auditoria during their design stage. The cheapness and flexibility of modelling at this scale are clear advantages and testing such models seems relevant to the majority of medium to large size auditoria.'

Part 2. Buildings and environment: symbol and anonymity

1   Leo Marx, 'Between Two Landscapes', *RIBA Journal* (Aug. 1973), pp. 422–4 (review of *The Country and the City* by Raymond Williams).
2   M. W. Beresford and J. K. S. St Joseph, *Medieval England* (Cambridge 1979), p. 214.
3   Laboratorio de Urbanismo, *Los Ensanches (1): El Ensanche de Barcelona*, ed. Manuel de Solà-Morales (Escuela Tecnica Superior de Arquitectura, Barcelona 1976).
4   Sir Leslie Martin and Colin St J. Wilson, 'New British Museum Library', unpublished report (Jan. 1964).
5   Leslie Martin and Colin Buchanan, *Whitehall: A Plan for the National and Government Centre* (London 1965).
6   Sir Charles Barry's 'General Scheme for Metropolitan Improvements' was exhibited in 1857. The chief danger to be avoided, he maintained, was the absence of some general scheme, 'which has in England especially wasted time and money on erections of isolated and often misplaced magnificence'. Alfred Barry, *Memoir of the Life and Works of the late Sir Charles Barry, Architect* (London 1870), p. 293.
7   See below, pp. 136–49.
8   See below, pp. 128–9.
9   See below, pp. 130–5.
10 Martin and March, 'Land Use and Built Forms'.
11 'Housing Developments, St Pancras'.

5. Structure and growth: university plans

1   Martin, 'Science Buildings', p. 602.
2   Martin and March, 'Land Use and Built Forms'.
3   Lionel March and Michael Trace, 'The Land Use Performances of Selected Arrays of Built Forms', *Land Use and Built Form Studies*, Working Paper no. 2 (Cambridge 1968).
4   Computer techniques for this purpose are at present being developed in Cambridge.
5   See 'Department of Zoology' in the handbook for the opening ceremony of the building, 12 July 1971. Oxford University Press.

8. 1933–1956; work in retrospect

1   Frank Jenkins, *Architect and Patron* (Oxford 1961).
2   *Ibid.*, p. 200.
3   Patrick Abercrombie and J. H. Forshaw, *A County of London Plan* (London 1943).
4   Leslie Martin, 'Science and the Design of the Royal Festival Hall', *RIBA Journal*, (April 1952), pp. 196–204.
5   See n.4 to Chapter 3 above. The Royal Festival Hall was designed purely for musical performance. Within a year, at Christmas time, it was being adapted for ballet. That kind of adaptation, had it been known, could have been taken into consideration at the design stage. The effect, however, could not have been predicted by our acoustic advisors in the way that is now more possible.
6   A series of photographs record dramatically the progress during the two years of building work. On 12 July 1949, the excavation, with its fence of de-watering pipes to lower the water table, had given us a clear dry site. On 29 September, the basement walls are under construction and pipe lines for pumping the liquid concrete are laid to various areas of the site. By 20 November, the shuttering to the floor of the foyer is in position and by 17 January 1950 the formwork for the raking floor of the auditorium is there. By 22 June 1950, the main skin to the auditorium roof was waterproofed and the internal finishes were in hand.
7   See *Architectural Design* (Jan. 1957), p. 25, for illustrations of this scheme. Alternative proposals for the building as it now stands were carried into effect later during the time of my successor as architect to the Council, Sir Hubert Bennet.
8   *Architect's Year Book*, no. 7 (London 1956).

9. Notes on a developing architecture

1   H. Muthesius, *Das Englische Haus* (Berlin 1905).
2   Catherine Bauer, *Modern Housing* (London 1935), pp. 176–81.
3   Thomas Sharp, 'The English Tradition in the Town: III Universal Suburbia', *Architectural Review* (March 1936), pp. 115–21.
4   Including Wells Coates, not yet practising as an architect, Jack Pritchard and Morton Shand. I first saw Le Corbusier's building with Oscar Stonorov in 1929.
5   J. H. Napper, 'The Long Weekend', *RIBA Journal* (Nov. 1975), pp. 26–32.
6   For an excellent outline of the development of housing policy see J. B. Cullingworth, *Housing and Local Government* (London 1966).
7   *Ibid.*, p. 24. See also Bauer, *Modern Housing*, for a pioneering comparative study of housing in Europe.
8   M. W. Beresford, 'The Back to Back House in Leeds 1787–1937', in *The History of Working Class Housing* (Newton Abbot 1971).
9   See Dean Hawkes, 'Garden Cities and New Methods of Construction: Raymond Unwin's Influence on Housing Practice, 1919–1939', in *Transactions of the Martin Centre for Architectural and Urban Studies*, vol. 1 (Cambridge 1976), pp. 275–95.
10 Gerald Heard, 'Science and Society 1901–1934', *Architectural Review* (May 1934), pp. 165–9.
11 Martin Mayer, 'Underground Architect', *Building Design* (11 April 1975), pp. 12–13. For some discussion of Holden's early work see J. Summerson, 'British Contemporaries of Wright', in *Studies in Western Art*, vol. 4: *Problems of the 19th and 20th Centuries* (Princeton 1963).
12 For an exposition of the ideas around it see R. Banham, *Theory and Design in the First Machine Age* (London 1970).
13 I leave aside for the moment the reinforcement that came from abroad between 1935 and 1937 when Mendelsohn joined Chermayeff, Gropius became associated with Max Fry and Breuer with F. R. S. Yorke. And on a broader front we should not overlook the arrival of Moholy Nagy, Gabo and Mondrian. But all that is later.
14 H. Wölfflin, *Principles of Art History* (New York 1932).
15 The *Calendar of Modern Letters* was edited by E. Rickword and D. Garman between 1925 and 1927. For an assessment and selection from its contents see F. R. Leavis, *Towards Standards of Criticism* (London 1933).
16 I. A. Richards, *Principles of Literary Criticism* (London 1926).
17 Wells Coates, 'Response to Tradition', *Architectural Review* (Nov. 1932), p. 165.
18 F. R. S. Yorke, *The Modern House* (London 1934).
19 For the limits of town planning legislation at that time see J. B. Cullingworth, *Town and Country Planning* (London 1964).
20 See Wells Coates, 'Planning in Section', *Architectural Review*, (Aug. 1937), pp. 51–8. Also *Focus*, no. 2 (1938).
21 See 'Housing Development, St Pancras'.
22 *Circle*, edited by J. L. Martin, B. Nicholson, and N. Gabo (London 1937, reprinted 1971).
23 These ideas were of course entirely tentative. Some indications can be given by the inclusion of the article by Bernal (the crystallographer who was at that time revealing so brilliantly some of the ordering forces in nature) or the note on Bio-Technics by the architect Karel Honzig. The work of art, we might have argued, was not the direct representation of the external form or the internal structure within nature. It moves through intuition towards those forms that may produce some kind of *equivalent*. If it is of value its power rests in the fact that it is an image: it carries meaning.
24 For some account of this see Sherban Cantacuzino, *Wells Coates* (London 1978).
25 For a selection see Trevor Dannatt, *Modern Architecture in Britain*, with a foreword by John Summerson (London 1959).

10. A sketch by Leonardo

1   J. P. Richter, *The Literary Works of Leonardo da Vinci* (2 vols. London 1883), vol. 2, pp. 41–57.
2   Rudolf Wittkower, *Architectural Principles in the Age of Humanism* (London 1949, 2nd edn 1952), pp. 12–18.
3   Cf. Richter, *Literary Works*, and for a descriptive reference Frances Yates, *Theatre of the World* (London 1969), p. 122.
4   Edward MacCurdy, *Notebooks of Leonardo da Vinci* (2 vols. London 1938), vol. 1, pp. 279–84.

11. Extracts from papers

1   Extract from 'An Architect's Approach to Architecture', *RIBA Journal* (May 1967), pp. 191–200.
2   Colin St J. Wilson and Colin Rowe, Contributions in *Journal of the Society of Architectural Historians* (March 1965), pp. 79–93.
3   James Marston Fitch, 'The Rise of Technology: 1929–1939', *Journal of the Society of Architectural Historians* (March 1965), pp. 75–7.
4   *Ibid.*, also contribution by Catherine Bauer Wurster in the same journal, pp. 79–93.
5   A. N. Whitehead, *The Function of Reason* (Princeton 1929).
6   *Ibid.*, pp. 42ff and Chapter 3.
7   Extract from 'An Architect's Approach to Architecture', p. 193.
8   Le Corbusier, *Urbanisme* (Paris 1925).
9   Edgar Wind, *Art and Anarchy* (London 1963), p. 52.
10 Extract from 'The Grid as Generator', in Leslie Martin and Lionel March (eds.), *Urban Space and Structures* (Cambridge 1972).
11 For example Lionel March, 'Homes Beyond the Fringe', *RIBA Journal* (August 1967).
12 R. Unwin, 'Nothing Gained by Overcrowding!' (1912) in W. L. Creese (ed.), *The Legacy of Raymond Unwin* (Cambridge, Mass. 1967).
13 Martin and March, 'Land Use and Built Forms'.
14 From Introduction to the Catalogue of the Circle Exhibition, Kettle's Yard, Cambridge (March 1982).

About the author

Born 17 Aug. 1908. Son of late Robert Martin FRIBA. Married Sadie Speight MA ARIBA 1935.

Professional education. School of Architecture, University of Manchester. RIBA recognised Schools Silver Medallist 1929. Soane Medallist 1930. MA PhD. Travel in France, Italy and Spain 1930. Member RIBA 1931. Practice from 1933.

Appointments. Head of the School of Architecture, Hull, 1934–9 and in private practice.
Architects' Department, LMS Railway, 1939–48: war-time building; post-war projects etc.
Deputy Architect to the LCC, 1948–53; Architect to the LCC, 1953–6.
Appointed first Professor of Architecture, Cambridge, 1956–72 and private practice from the Studio, The King's Mill, Shelford, Cambridge, 1956 onwards.
Slade Professor of Fine Arts, Oxford, 1965–6; Ferens Professor of Fine Art, Hull, 1967–8; William Henry Bishop Visiting Professor of Architecture, Yale University, 1973–4; Lethaby Professor, Royal College of Art, 1981.
Member of the Royal Fine Art Commission, 1958–72.

Lectures. Gropius Lecture, Harvard, 1966; Cordingley, Manchester, 1968; Kenneth Kassler, Princeton, 1974; Annual Society of Architectural Historians, 1976; Townsend, University College, London, 1976; Convocation, Leicester, 1978; Albini Memorial Lecture, Milan, 1981; Lethaby, RCA, London, 1981.

Honours, Honorary Degrees, Awards etc. Knight Bachelor, 1957. MA Cantab; MA Oxon; Hon. LLD, Leicester, Hull, Manchester; D. Univ. Essex. Fellow Jesus College, Cambridge, 1956 (Hon. Fellow 1973). Hon. member Finnish Association of Architects. Accademico correspondente Nat. Acad. of S. Luca, Rome; Comdr Order of Santiago da Espada, Portugal. RIBA Dist. Town Planning, 1956; Civic Trust Award Oxford, 1967; Commend. Cambridge, 1972; Conc. Soc. Award Oxford, 1972; Royal Gold Medal for Architecture, 1973.

Chronological list of work

To avoid the problem of applying exact dates to buildings which may take several years from design to completion, the work has been grouped in five year periods.

1935–9 Extensions to a house at Brampton, Cumberland
Morton House, Brampton, Cumberland
Robinson House, Ferriby, Yorks
Sutherland House, Dockray, Cumberland
Nursery School, Northwich, Cheshire
Unit Furniture for Messrs Rowntree, Scarborough

1939–48 Principal Assistant Architect LMS Railway. War-time building work etc., studies for station reconstruction, unit stations etc.

1948–56 Deputy Architect and Architect to the London County Council (1953–6). Principal work on Royal Festival Hall and proposed developments for the Crystal Palace site

1956–60 Own house at the King's Mill, Shelford
Development plan for the University of Leicester
College Hall, Knighton, Leicester
Development plan, University of London
Harvey Court residential building, Cambridge
Various housing studies

1960–65 Development plan, University of Hull
Group of library buildings, University of Oxford
Development plan, Royal Holloway College, Egham
Science Area, University of Oxford
First designs for buildings for Zoology/Psychology, Oxford
Small houses abroad
Residential building, Peterhouse, Cambridge

1965–70 Middleton Hall and Arts building, University of Hull
Consultant to the Gulbenkian Foundation, Lisbon
Wellington Square development, University of Oxford
New Concert Hall etc., Glasgow – preliminary investigation and proposal
Balliol and St Anne's, postgraduate residence, Oxford
Walston house, Thriplow, Cambridge

1970–75 Government building, Taif, Saudi Arabia
Housing studies etc., Saudi Arabia
Music School, Cambridge, Stage I
New Civic Halls, Glasgow, development stage

1975–80 Library and residential development, Pembroke College, Oxford
Music School, Cambridge, Stages II and III
Revised designs, halls and shopping centre, Glasgow
Scheme for a college social building
Competition scheme, linked auditoria

Extension to Kettle's Yard Gallery, Cambridge
Own house, The Barns, Shelford

1980– Gallery for Contemporary Art, Gulbenkian Foundation, Lisbon (in construction)
Children's Pavilion as above
Final design, Royal Scottish Academy of Music and Drama (working drawings)
Music School Library, Cambridge, Stage IV (in construction)

Publications

Circle, joint editor with Ben Nicholson and Naum Gabo (London 1937; reprinted 1971)
The Flat Book, joint editor with Sadie Speight (London 1939)
Whitehall: A Plan for the National and Government Centre, with Colin Buchanan (London 1965)
Urban Space and Structures, Cambridge Urban and Architectural Studies, joint editor with Lionel March (Cambridge 1972)

Papers

'Science and the Design of the Royal Festival Hall', *RIBA Journal* (Jan. 1950)
'An Architect's Approach to Architecture', *RIBA Journal* (May 1967)
'Education without Walls', *RIBA Journal* (Aug. 1968)
'The Framework of Planning', Inaugural lecture, Ferens Professor, University of Hull, 1969
'Education around Architecture', RIBA Conference, Birmingham 1970, *RIBA Journal* (Sept. 1970)
'Bridges between Cultures', Address on receiving the Royal Gold Medal, *RIBA Journal* (Aug. 1973)
'Notes on a Developing Architecture', *Architectural Review* (July 1978)
'Fifty Years after Lethaby', lecture as Lethaby Professor, Royal College of Art, London (1981)

Various short articles

'Architecture and the Painter: with special reference to the work of Ben Nicholson', *Focus*, no. 3 (1939)
'A Note on Science and Art', *Architect's Year Book*, no. 2 (London 1947)
'A World within a Frame: Ben Nicholson', *The Listener* (27 Jan. 1947)

Articles on work

These include various publications referred to in the general bibliographies and citation for the Royal Gold Medal, RIBA 1 Feb. 1973. See also *RIBA Journal* (Feb. 1973); *Building Design* (2 Feb. 1973); Trevor Dannatt, Speech at the Presentation, *RIBA Journal* (Aug. 1973); 'Leslie Martin: Selected Works', *Architectural Design* (Sept. 1965); Thomas Stevens, 'The Third Force in English Architecture', *Architectural Design* (Sept. 1965)

Acknowledgements

I would like to acknowledge the kindness of Mme Elissa Aalto who allowed me to reproduce the illustrations of Alvar Aalto's work. Marco Albini kindly granted permission to illustrate the work of his father, Franco Albini. Dean Hawkes allowed me to use illustrations of auditoria from his article in the *Transactions of the Martin Centre for Architectural and Urban Studies*, vol. 4 (Cambridge 1980). H.E. the Minister of Finance kindly gave me the original permission to illustrate plans and models of the Government Centre at Taif.

It was Marcial Echenique and Manuel de Solá-Morales who first brought to my attention the work of Ildefonso de Cerda, and the reproductions of his plans for Barcelona come from the monograph of studies edited by Sr Solá-Morales under the title 'Laboratorio de Urbanismo' and published in Barcelona. The early plans and illustrations of Glasgow are reproduced by kind permission of the Mitchell Library, Glasgow. My friend Peter Moro provided the illustrations for my reference to his work on variable auditoria. The article 'Notes on a Developing Architecture' was first published in the *Architectural Review* and I am grateful for permission to republish this and its illustrations in its original form; also for various photographs

Photographs of all the models and many of the plans produced by the Studio are by Edward Leigh and more recently, John Leigh of Cambridge. The *Architectural Review, The Architects Year Book* and *Architectural Design* have described and illustrated buildings included in this volume. Other photography includes that of Mann Bros and Edgar Hyman (College Hall, Knighton); Sam Lambert (Leicester and the King's Mill); the University photographer, Hull; the University photographer, Oxford (Zoology/Psychology building); Richard Einzig (Zoology/Psychology building, Oxford, the Stone Building, Peterhouse, and the Walston House, Cambridge). Finally John Donat is responsible for Harvey Court, Cambridge, the libraries, Oxford, the Music School, Kettle's Yard and the Barns, Cambridge. Margaret Harker and de Burgh Galway took the photos of the Festival Hall that I have used and which were first reproduced by the *Architectural Review*. One illustration of the interior of the Music School is used by kind permission of the *Illustrated London News*.

232

Index of architects, authors and buildings